TREASURES FROM HEAVEN

Relics from Noah's Ark to the Shroud of Turin

Steven Sora

WILEY

John Wiley & Sons, Inc.

To my father and mother, Anthony and Lillian Sora

Published by John Wiley & Sons, Inc., Hoboken, New Jersey
Published simultaneously in Canada

For general information about our other products and services, please contact our Customer Care Department within the United States at (800) 762-2974, outside the United States at (317) 572-3993 or fax (317) 572-4002.

Wiley also publishes its books in a variety of electronic formats. Some content that appears in print may not be available in electronic books. For more information about Wiley products, visit our web site at www.wiley.com.

Library of Congress Cataloging-in-Publication Data:

Sora, Steven, date.
   Treasures from heaven : relics from noah's ark to the shroud of turin / Steven Sora.
     p.   cm.
   Includes bibliographical references and index.
   ISBN 0-471-46232-2
   1. Relics.   I. Title.
   BV890.S66 2004
   235'.2—dc22

2004007049

Printed in the United States of America

10 9 8 7 6 5 4 3 2 1

CONTENTS

Acknowledgments   v

Introduction   I

  I: The Enigma of the Holy Shroud   13

  2: The Sacred Face: The Veil of Veronica and the Sudarium
of Oviedo   39

  3: The True Cross and the Relics of the Crucifixion   51

  4: The Spear of Destiny   65

  5: The Skull of St. John the Baptist   80

  6: The Blessed Virgin Mary   90

  7: Christianity's Most Sacred Women   100

  8: The Bones of Contention—the Relics of the Apostles   118

  9: The Gospel Writers (Mark, Matthew, Luke, and John)   144

10: The Miracles and the Relics of the Saints   152

11: Noah's Ark   167

12: The Ark of the Covenant   184

13: The Holy Grail   206

14: The Modern Relic Trade   215

Epilogue: Relics—the Last Word   223

Notes   225

Bibliography   235

Index   240

ACKNOWLEDGMENTS

As always, thanks are to my wife, Terry, for her active and constant support. Thanks to my son Mike for technical assistance and my son Christian and Tara Albergato for firsthand research in Rome. Special appreciation to Gary Festermacher and Terry Hamlin for an early critical review. Thank you to the librarians at Bethlehem Library in Bethlehem and at Moravian Academy Library also in Bethlehem. Thank you to Kevin Pursglove at Ebay.com, to Carol Myers of the shrine of St. Nicholas, to Steve Mallinger in Virginia, and Larry Haptas from the Shrine of St. Anne de Brighton.

At Wiley, I would like to thank Stephen S. Power, my editor; Kimberly Monroe-Hill; Shelly Perron; and Michael Thompson.

INTRODUCTION

For two thousand years the Catholic Church has amassed a collection of religious articles, from the unforgettable Shroud of Turin to the mundane and often macabre bones, blood, and body parts of the saints. The central storage for the collection is the Apostolic Palace in Rome, which, despite its name, more closely resembles a warehouse. Cabinets and filing drawers hold thousands of sacred artifacts. The palace does not keep the collection to itself, and on a regular basis it serves as a shipping department, packaging relics of saints in boxes or even envelopes and sending them on their way to churches all around the world. And yet the collection keeps growing.

Recently Pope John Paul II seized the opportunity to make a gift of an unspecified body part of Pope John XXIII to a cathedral. The body of the Good Pope, interred in 1963, is considered in pristine condition, adding weight to the case for his canonization. In California proponents for the sainthood of Father Junipero Serra shave his bones into minute fragments, creating thousands of relics. The hope is that each new wearer is one more miracle waiting to happen, making sainthood more possible. In Central America the blood of Archbishop Oscar Romero, shot dead while saying Mass, was preserved in vials, as martyrs are almost certain to attain canonization.

For millions such relics have meaning; they can save souls and heal bodies. The bones of St. Theresa have completed a world tour that included chapels of cathedrals and the death row of an infamous prison. Her reputation as a healer of both body and soul is given credit for miraculous healing as well as death row conversions. Seeking miracles or just to be closer to the sacred, thousands make pilgrimages to the places of apparitions. From Fatima and Lourdes to Australia and even Massachusetts, religious tourism is an industry within itself.

At the same time science has amassed an arsenal to challenge and deny the authenticity of relic objects, relic bones, and the manifestation of phenomena like stigmata, incorrupt bodies, weeping statues, and apparitions of the Blessed Virgin. Using crime-scene-investigation thoroughness and breakthrough methods, scientists are studying bones that have oozed powder or liquid substances for centuries, blood that liquefies on cue, and corpses that are lifelike after centuries of interment.

The Shroud of Turin itself has been scrutinized by doctors, scientists, physicists, and anatomy experts using carbon dating, textile testing, and pollen sampling. To date no conclusion has been agreed upon. One researcher still claims it was painted, and others believe the Shroud is nothing short of evidence of the Resurrection.

The wide range of newly developed scientific techniques can be called upon to date and authenticate objects that for centuries have been taken for granted as real. The Veil of Veronica, the wood of the True Cross, the nails and thorns of the Crucifixion can all be investigated and subjected to new conclusions. Forensic evidence can be used to challenge or corroborate historical texts.

People have always had a love for relics. Baby's first tooth, a lock of hair, and the ashes of the departed become treasured collections of millions. Relics of important people from presidents to movie, sports, and music stars are also treasured and take on commercial value. From John Kennedy's golf clubs to the baseball cards of Mickey Mantle, much money has chased objects that have no intrinsic value other than they give the owner a sentimental connection to a person they admire. For this reason the matter of authenticity is rarely controversial.

But religious relics go beyond sentimentality and admiration; they are called upon to bring us closer to God, to provide favors, to grant protection, to heal sickness, and in some cases even to perform miracles. Witnesses will testify that statues of the Blessed Virgin cry, hosts used in the Mass bleed, and a saint's bones cure the sick. The True Cross is said to have raised the dead, and the spear that pierced Jesus' side is said to be a source of unlimited power for the holder. In the hour that it passed from a German vault to a liberating army of Americans, the spear's former owner, Adolf Hitler, committed suicide. The new owner then unleashed the world's most destructive weapon ever on its remaining enemy. Are such traditions true? Are these relics authentic?

The Roman Catholic Church has amassed, over the centuries, a collection of relics that can fill more than one palace or warehouse. Since it has been a requirement that each altar must contain two relics, the proliferation of saints' bones and the trade in the sacred has not slowed. At least once a month a new church is dedicated somewhere in the world and relics are housed within each altar. No longer as fevered as "relic mania" became during the Crusades, the trade is active, although more reserved.

Now science can attempt to provide answers. The church's massive collection of relics, great and small, is coming under scrutiny. Just which one of the multiple skulls of John the Baptist is real may be determined by a combination of the sciences. Beheaded by Herod after the dance of Salome, St. John's head is, depending on the believers, revered by Christians in two separate cities in France, revered by Muslims in Damascus, or recently unearthed near the Dead Sea. But before various data can be analyzed, science must first gain the cooperation of religious authorities. This was not easy in the past, but the attitude of the church has recently become more hospitable to putting its collection under the microscope.

The bones and teeth of St. Luke the Gospel writer recently passed several tests that concluded the surviving parts of the saint were at least from a Syrian man who survived to a very old age. The blood of St. Lawrence was recently tested on national television in Italy. Next may be the blood of St. Gennaro, which turns from solid to liquid three times a year in front of the faithful. In some cases explanations, though not always conclusive, are offered. Incorruptible bodies, stigmata, apparitions, and weeping statues may have rational explanations. Other phenomena remain unexplained—such as the ability of the bones of St. Nicholas and other saints to produce seemingly forever what the church calls "manna," a powder, or in other cases, an oily liquid substance. Also inexplicable is the ability of holy men and women to survive for months on no food and occasionally even gain weight.

The intrusion of modern science is not always welcome. And the Internet is one outgrowth of new technology that is specifically unwelcome. The relic trade, after having assumed a more dignified role since medieval times, has just begun to face the glaring world of the online auction. Saintly bones, artifacts of the Crucifixion, and rare reliquaries are traded alongside Beanie babies and Barbie dolls. Armed with better tools and technology, tomb raiders in Italy, icon thieves on Cyprus, and cathedral robbers in England can take advantage of the new market for religious relics. They have created a threat not seen since monks raided one another's collections centuries ago.

The Italian police, the American FBI, and the borderless police of Interpol are now regularly relied upon to curb such modern threats to sacred valuable artifacts.

Even the CIA and the NSA (National Security Agency) have been enlisted in assisting the search for the sacred. Declassified spy satellites have identified a boat-shaped object on the slopes of Mount Ararat in Turkey. Agents of the CIA, scientists from the NSA, and even a former astronaut have been linked in the search since it appeared in a photograph during the height of cold war spy operations.

The world of science has only begun to encroach on the world of the sacred, and some scientists appear eager to avenge the judgment of the Inquisition on Galileo. For others it is just as much a crusade to verify long-held beliefs that the Bible is grounded in reality and not just in traditions and myths.

Early Veneration of Relics

It is impossible to date the early Christian veneration of relics. In the first century many Christians were often Jews who shared prohibitions against images and sacred items. As Christianity spread into Asia Minor, an area that was a melting pot of culture and religion, the prohibition was not shared by all. After the public execution of St. Polycarp, the bishop of Smyrna, circa A.D. 150, his disciples attempted to collect his remains. The Jews asked the Romans to stop them, as it was feared Polycarp's following was so large there was danger he could become another Jesus. The rescuers of his remains gathered his bones, which they regarded as "more valuable than precious stones and finer than refined gold," and brought them to a place of worship.[1] Before two more centuries would pass, even flowers and water from the Jordan River brought home from the Holy Lands could be items for veneration and even by themselves responsible for miraculous cures.

In the early fourth century the mother of the Roman emperor Constantine mounted an expedition to the Holy Lands. After Helena brought home her treasures, the collecting of Christian relics began to reach a fever pitch. While collecting relics had always been a part of older traditions, it was never as widespread as it became during and after Helena's time. Before the end of the century Bishop Ambrose, a church writer, discovered the relics of two martyrs, Gervasius and Protasius, and brought them to the church in the center of Milan, Italy. Miraculous events followed, including the curing of a blind man. It was not the first time a Christian relic that wasn't directly from the Holy Lands had received attention and was venerated; however, the accompanying miracles and the statues of Ambrose in the church gave the miracles a stamp of authenticity. The relics created widespread interest, which led, in turn, to the discovery and collection of more relics. Ten years later Bishop Victricius wrote on how much church attendance had increased after bringing the relics of martyrs into the church. The saints had always been in the hearts of the faithful; now they were physically present in the altar.

The statues of Ambrose in the church cannot be underestimated. He was a practicing attorney in the Roman court when the people elected him bishop. This was unusual because he was not yet baptized. But he soon became both baptized and a church leader. It was he who told St. Augustine, when questioned by him on the celebration of feast days, "When in Rome, do as the Romans do"—a lesson that survives today. While he gave such advice to others, he himself changed custom. When Emperor Theodosius I ordered a massacre to punish rioters, Ambrose ordered him to do public penance for the act. He declared, "The Emperor is within the Church: he is not above it." Theodosius submitted.

Clearly the power of the church doctor Ambrose and the emperor Constantine's mother carried great weight. Ambrose and Helena created the cult of relics, and for eight hundred years it grew. Rome let it be known, immediately after their discoveries, that they had Saints Peter and Paul; Constantinople was proud to have Andrew, Luke, and Timothy. In Jerusalem the body of St. Stephen, the head of John the Baptist, and the chair of St. James were discovered.

Relics too had a remarkable power of growing. Despite a body being dismembered, the power that was held in the separated parts was not diminished. The hand of a saint who was revered was not any more powerful than each finger. The intercession of the saint for the owner of the relic might be granted through the smallest relic. Each saint, with two hundred bones, not to count objects he owned, provided a source of closeness to divinity. Each saint also provided an opportunity to make a profit.

When the body of St. Nazarius, a church martyr, was brought out of his tomb, it was discovered that his blood was as fresh as if he had just been killed. Cloths were dipped in the blood and sent all over Europe.[2]

Medieval times are noted for the mania that surrounded relic collecting, but it was much earlier that buying, selling, stealing, and faking sacred objects spread throughout Europe. Around A.D. 400, St. Augustine, who like Ambrose is considered a church doctor, would criticize the relic market, which was dominated by monks. Another church writer would consider the veneration given to the items themselves as idolatry.

Ambrose, however, had the final say, and the practice was not curbed, not even by the laws of the state. When Theodosius laid down a law that said relics could not be bought and sold, the practice of trade in sacred objects hardly changed. When relics changed hands with a contract, the "seller" would be described as freely giving the relic. The buyer would then freely give his own gift in exchange. Usually, the freely given gift was money.

From the fourth century the collecting of relics became an important aspect of the church. The Roman Catholic Church did not invent the veneration of relics. Followers of Buddha and Confucius would venerate the body parts and even the hairs of the masters, a practice that remains active in modern times. In December 2002 a relic in the form of the tooth of the Buddha was given a warm welcome during a seventy-six-day visit to Thailand.[3]

From primitive hunter-gatherer societies, where bear skulls and painted images played a role in ceremony and magic, until modern times, even organized religion cannot claim a monopoly on preserving and venerating any items that were the body parts of, or touched by, an important person. In Scotland the tomb of the heart of Robert the Bruce is located in the yard of Melrose Abbey. It had been carried into battle against the Moors in Spain, recovered, returned to Scotland, and finally laid to rest in one of that country's holiest shrines. In America, General Stonewall Jackson has the distinction of being buried in two locations, one for his body and another for his arm. Pilgrims of a modern sort make journeys by the thousands to visit the home of Elvis Presley at Graceland or the tomb of Jim Morrison in Paris. Devotees pay thousands for Judy Garland's shoes from the *Wizard of Oz* and for the graven images of baseball's Yankee idols that once sold for pennies (and included a stick of gum).

The Viewpoint of the Church

In early years there was no reason for the church to curb the practice of venerating and collecting relics, although the church leaders considered it important to define the use and worship of relics. The position of the church is that the relic is not the object of veneration; the relic merely represents the intercession of the saint or the martyr. The church did not want the relic itself to be given credit for miracles. Even the saint was not given credit. It was the intercession of the saint to the Blessed Virgin or Jesus himself, who can then be given credit.

Over time the church did make attempts to classify such relics and define them more specifically. Today relics are divided into three classes. A first-class relic includes almost any article that can be attributed to Jesus or any bone or body part of a saint. A second-class relic is an item that a saint used. This can include a Bible, an item of clothing, or if he was killed, an item used in his or her death. A third-class relic is an item that has touched a first- or second-class relic. The act of an artist placing their own painting of Jesus against an item as sacred as the Holy Shroud instantly conveyed a much greater status to the work. No longer simply a work of art, it now had status as a relic.

It also became a church law that all altars had to have at least two relics. This amazing interpretation only served to increase the trade. Relics were valuable, as they radiated power, provided protection, and could on occasion provide cures, and now they were indispensable for the Christian mass.

Because they were required in churches, they soon became the reason for building churches. The more important the relic, the more important the church. The churches that housed important relics attracted pilgrims. Relics were also often the centerpiece at the trade fairs that existed in many cities several times each year.

Every cathedral with any status had to have at least one part of the True Cross, and soon Rome, Venice, Ragusa, Paris, Brussels, Ghent, Limbourg, and Mount Athos in Greece would all have cathedrals with the most sacred of relics. Over the centuries the number of churches and cathedrals holding a piece of the True Cross would continue to expand. A large piece of the Cross is at the Cistercian monastery of la Boissiere in France. Another piece of the Cross found its way to Scotland.

Relics also became a form of wealth, in a simple monetary sense. They could be given to provide favor, to found new churches, and simply to sell in times of need. Returning Crusader kings who incurred debts sold relics to those kings who stayed behind. The religious objects in Charlemagne's treasury were a source of great wealth. His monks even knew how to create such treasures. Waters from Aachen would be bottled and sold to pilgrims to serve as curative aids or talismanic items back home.

The Power of Relics

When the first saints were unearthed, there were often accompanying miracles, including the curing of the blind, the healing of the sick, and even more miraculous phenomena. The reason why cloths were dipped in the blood and carried home when St. Nazarius was brought out of the tomb was that they were believed to have the ability to heal.

Relics could heal sickness, cure blindness, exorcise demons, and bring luck. While modern science and skeptics scoff at such claims, during the life of Jesus, religion and healing were not separate. In 600 B.C. Pythagoreans attributed the power of healing to music. Followers of the healing god Asclepius believed healing was a mental process, often accomplished by a visit to the temple. The Chinese placed more stock in healing through their gods, as they were taught as children the positive role of faith. Only today does science provide terms like biofeedback for what Indian Sufis have exhibited for thousands of years—the ability to slow their hearts, to be unresponsive to pain, etc.

As Jesus and his apostles could heal, so could holy men and women through the centuries. Some saints in particular have enormous healing power. One needs only to visit the shrines of St. Anne, the grandmother of Jesus, for evidence. Just outside of the city of Quebec and in the south side of Chicago, two important shrines that house the saint's bones, exhibit a multitude of canes and crutches that the recipients of her blessings no longer needed. While skeptics attribute such miracles to the power of suggestion, or imply that many recover from illnesses naturally, those who are healed ignore the semantics. They are healed.

In some medieval cases it is not unlikely that even gradual healing was attributed to the miraculous. The possibility of spontaneous remissions and misdiagnosed illnesses in modern times can also lead to the conclusion that a miracle has occurred. Science has little basis for proving a miracle did not occur, and religion has only faith to prove it did.

An inability to correctly assess a patient's death may have occasionally resulted in a "resurrection." The circumstances of medieval medicine were aided by church fathers like St. Ambrose, who declared that in terms of healing, the belief in prayer was stronger and would prevail over that of any medicines. Today Western medicine may claim to "know" better, with a medicine for every ill. But the power of belief, however, may be at least as strong. Each February, on the third day of that month, Catholics still visit church to get the blessing of St. Blaise, who protects against illnesses of the throat.

Other Powers of Relics

The relic bones of saints could be counted on for blessing the crops. In the Champagne district of France the bones of St. Julian were carried through the fields to guard against crop failure. In his life Julian could cure a man of possession with one word. In his afterlife his bones were still accorded great power.[4] The English patron saint of farmers is St. Botolph. In his life he turned scrub and marshland into productive fields. After his death his relics were carried in procession to end droughts. The town named for him, Botolph's Town, grew to be called Botulphston, and later Boston.

Relics provide victory and protection. The bones of St. Cuthbert were carried into battle by William the Conqueror's army at Hastings in 1066. The battle of Bannockburn, which secured Scotland's independence for centuries, had help from St. Fillan, whose arm was carried into battle against the English. Relics were used in both attacks upon, and defense of, cities. St. Genevieve foresaw the coming of Attila to Paris, but her prayers and fasting induced him to change direction. The relics of this patron saint of Paris continue to protect France from epidemics and disasters.

And sometimes they don't. The relic bones of St. Theresa were brought to Baghdad in November 2002 at the urgent request of the city's archbishop to save the country from impending war.

The Trade in Sacred Objects

Both the trade in relics of the faith, as well as their preservation and use, are not without controversy. While one church doctor's arguments against the trade were countered by another's, the intensity of the antirelic side has never dwindled. It was one of the serious abuses of faith against which reformers took issue. Martin Luther made it one of the serious points of his anti-Rome theses that he nailed to the door of the Castle Church in Wittenberg, Germany. That church had gathered nineteen thousand relics of saints to display. The relics were sure to draw crowds and to assist in no small way in raising funds for the church.[5] Those who visited, viewed the relics, and left a donation that could earn a "quarantine," which meant a 111-year indulgence. To those with more than their share of sins, a visit to such an exhibition, which Wittenberg held seven times each year, could knock off a great deal of time in purgatory, where Catholics believe they must wait before entering heaven.

From Martin Luther's time to the present day, Protestant churches are still very much opposed to the trade in relics. The Catholic Church has no such qualms. The church cautions that the worship of the relic and the worship of a saint should not be confused. If a relic of a saint draws the faithful closer in focusing worship on that saint, it is a positive thing. While indulgences are no longer earned by visiting relics and leaving a donation, who is to say that no intercession by the saint worshipped will be acquired.

On occasion the church is concerned about just how the trade is conducted. In the Middle Ages the "trade" in relics would be very expensive, and often a church could not afford a relic or possibly only be able to afford a minor relic. Relics were "found" thanks to miracles, invented, created by touching one not-so-sacred item to another very sacred item, and—not as a last resort—stolen. The church did not frown upon such initiative, and there was a name, *furta sacra,* for stealing the holy. An English word for the taking of a relic was *translation.* When a relic could not be bought, it might be *translated.* Despite the prohibition "thou shall not steal," it was justified, because if the relic could be taken, it was divine will that allowed the act.

Alfred, the canon of Durham, piously visited a church at Jarrow each year until one day he simply stole the bones of his favorite saint, Bede. Stealing was not called stealing, but instead, translating.

Not only was translating the body of a saint somehow sanctioned, but the finder was actually doing God's work, as the loser must somehow no longer be good enough to house the saint that it had been unable to keep. St. Martin is the patron saint of Tours. He died in Candes near Tours, but his followers had no intention of leaving him there. They took him from that town's church and transported him down the Loire River. To commemorate the event, a painting depicting him being passed through a window was commissioned.

St. Benedict, a highly regarded saint in Italy, was stolen from Montecassino in that country and brought to Fleury in France. The theft was regarded as a "pious theft" and not a sin.

From the earliest years of Christianity, when Rome and Constantinople engaged in confiscating important relics, to more than a thousand years later, items not offered for gift or sale were regularly stolen. Churches and kings competed to build collections and drove up both prices and the risks necessary to obtain suitable items. Relic forgery, relic theft, and relic selling were all by-products of this sacred industry. The abbey at Reading had 242 sacred items, including the Lord's shoe, his swaddling clothes, blood and water from his side, the bread from the feeding of the multitudes and the Last Supper, the Blessed Virgin's hair, her bed, and her belt. The archbishop of Mainz had nine thousand items, including whole bodies of saints, a bone from Isaac, manna from the wilderness, a piece of the Burning Bush, a stone that was used to kill Stephen, the first martyr, and a jar of wine from the wedding of Cana. It was still filled with wine. The Cathedral at Aachen has the loincloth worn by Jesus on the Cross, his swaddling clothes, part of the sponge used to wipe him, a shroud of the Blessed Virgin Mary, the arm of St. Simeon, and relics of St. Anne, the grandmother of Jesus. The Cathedral at Trier has the seamless coat of Jesus, a piece of the True Cross, a thorn from the Crown of Thorns, a nail of the Crucifixion, and the head of St. Andrew. The list of relics at the Vatican runs several pages. Not all of the church's religious articles are strictly for the faithful. The Cathedral of Our Lady of the Pillar in Saragossa, Spain, has a crown made of twenty-five pounds of gold and loaded with diamonds. In the same cathedral are six other crowns made of gold, diamonds, and emeralds as well as 365 mantles embroidered with gold and roses of diamonds. There are six chains of gold set with diamonds. There is a five-foot silver statue set with precious stones and a diamond-studded golden crown.

The race to visit such sites and even go on multicountry pilgrimages spawned the early tourism industry. Thousands entered Rome every day. Business and trade fairs were organized around the dates certain relics would be displayed. Inns and taverns were built to accommodate the traffic. It is said that in one day in 1496, 140,000 passed through the Cathedral at Aachen to view the sacred relics and leave a gift. Tourists then, as today, were accommodated in their need to bring home a souvenir, or worse, considered targets to be fleeced. While some relics could not be bought to bring home because of prohibitive prices, religious pilgrims themselves were free to bring home what they could. Dirt and stones from the road that Jesus or the saints walked, water from the Sea of Galilee or the Jordan River, would serve the purpose.

The value of possessing relics remains a powerful influence today. In a personal sense relics can bring the owner closer to patron saints and to God. In a larger sense artifacts such as the Shroud of Turin have forced the scientific community to seriously debate the Resurrection of Jesus Christ.

1

THE ENIGMA OF THE HOLY SHROUD

The Shroud of Turin is the holiest object in Christendom. To those who believe, it is proof not only of Jesus the man, but it is also evidence of the Resurrection, the central dogma for hundreds of millions of the faithful. Regarded as the winding sheet, the burial cloth of Jesus, it is revered by many, and on the rare instances when it is displayed, the lines to view the Shroud go on for hours.

The Shroud measures fourteen feet three inches long and three feet seven inches wide. It depicts the full image of a six-foot-tall man with the visible consequences of a savage beating and cruel death on the cross, in other words, crucifixion. Belief in the authenticity of the Shroud is not universal. To critics it is a medieval production, created either by paint or by a more remarkable process not to be duplicated until photography was invented in the nineteenth century. Nevertheless, a fake.

Despite the debate about the Shroud's authenticity, it has been described as "one of the most perplexing enigmas of modern time." This enigma has been the subject of study by an army of chemists, physicists, pathologists, biblical scholars, and art historians. Experts on textiles, photography, medicine, and forensic science have all weighed in with an opinion.[1] Had the image on the burial cloth been that of Charlemagne or Napoleon, the debate might have proceeded along scientific lines. But the image is that of the crucified Jesus, so to some it means that the religious biases of each scientist and expert are grounds for suspicion. To others the stakes are even higher. The reality of Jesus and the Resurrection may either be confirmed or challenged by an ancient linen cloth.

Officially, the Catholic Church is neutral and, while guarding the Shroud from overzealous poking and prodding, has made it available on occasion for study. Recently this study has come to include carbon 14 dating. The results of this caused quite a stir in the months preceding the most recent exhibitions, as that process declared the Shroud itself to date to the same time it appeared in France. For some the jubilee celebration was a bit chilled because of the controversy of the latest test. For others science simply didn't matter. Crowds waited for hours to get a chance to view the image of Christ on his burial sheet. Scientists retreated and regrouped for a battle that was not decided by that last test.

The Shroud had passed other challenges before carbon 14 dating came along.

For centuries, the Shroud had been the property of the House of Savoy, who treated it as a most sacred object and stored it in the Chapel of the Holy Shroud in the Cathedral of St. John the Baptist in Turin. While some had regarded it as a painting, just one of many depictions of the crucified Jesus, others regarded it as being the true cloth that was used to prepare Jesus for burial. It was not until 1898 that science would enter the mix in the form of the photographer Secondo Pia.

Pia had been given permission to photograph the Shroud twice, once in daylight. The Shroud itself is on a very thin material, although a backing had been sewn onto it to protect it from handling. When one is thirty inches away from the cloth, the image of the man depicted is visible. As one gets closer, the image is hard to see.

Photography in Pia's time was still in its early stages of development. He set up his boxlike camera in front of the altar. He had no automatic focus or guide to shutter speed, and worse he was given a short time to take his photographs. He took two photographs, one with a fourteen-minute exposure, the other lasting twenty minutes. Then he rushed back to his darkroom to develop the images.

The results were unbelievable. Through the relatively new art of photography, he showed that the Shroud was not a painting, as critics had branded it much earlier, but a negative image. It was a photographic image of Jesus created long before photography and the negative process were invented. Light and dark shadings provided depth to the image. Pia was at first relieved that his pictures were developing, then he was astonished by the image. He had no question that he was among the first to see a likeness of Jesus Christ, hidden to the rest of the world for nearly two thousand years.

The results of Pia's images would change the way the world viewed the

Shroud. It now showed an image that could be studied to see the real Jesus, as no one had for two thousand years.

For such an important relic, the key to declaring its authenticity rests in the available science and in the provenance. As in the art world, a broken provenance, or chain of ownership, is a reason to be suspicious. Police use a near-similar term, chain of custody, to keep track of evidence. The authenticity of the Shroud rests in passing the available testing methods and in proving to have a point of origin that dates to the first century.

The Travels of the Holy Shroud

The Gospels are invaluable in providing an eyewitness account to the Crucifixion. Jesus was taken by the Romans from the Garden of Gethsemane. In rapid succession he was arrested, interrogated by Pilate, condemned to death, scourged, and delivered to be crucified. After his Crucifixion he was placed in a tomb secured by Joseph of Arimathea.

When the women returned to possibly administer to the body of Jesus on Sunday, it was no longer in the tomb. Jesus had been resurrected from the dead, the premise of the new religion that would soon develop. The winding clothes were left behind.

John describes St. Peter and "the other disciple whom Jesus loved" heading toward the tomb.[2] The other disciple is most likely John, the author of that Gospel, who may have felt it was modest not to name himself. The "other disciple did outrun Peter" and was first into the chamber. He noticed "the linen cloths lying" and mentioned them three times. Luke, too, mentions "the linen cloths laid by themselves."[3] Neither recorded anything further about the linen cloth.

Early Gospel writers discussing the low point and the high point of the story of the life of Jesus may be forgiven for an imperfect accounting of his personal inventory, however, the lack of a record becomes problematic. Until recently, there is almost no mention until the fourteenth century of the winding clothes of Jesus or the imprint his body made in the cloth.

It was the author Ian Wilson who provided a great deal of evidence that filled in the gaps in provenance.

During the short ministry of Jesus, a king in the city of Edessa heard of his powers of healing. This King Abgar wrote a letter to Jesus requesting that Jesus travel to Edessa to cure the king. Jesus wrote back basically telling the king he had too much on his agenda at the time but would send an apostle. These letters are remarkable in themselves, as despite Jesus' education, nowhere in the Gospels is there a record of Jesus writing. While the Roman Catholic Church has not put emphasis on the Abgar story, both the story, the letters, and the subsequent travel of Addai or Thaddeus to Abgar is recorded. Eusebius, one of the church's first historians whose works survived, discusses Abgar in detail. He calls him "the monarch of the peoples in Mesopotamia" and claims that all records of the Jesus-Abgar correspondence were in the records office of Edessa.[4]

Today the Syriac Christian Church commemorates the correspondence in its Lenten liturgy.[5]

Edessa was not a backwater province, and its modern name, Sanliurfa, meaning Glorious Urfa, is not exaggerated, considering its history. Some believe the Garden of Eden was nearby. When the Seleucid rule followed the conquests of the Greek Alexander the Great, Urfa became Edessa. It would keep that name for the next two thousand years until the Ottoman Empire was formed.

In the century when Jesus lived it was a cultural crossroads where Persian and Indian thought met with the Western ideals of Rome and Greece. It became a crucible of strange heresies and exotic gnostic doctrine.

It was into this world that an apostle—not of the original twelve but of the wider circle of seventy—traveled, bringing his ability to cure without herbs and a remarkable gift. It is an image of Jesus, an acheiropoietoe, that is to say, an image made not by human hands. King Abgar V was suffering from an unknown disease, possibly gout or leprosy. Eusebius called it "a terrible physical disorder which no human power could heal." Since he is also known as Abgar Ukkama, meaning Abgar the Black, many believe it was some form of skin disease. Upon receiving his visit and gift he was presumably cured. He did have one problem, however, with the sacred object. World religion was in a state of turmoil, and the Middle East, then as now, was a friction point where politics and religion made a combustible combination. Jews regarded a burial cloth as unclean. Not only was it not an object of reverence, but it also was not to be handled period. Romans would regard an object of the charismatic rebel Jesus who challenged the authority of Rome as something to be destroyed. Pagans of Asia Minor, of which Edessa was part, regarded a portrait or depiction of a person, dead or alive, as bad magic. Again, it was something that needed to be destroyed. Abgar's decision to hide his prize in the walls of the city was a wise one. His successor was his rebellious son Ma'nu VI, who was threatened by the new Christianity. He would go on an anti-Christian rampage that included destroying any religious article.

Edessa would find its way back to Christianity when Abgar VIII took the throne in A.D. 177. He would mint a coin with his portrait on one side and the emperor of Rome's portrait on the other side. Since Emperor Commodus had married a Christian, he was not averse to the new religion. The coin is also remarkable as the first coin to depict a Christian symbol, a cross on Abgar's crown. When a new and less tolerant emperor took over for Commodus, succeeding coins were minted without the symbol.

The image of Jesus on the Shroud is not mentioned again until May of 544, when the Persians led by King Chosroes I Anushirvan attack Edessa. The Persian Army erected a huge rampart against the wall of the city. But the defending Edessans tunneled under their city wall, or perhaps through an existing secret passage, to set fire to the siege machine. With the rampart ablaze, the image was rushed out of the tunnel and splashed with water. The rampart burned, and Edessa survived the onslaught.

Sometime after Edessa's victory the *Acts of Thaddaeus* records the gift of the cloth, which is referred to as a tetradiplon, that is, folded into four. This may be the first time that the size of the cloth is determined. It distinguishes the Shroud from a burial napkin, or the handkerchief-size Veil of Veronica.

While the survival of Edessa itself is not critical to the Shroud's provenance, it is important to note that around the time of the Shroud's reappearance, the depictions of Jesus had changed. Byzantine art, which has done much to preserve the representations of Christian figures, had usually portrayed Jesus as being beardless. This was more common to Greeks and Greek gods but was not typical of Jewish men. After the emergence of the Shroud in the sixth century, Byzantine art took a dramatic turn and began picturing Jesus as the Shroud did, that is, full bearded and longhaired. Enigmatically a V at the bridge of the nose became almost universal in Byzantine paintings depicting Jesus and is mirrored on the Shroud.

Edessa managed to defend itself against the Persians, and it was claimed that the Shroud had protected the city. True or not, the Shroud was now known to the world and did make an impact. While many writers on the Shroud disparage the gaps in ownership, at least a handful of writers would record Edessa's sacred image. These include a French bishop, Aroulf, and St. John Damascene, who would both refer to the burial cloth in seventh- and eighth-century writings, respectively. The greatest impact, however, was in the art world. The Shroud served as such an inspiration that soon there was a flood of new art depicting Jesus in this new way. The sheer number of new paintings was so immense that later there would be a backlash against such art. In 726 Emperor Leo III banned the worship of images, and the painters of such icons were regarded as greedy swindlers. No doubt this was a reaction to paintings being fraudulently passed off as the real thing. Despite this, the Shroud itself was still highly regarded and revered. Leo, the lector of Constantinople, recorded his 787 visit to Edessa and seeing "the holy image made without hands."[6]

Edessa did not manage to hold onto the Shroud forever. When the rising Islamic threat became a reality, the city was soon invaded. Negotiations with the Arab conquerors allowed for the image to receive a new home, in the eastern capital of Christianity, Constantinople. The basilica of St. Mary of the Blachernae in Constantinople received the Shroud on the feast day of the Blessed Virgin, August 15, 944. In 1157 an Icelandic abbott, Nicholas Soemundarson, writing in his native Old Norse language, lists the relic among many he had been privileged to see in his travels to Constantinople, specifically citing it as "shroud with the blood and body of Christ on it."[7]

After the armies of Islam took control of Christianity's holiest city, a series of Crusades were launched to recover Jerusalem. On their way to Jerusalem, the Crusaders sacked the Christian city of Constantinople, which fell victim to their three-day rampage, which spared none in an orgy of pillage, looting, and rape. Anything that could be carried was plundered, anything that could not be taken was destroyed. The Historian Niketas Choniates who served as an eyewitness said, "Even the Saracens would have been more merciful." Steven Runciman, writing in the third volume of the *History of the Crusades,* said, "The sack of Constantinople is unparalleled in history."

In 1204 nine centuries of collecting works of religious artisans, relics of saints, and art objects, and of building libraries replete with volumes of history and science came to a disastrous end in a matter of days. Mobs rushed through wealthy homes and stately buildings, sparing neither libraries nor churches.[8]

Robert di Clari, a knight from Picardy, had arrived in Constantinople a year before the massacre. He would remark, "Neither Greek nor Frenchman knew what became of this Shroud when the city was taken."[9] Wealthy citizens were tortured to reveal the locations of their treasures, and after their rampage thousands of soldiers were ordered to turn over their loot to the Frankish nobles.

The Shroud had truly disappeared from history and would not emerge again for nearly 150 years. There is more than one theory of where the Shroud was in that missing century and a half. The author Ian Wilson[10] believes it was taken by Hugh de Lille de Charpigny and held by his family and heirs. Geoffrey de Charny was one of those heirs, and he and his wife, Jeanne de Vergy, are the next documented owners. Here, in France, it existed either to be protected, or even to provide protection to the Cathars, who were under siege by the Roman Catholic Church.

During that time there are hints that the Shroud became more known in Western Europe. Gervase of Tilbury mentions the crucified Jesus leaving an imprint of his entire body on a sheet of white linen. A few years later in the Holy Sepulchre Chapel of Winchester Cathedral, a fresco depicts a man with a large shroud meant to cover the full length of the body. Grail literature, too, recalls the story of the Holy Grail and the preservation of the blood of Jesus.

In 1353 Geoffrey and his wife showed the Shroud to the dean of a proposed abbey at Lirey in France, where they wished the image to be housed. The abbey would be built for that purpose. Geoffrey would die in the act of protecting his king from a lance at the battle of Poitiers. The year after his death, his widow, Jeanne, in reduced circumstances made the decision to display the Shroud.

At the time churches rivaled one another for attendance, and such an important item would bring Lirey both pilgrims and pledges of money from the faithful. Bishop Henri of nearby Troyes had his own church to protect. His church owned the body of St. Helen, which by comparison would be eclipsed by such an object of veneration as the Shroud. He launched an investigation. Allegedly he heard the confession of a man who painted the image. While the bishop ordered the display ended, the Charny family ally, Pope Clement VII, not only allowed the display but also ordered the bishop to silence.

A generation later a new bishop of Troyes, Pierre D'Arcis, called for the end to the image's exhibitions, claiming the motive was profit not piety. Again, Charny connections won the day. The attack on the Charny family by the rival bishops of Troyes may be chalked up to jealousy, but one point was made that is used by modern critics of the Shroud. The Charny family had steadfastly refused to answer the question on just how they came to own such a relic.

There may have been good reason. Barely sixty years had passed since another Geoffrey de Charnay, note the spelling variance, was burned at the stake. This Geoffrey was the precept of the Knights Templar in Normandy and possibly the second-highest-ranking survivor of a vicious attack on the sacred order. Along with Geoffrey was Jacques de Molay, the grandmaster of the Order. It is said that as the two men burned, de Molay had cursed both the French king and the current pope, who had betrayed the order. Neither, he said, would live a year. Neither did.

The story of the Knights Templar begins in 1118 when nine French nobles pledged themselves to guard the highways surrounding Jerusalem, to make them safe for pilgrims. Two hundred years later they were a most powerful organization, second only to the church itself. Having lost Jerusalem while amassing great wealth, the Knights Templar made many enemies, such as the king of France. He would create evidence of heresy to destroy the order. The Templars were the subject of mass arrests, cruel tortures, induced confessions, and finally for many, execution. They were ordered to disband.

Though the Knights Templar had been officially disbanded by both church and state, in their place rose other elite orders. Geoffrey himself, born too late to have been a Templar knight, was a member of a small elite Order of the Star, which like the Templars was a religious military order.

Heirs of Geoffrey may have deemed it wise to wait the half century before revealing their sacred treasure. In fact, during the trials of the Templars and the cruel tortures of medieval investigators, many knights confessed to "worshipping" a bearded head. Ian Wilson believes it is more than coincidence and points to a Shroud-like depiction at Templescombe in England as evidence that the Shroud and the bearded head were the same. He believes the Templars had come into possession of the image in 1204 and retained ownership until de Charnay became the guardian of the image. The dropping of the vowel in the name is typical of medieval spelling.

The last of the de Charnys was Margaret, who would give the Shroud to the wife of Louis I, the duke of Savoy. While the church forbids the sale of relics, the House of Savoy reciprocated the gift with their gift of two estates, complete with a castle and ongoing revenues.

What is less well known is that the Savoy family and the family of de Charny and de Vergy are related. It was Ian Wilson who had speculated that Charny and Charnay were the same. He was proved correct in 1987 when Noel Currer-Briggs, a genealogist and a member of the British Society for the Turin Shroud, proved that the Geoffrey of Lirey was the nephew of the Geoffrey who was burned at the stake. Currer-Briggs, who has worked for *Debretts* and *Burke's Peerage,* the two most distinguished journals in the world of heraldry and genealogy, would also show that the younger Geoffrey had a second cousin who had been a Templar grandmaster. Geoffrey and Jeanne de Vergy both had grandfathers who were seneschals of Champagne and Burgundy. It was the seneschels who were given secret orders by the king of France to arrest the Templars on Friday, October 13, 1307. An early tip-off may have allowed the commander of the Paris Temple, Gerard de Villiers, to escape with the treasure of that temple just ahead of the king's men.[11]

The Shroud became better known under the control of the Savoy dynasty, and in 1464 Pope Sixtus IV believed it was the authentic burial cloth of Jesus. While the Savoy family traveled extensively with the Shroud, in 1502 it was given a permanent home. The dukes built a special chapel at Chambery to house their relic.

It was here that on December 4, 1532, a fire broke out in the Sainte-Chapelle at Chambery. The Shroud was protected in a grill that required four locks to be opened. The problem was that four separate men held those keys. The fire was so hot that silver, which does not melt until 900 degrees Celsius melted on the folded cloth and burned through the folds. The fire was doused with water but not before doing irreparable damage to the cloth. The image itself survived almost untouched, though the cloth bears the scar of this fire. A little over one year later repairs would be done by sisters of the Poor Clares convent. The Shroud was stretched out and sewn onto a holland cloth. Patches were applied to the damaged areas. After the repairs the Shroud was then exhibited in several cities. The family of Savoy moved their capital to Turin, and soon the Shroud would be housed in that city. It would remain there until modern times.

Fairly regularly the Shroud was displayed both for the public and often for private audiences with holy men and European royalty. After the defeat of Napoleon it was hung out over a balcony in celebration.

In addition to being regularly exhibited, it was also subjected to more than one alteration. In 1868 it is known that Princess Clotilde of Savoy would change the lining of the Shroud, replacing it with crimson taffeta.

In September 1939, following the outbreak of war, the Shroud was removed from Turin and brought south to the Benedictine Abbey of Montevergine. Only the vicar general, a prior, and two monks were told just what treasure they were holding. In October 1946 the monks were shown the Shroud, and it was returned to Turin.

Months before, the people of Italy had voted for an elected government, and the king who was the owner of the Shroud was no longer a king. Umberto II lived until 1983, and in his will he officially made the Vatican the owner of the image.

The Science

From the day in 1898 when Secondo Pia took his photographs, the Shroud became subject to a massive number of tests, debate, and more tests. The man depicted on the Shroud, according to Dr. Robert Bucklin, the deputy coroner and a forensic pathologist of Las Vegas County, is described as being five foot eleven inches tall and weighing 178 pounds.[12] Height is something that forensic scientists can determine with very little trouble and a high degree of accuracy. There are 206 bones present in the human body. Provide a femur, a tibia, or a fibula, and with a simple calculation the scientist has the full height. The sex of a person, as well as the race, can also be determined by the bones.[13] The man on the Shroud was above the average height and weight of most men at the time and place in history. The Harvard professor Carleton Coon stated, "He is of a physical type found in modern times among Sephardic Jews and noble Arabs."[14] Archaeologists who studied skeletons of the area have established that the average build of a Semite male at the time of Jesus was five foot one inch and the average weight was 110 pounds.[15]

The combination of the then new art of photography and forensic science would also help scientists learn more about their subject. Dr. Bucklin, whose career has been spent mostly in California and Nevada as a medical examiner, and who is now an active expert witness in many modern murder cases, would determine the cause of death of the man wrapped in the Shroud. He had lesions on the head, including numerous puncture wounds, swelling over one cheek, most likely a black eye, a wound in the left wrist, and swelling of both shoulders.[16] The actual cause of death may have been the severe scourging. The final blade wound did produce both blood and water, as one Gospel recalls. It is the effect of both the lung and heart area being punctured.

The early photographs convinced many that the man on the Shroud had been crucified, and this conviction would only grow as science improved.

Future photographers would have their chance. In 1931 Giuseppe Enrico, chosen by Victor Emmanuel III of Savoy, the king of his country and the owner of the Shroud, would be allowed to work without the glass covering the cloth and to take advantage of the newer developments in photography. In 1969 the first color photographs were taken, and more recently even X-radiographs (images created using short-wave radiation) and high-quality color photographs were taken, allowing life-size transparencies to be made. All would be valuable tools in further research, although it was the first photographs, by Pia, that were the most instrumental in creating new interest for the Shroud.

Soon after the photographs were published, Yves Delage, a professor of anatomy at the Sorbonne who reviewed the photographs in detail, declared he was convinced that the man on the Shroud was Jesus. He presented his findings in a professional paper and pointed out that he was an agnostic. His paper met with the derision and outrage that greeted many scientists as most regarded the Shroud as a fake. Despite his credentials, he was ordered to rewrite his paper and limit it only to actual science. But he became a believer, and over the years the Shroud would claim other believers as well.

After the early photographs became more widely known, Pierre Barbet, a French doctor, traveled to Turin to see the 1933 exposition. On the final day, the Shroud was taken outside the cathedral and could be viewed in sunlight. Barbet was able to view the cloth from less than three feet away and was moved by the visible difference in color that the blood made. After his own lengthy investigation he went on to write *A Doctor at Cavalry*, detailing his findings. Medical examination now had more evidence than before to discuss the Crucifixion. Up until the most recent times, the nail wounds in the hands of Jesus were depicted as having pierced his palms. Yet the palms alone could not support the weight of the body; the nails would have simply ripped through the hands. The Shroud, however, depicted the nail wound on the left wrist. (The right wrist is covered by the left and so cannot be seen.) In the wrists is an area called "the space of Destot," an opening not known about by anatomists until the nineteenth century. This opening through the bones was apparently known to the Roman executioners.

Barbet's experiments with fresh corpses proved that a hole in the palm could hold 100 pounds. A hole in the wrist through tightly packed carpal muscle could hold 240 pounds.

A nail driven through this space would sever the median nerve and pull the thumbs tightly to the hand. This too is shown on the Shroud, where the thumb of the left hand is not shown at all. This is considered evidence that the Shroud is not a medieval creation, as such anatomy would not have been common knowledge, if it were known at all in that period.

The collection of evidence by medical and forensic experts would all weigh in on the side of declaring the Shroud authentic. In addition to the nail wounds there are three sets of major wounds, those made from the Crown of Thorns, the brutal scourging, and what may have been the final death blow made by the lance. Commentary on the blood flow from the various wounds indicates that a forger would need to have done a great deal of research in blood flow. While Dr. Barbet had the advantage of studying cadavers, it would be unlikely that an artist would be presented with such an opportunity.

Crucifixion was a common practice during Roman times. Capital punishment was common, and crucifixion is its cruelest form. The slave revolt of Spartacus ended with six thousand crucifixions. While putting down the rebellion in Jerusalem in A.D. 70 Titus crucified five hundred Jews daily. When an individual was targeted for death by crucifixion, he would first be subjected to flogging. Hebraic law limited the number of lashes to thirty-nine. Roman law dictated a slave could receive a maximum of forty lashes. While flogging on English ships in the eighteenth and nineteenth centuries could see men die of 40 lashes, the man on the Shroud would suffer 120 lashes. Surviving such a beating would have certainly left him in poor shape to carry the hundred-pound crossbeam of the Cross through the city streets up to the place of execution. Testimony of Gospel writers regarding a man being ordered to help, as well as knee bruises evident on the legs of the man on the Shroud, concur that the Cross was carried with great difficulty.

Just how the image came to be on the linen cloth was for years the greatest source of debate. The world of religious artifacts is rife with forgery and fakes, and many dismissed the Shroud as one more man-made creation. Many scientists had a built-in prejudice that the Shroud was simply a painted cloth.

Between 1976 and 1977 a handful of scientists began corresponding about the Shroud. In March 1977 they would participate in the U.S. Conference of Research on the Holy Shroud. Many who attended would come together in the next year to create a Shroud of Turin Research Project, more commonly known as STURP. Others left the conference to create the BSTS, the British Society for the Turin Shroud. Over several years it would be STURP that took the lead in requesting and performing numerous tests on the Shroud, while attempting to stay objective about both religion and politics. Because the majority of STURP members were Christians, they would be considered to have a built-in bias, although even critics admitted "we could not ignore the sterling work of STURP and other scientists."[17]

One of the early tests was to determine where the Shroud had been. Dr. Max Frei of Switzerland had taught microscopic techniques at the University of Zurich and set up a crime lab for police. In 1973 he was given permission to take samples. He took sticky tape and lifted residue from the Shroud's frontal end. His twelve samples yielded nearly fifty different types of pollen. From this he determined that the pollen on the Shroud was consistent with that of an object exposed to the air in Palestine, Turkey, and France. Every grain of pollen has a very hard outer shell that can survive for tens of thousands of years. This shell, called the exine, can attach itself to a suspect's clothing, and detecting the presence of various exines is a method used to provide evidence for or against a suspect being in a certain location. While Frei had traveled to these various areas to collect pollen at different times of the year, not everyone agreed with his conclusions, which were published in 1976. Those who agreed with Frei's conclusions would admit that pollen alone could not provide firm evidence of just where the Shroud had been, but it would take an inventive forger to even think of gathering such pollen.[18] Those who disagreed pointed to evidence that the Shroud in numerous exhibitions was touched, kissed, and handled by many whom had come from all over to view the object.

While such corruption of evidence would make a modern crime scene investigator cringe, there was worse news. The Shroud was actually vacuumed to remove dust particles after Frei's test. Some of the minute particles removed turned out to be paint, which led to serious debate. Though it would later be proven without a doubt that the Shroud was not painted, the evidence of these paint particles had to be accounted for. It was discovered that religious painters would travel to Turin to touch their artwork to the Shroud. Since the Shroud itself is a first-class relic, this immediately raised the status of the new painting to a third-class relic. An example is found in the Royal Monastery of Guadeloupe near Toledo, Spain. Here is preserved a copy of the Shroud with an inscription stating it was "laid upon" the Shroud of Turin.[19] STURP exhaustively covered the paint controversy, and the majority of scientists working on the project team concluded that while a substance found in paint may have touched the

Shroud, it did so well after the original impression on the Shroud was made.

In 1978 scientists put in over 100,000 hours of time and spent over $5 million examining the Shroud. They performed tests using infrared light and ultraviolet light. They examined the results of X-rays. They put the Shroud cloth under a microscope and in all were not able to find any evidence of artificial means of coloration.

Nevertheless there was still at least one debunker, Dr. Walter McCrone, who said the winding sheet had been painted. Numerous materials had collected on the Shroud over the years. In addition to pollen and black and red paint particles, it held insect parts, wool, wax, silk, and even modern synthetic fibers, which may have been from the vestments of priests. The chemists John Heller, of the New England Institute of Medicine, and Alan Adler, of the University of Western Connecticut, were among the first to conclude that the image "was not caused by applied pigment or any other foreign substance."[20] In an exhaustive series of chemical tests no sign of any medium that an artist could have used was found. Visible light examination, X-ray fluorescence, and microchemical studies all pointed to the conclusion that while iron oxide was present, it was not used to create or enhance the image. It was simply part of the accumulated material that had been acquired by the cloth.

McCrone would not give up, however. He insisted the Shroud was a painting, and despite being at odds with the many scientists who had studied the image, he had a formidable reputation. When Yale University bought what came to be known as the Vinland Map, it was McCrone they hired to review its authenticity. The importance of the map went beyond the map itself. If it was real, then the Vikings had reached North America, as the map depicted their early knowledge of the North American Atlantic Coast. If it was a fake, the prevailing thought that no Europeans had been to America before Columbus would remain intact.

He told the university they had been taken, bluntly declaring that the map being authentic was as likely as "that of Admiral Nelson's battleship at Trafalgar being a Hovercraft."[21] His reason was based on what he said was a significant amount of titanium anatase in the ink, which was not in use until after 1920.

Regarding the Shroud, he claimed the particles of iron oxide and cinnabar were evidence of a base to make paint. What he called paint, Drs. Adler and Heller demonstrated was blood. The scientists discovered serum, blood clots, blood protein, and hemoglobins. Finding a high concentration of bilirubin, Adler, whose specialty was blood chemistry, determined it was the blood of someone who had died under great stress or trauma. Despite the scientific evidence, Heller and Adler were young and McCrone was the old master. In a showdown Heller asked McCrone how he knew the red dots to be iron oxide. "Experience" was McCrone's answer. Heller asked, "Did you test them chemically?" The answer was "I don't have to: experience." [22]

When confronted with the X-ray analysis that proved otherwise, McCrone simply said it was wrong. Many would regard McCrone's speculations as impossible, but his reputation plagued STURP, as it was hard to put the paint issue to bed. Regarding the Vinland Map, Dr. Thomas Cahill would later show that the amount of titanium present occurred naturally and that the map was no different from 150 other medieval manuscripts he had studied. While McCrone's reasoning for branding the Vinland Map a fake might have been correct, his ability to provide an accurate test was thrown into question. He had determined that the amount of titanium was one thousand times what it would actually prove to be. The unearthing of a Viking farm at L'Anse aux Meadows in Newfoundland would resolve the issue.

The linen of the Shroud too would be tested. It was a linen fiber that had been woven on a loom that was also used for cotton. The cotton was a Middle Eastern variety, and traces of the cotton could be detected under a microscope. The weave was a three-to-one herringbone twill, which is still used today in denim jeans. In its day it was regarded as expensive linen, but this would not be out of line, as it was provided by a wealthy man who had also provided a large tomb for Jesus.[23]

Next, a most remarkable test was then done by the Jet Propulsion Laboratory of Pasadena, California. Dr. John Jackson had earned a Ph.D. in physics while in the navy. His first assignment was in the Albuquerque Weapons Laboratory, where he worked with sophisticated, almost futuristic weapons systems such as laser beam and particle beam weapons. He teamed up with a civilian expert in image enhancement, Don Devan, who was consulting for the air force at the time. To begin to create a three-dimensional picture of the Shroud, they used a densitometer, which measures degrees of darkness and density. After an incredible 750,000 measurements were taken by hand, a digital computer analyzed the data. Dr. Eric Jumper, of the Weapons Lab, wrote a program to sort through their data. Their team grew and soon included members of the Jet Propulsion Laboratory, which is sponsored by NASA. Normally they were responsible for assembling images of moons, planets, and their rings. Computers can be used to remove any irrelevant material, which helps present a final image. After lifting away the damage left by a sixteenth-century fire, they were left not only with a cleaner image but also with a startling deduction. There are no brushstrokes anywhere on the Shroud.

Jumper's conclusion implies that an artist would have had to color each thread prior to weaving the cloth. This is a feat that not only has never actually been performed but is also impossible without a computer.

Their next test employed what is called a VP-8 image analyzer. This is generally used to decipher the "pictures" sent home by space probes. These craft do not employ cameras, instead using a device that picks up light signals. At the Sandia Lab in New Mexico, Dr. Jackson and his colleagues placed a photo of the Shroud in the VP-8. The result: a three-dimensional image as different from the photograph as a statue is from a painting. Their reaction was similar to Secundo Pia's; they were gazing at the face and body of Jesus from two thousand years before.

Evidence for authenticity mounted. Dr. Frei's pollen testing was a positive indicator of authenticity. Dr. Jackson and his colleagues at Sandia provided evidence that the image was not a painting. Next, more detailed testing on the area perceived as blood was done using a microspectrophotometer. This test determined the presence of hemoglobin, indicating that what was perceived as blood actually was blood. From there, the Italian forensic medical expert Professor Pierluigi Baima-Bollone claimed that the blood identified was of the type AB.

There are several different blood types, including the rare type AB.[24] In the general world population AB occurs in 3.2 percent of the population. In Northern Palestine and among "Babylonian Jews" the occurrence of AB is much more common, with 18 percent of the population having that normally rare typing.

Later Marcello Canale, a professor from Genoa's Institute of Legal Medicine, reported that DNA had been extracted from a thread. The blood that was originally thought to be only iron oxide and paint now provided meaningful results for the presence of DNA. Enough DNA was present to be replicated, that is cloned, by using an enzyme that would provide enough characteristics to identify an individual or possibly a relative.

This additional blood evidence continued to favor authenticity.

• • •

The forensic evidence of blood spatter and whip and thorn damage was realistic rather than artistic. The correct placement of the nail holes was equally consistent with the description of the execution of Jesus. The location of the nail in the wrist seemed to preclude a medieval forger. The linen was of both a type and a pattern known to be used during that period of time and was considered to be an expensive weave in comparison to most. The pollen evidence fit with the known history of the Shroud. And excluding the opinion of Dr. McCrone, there was nothing to indicate that the Shroud was not what it was believed to be. Many scientists in fact had felt they had been drawn into an investigation that could only yield a supernatural explanation.

The Carbon Dating Affair

Proving the Shroud to be authentic would suffer a sharp reversal after it was subject to carbon 14 dating. The technique had been available for years, and several STURP scientists and outsiders had suggested it be performed. Finally in 1988 permission was given. To avoid further damage to the Shroud, a sample was taken from a corner that had already been used, back in 1973, to provide a sample. It was argued by STURP that samples be taken from several locations on the Shroud, that a blind test be used, and that the tests should be performed by seven labs. As early as 1981 they gave authorities a list of the labs they wished to be included. One was the Rochester lab of Dr. Harry Gove, who had pioneered the science of carbon dating. Another was New York's Brookhaven Laboratory. The Catholic Church resisted for several reasons.

The reasons for the church's hesitation were based not on an aversion to science but in concerns about the methodology that would be used. For example, in 1985 an Egyptian mummy was tested by the new method of carbon dating, and the findings were off by one thousand years. This was the result not of faulty science but of a faulty protocol. It would not be until 1987 that Cardinal Ballestrero of Turin gave his permission. At the last minute, however, Professor Luigi Gonella, the cardinal's scientific adviser, turned the tables. Cloth from only one part of the Shroud was given, and only three labs were allowed to play a role in testing.

The sample was divided into three, and these parts were sent to the Oxford Research Laboratory, in England, to the University of Arizona, in Tucson, and to the Institute of Technology, in Zurich. The Zurich lab is where the mummy error had occurred.

The results would disappoint many. All three labs had dated the cloth as originating between 1260 and 1390, a date that would fit perfectly with the Shroud's emergence in Lirey, France. Despite the varied strong evidence that indicated the Shroud to be authentic, the carbon dating appeared to be the critical issue. The media cried hoax. The American media singularly pointed out that carbon dating proved the Shroud was a medieval forgery. Dr. McCrone, whose conclusions and comments were at odds with the scientists of STURP, was sought after for interviews by the press. The anti-Shroud camp was as zealous in debunking the Shroud as they claimed the pro-Shroud crowd was in attempting to authenticate the image. One went so far as to call anyone not convinced that the Shroud was a fake a Flat-Earther.

The media spin threw out three decades of research by dozens of experts in an instant. Many of the scientists, however, dissented from the carbon 14 date, claiming the cloth had been handled wrong, tested in a manner inconsistent with even STURP's guidelines, and the labs involved had never even used a blind test to check their accuracy. They made a strong case. The Zurich lab had missed the mummy's age by a thousand years. The Oxford lab dated a painting as 1,200 years old that had been done eleven days before. The agreement of these three labs, however, carried serious weight, despite their past mistakes.

Carbon 14 is a natural product of the atmosphere and is absorbed by all living organisms and can be measured. It is found in plants, which ingest carbon dioxide directly. It is found in animals and in humans as a result of their eating plants. When alive, organisms are constantly ingesting. After the living organism dies, the ingested C 14 decays. It is the rate of decay that is measured in radiocarbon testing.

The method by which the Shroud was tested was done by accelerator mass spectrometry, a relatively new method that was still experimental ten years before the test was done. The test compares the level of C 14 to C 12, which is supposed to be a constant. After the organism dies and the C 14 turns to nitrogen, the ratio of C 14 to C 12 changes. The new ratio, which determines the length of time of decay in the C 14, is what indicates the date. There are problems in the system. One is that shorter and longer cycles of sunspot activity can throw off the test.[25]

Rodney Hoare described just how serious errors in carbon 14 dating can be, even on matters of great import.[26] In 1984 a well-preserved body of an Iron Age man was discovered in Lindow Marsh in Cheshire, England.

Two labs did the testing; one of them was the Oxford lab that had tested the Shroud. The difference between the results of the two labs was a gaping 400 years. It was the Oxford lab that was told it was testing a painting done by an African bushman and dated the artwork to be 1,200 years old. The painting in question was actually done eleven days prior to the test.

Discounting the chance that all three labs could have produced serious errors, there are other factors that could show the carbon dating of the Shroud to be expected to produce inaccurate readings. A paper presented at the August 2000 Worldwide Congress "Sindone 2000" in Orvieto, Italy, says the sample taken contained one of the numerous patches that had been applied over the centuries to repair the damage from fire and dripping molten silver. While there are several documented repairs, the authors Joseph Marino and M. Sue Benford believe that other undocumented repairs had also taken place. The sample is very likely to be part of a patch, and Marino and Benford quote the Italian author Giorgio Tessiore as saying part of the sample had to be discarded because of the presence of color threads. This patch job would have taken place before 1534, when a backing cloth was sewn on to reinforce the damaged Shroud. The authors quote other scientists who not only concur but also point to a nearly 98 percent variation between the sample and the main Shroud cloth.

The chemist Alan Adler was quoted in a *Time* magazine story on the Shroud as saying "the sample used for dating came from an area that is water-stained and scorched, and the edge is back-woven indicating repair."[27]

Scientists soon began to weigh in further evidence. The most dramatic may be the fire that had nearly destroyed the Shroud in 1532. Silver melts at 900 degrees Celsius, so the heat of the molten silver that then poured onto the Shroud exceeded that temperature. Cloth burns at a much lower temperature, and it might be tempting to claim miraculous intervention as the reason the Shroud, a thin linen, survived at all. It had escaped Roman Jerusalem, been stuck in a wall in Edessa where it survived a flood, been rescued from Arab Constantinople at the last minute, survived a fire in Chambery, and even survived a 1997 fire in Turin's Royal Chapel. The latest fire had the firefighter Mario Trematore risking his life to smash open the bulletproof case with a sledgehammer to rescue the sacred object. (This last fire was after carbon dating samples were taken.) Less dramatically, it survived being sewn and unsewn, doused with water, and if one medieval record be true, washed in oil after the 1532 fire. Could any of this—from intense heat to medieval oil—affect the results?

The conclusions of Marino and Benford and others will no doubt be taken seriously. A European-trained American tailor agreed that "it is definitely a patch," pointing out that medieval weavers, not unlike modern weavers, would attempt to match the original cloth.[28]

Another research team, led by Leoncio Garza-Valdes and Stephen Mattingly, believe that microbes skewed the results. Garza-Valdes, a doctor from Mexico, had trained himself in the forensics of Mayan objects. By performing optical microscopy studies on one disputed item, he discovered that millions of "gram-positive bacteria . . . and fungi" had formed a plasticlike coating, which he dubbed bioplastic. This was what the carbon dating have been measuring, not the actual artifact. Because this varnish of biogenic material adheres to objects at a faster or slower rate, depending on exposure, it can cause havoc in the dating process. This varnish was present on the Shroud.

Tests using infrared spectroscopy and mass spectroscopy were done that indicated the linen cloth was not pure cellulose, which is the main property of linen. Instead, by using natron, which is a bleaching element, in cleaning the cloth, microbes were attracted. The cloth was not only patched on more than one occasion, but it was also cleaned more than once. The test then is not on the linen alone but also on the age of the varnish that has built up on the linen. The best results then might be inconclusive.[29]

Creating the Shroud

While scientists review the evidence from two viewpoints, the most important question remains: how then was the Shroud created? The Shroud is consistent with the winding sheet of a man in either a near-death or coma state or according to others an early state of rigor mortis. Several theories have been advanced on just how the image could adhere to the cloth.

The first is that the cloth simply touched the man, and through contact with blood and sweat, the image was then created. This theory can almost be dismissed out of hand, as this type of image would not allow for such an exacting imprint. There would be smears and places where the cloth simply would not touch unless forced. And if the cloth was purposely forced to touch every inch of, for example, the face, areas such as the nose would appear much larger.

A second theory is what scientists call a vaporograph—an image created by the emanation of gases from a still warm body who had suffered a cruel execution. The unique image that the body of Jesus may have created was a result of his own sweat and blood, intermingled with healing agents such as myrrh and aloe that had been used to prepare the body for burial. This conclusion had long been accepted by many. The claim that a gas mixture created the "negative" proved to be consistent with sweat and urea mixed with myrrh and aloe, which would be present on the body of a crucified man that was afterward treated with such substances. However, in a post-STURP survey half of the scientists who would provide their personal opinions believe that while this conclusion appears valid on the surface, even gas diffuses. Diffused gas would produce something akin to the pressed-cloth theory and not be as sharp and distinct as the Shroud's image.

Carbon dating casts doubt on the authenticity of the Shroud by dating it to medieval times. This leads to some creative theories about how the image on the Shroud supposedly was made. If the date was wrong, then the person depicted on the Shroud could not have been Jesus. So several new theories on just how the Shroud was produced went into publication.

Novel Theories

One theory is that the image is a negative produced by an early photographic process. Scientific inventions do not become reality until they are completely developed, but the concept for an invention begins much earlier. From flying machines and electric light to the telephone and the modern camera, multiple stages and a great deal of time separate concept and completion. Artists and creators like Leonardo da Vinci are responsible for proposing items such as flying machines complete with landing gear, armored vehicles with scythes, diving suits with breathing apparatus, and even contact lenses centuries before these ideas became both reality and commonplace. Da Vinci, born in 1452, would serve as his king's painter, sculptor, architect, and hydraulics expert. He would design and build siege weapons, battering rams, rope ladders for assaults on walls, dredging machines floated on pontoons, and hydraulic pumps.

At the same time he produced paintings of great religious significance, including *The Last Supper* and the *Madonna with the Baby Jesus*. Many believe he used an occult symbolism in his art. His *Virgin and Child with St. Anne* is considered to be a "treasure trove of esoterica and occult wonders," and even Dr. Freud detected a vulture lurking in the Virgin's cloth.[30] There is no doubt that science and religion were at odds in his lifetime. What today is regarded as chemical engineering would then have been considered alchemy. Today's genetic scientists would be the nineteenth-century's Dr. Frankenstein and the sixteenth-century's Devil. So the maestro had no way to reconcile his foresight with the suspicious age he lived in.

One can only imagine what he had to do to produce his *Treatise on Anatomy,* complete with much of what is known of the human body and detailed sketches that accurately represent organs, tissue, muscle, and bone.

Lynn Picknett and Clive Prince, the authors of *The Turin Shroud, In Whose Image?,* believe da Vinci used that knowledge together with his advanced work on optics to create a prototype camera. His *Codex Atlanticus* contains a diagram of the early camera, with an artificial eye to let in light, which then can be used to produce an image on white paper or thin white cloth.[31] Capturing the image, however, was much harder. In fact the first images that were considered permanent did not appear until the nineteenth century, when Louis Daguerre showed the development process to be a two-step chemical process. The first step has light striking a sensitive emulsion solution and producing an electrochemical effect on silver halide crystals within the emulsion. The action of the light alters the charge within the silver halide crystal, and a latent image, however invisible, is processed with further solution. The trick is removing the halide before any further exposure. This is done by using a fixing agent, which is another chemical solution. An imperfect fixing agent would not allow the negative to develop correctly. This key element of the process is today solved with proprietary chemicals that were patented and produced by Eastman Kodak. Getting to the point where a negative is evenly cleaned of the image-producing chemicals entailed a long, hit-or-miss process in the development of the camera and the creation of the negative. Picknett and Prince believe that da Vinci had mastered the technique long before Daguerre, although there is no evidence. They believe that da Vinci used at least his own head and the body of another person to make a composite early photograph. But according to medical professionals who viewed the Shroud, the other man would have to be someone who was scourged, crowned with thorns, speared through a lung and the heart, and correctly pierced through the wrist. Would any artist inflict such cruelty on a living person to produce such an effect?

There are other problems with their conclusions. One is that in all his depictions of Jesus, da Vinci painted him beardless. If da Vinci painted the Shroud, then why would he produce a bearded Jesus? A second problem is that the Shroud had been displayed a hundred years before da Vinci was born. The authors claim that the Lirey shroud was a painting, as Bishop Pierre D' Arcis said it was. The "real" Shroud, the da Vinci prototype, would later be a substitution. A third problem is that in their own re-creation, they admit the ingredients necessary to have created the Shroud were not yet available. They hypothesize that it is possible they were available but no record has been made.

Another theory of just who the Shroud depicts was proposed by Christopher Knight and Robert Lomas. They claim that the man on the Shroud is no other than the last grandmaster of the Knights Templar. Though Jacques de Molay was indeed bearded, the remaining evidence appears to be contrived. They claim that the Freemasons do have a Shroud ritual and the carbon 14 dating is in line with de Molay's death. Such a shroud would have been kept at the Paris Temple. Their theory requires the grandmaster to have been crucified, and they admit there is no evidence leading to that conclusion. History records him being burned at the stake on a small island in the Seine River. Knight and Lomas theorize that the Inquisitors would have privately crucified de Molay, as his greatest crime was heresy.

The question of just how de Molay might have left a miraculous impression in the linen is unanswered, as is other scientific evidence.

A third novel theory was proposed by Holgar Kersten and Elmar Gruber in *The Jesus Conspiracy*, which claims that the plan all along was for Jesus to survive his Crucifixion. The Vatican then plotted to have the Turin Shroud declared a fraud, as it is proof Jesus survived his Crucifixion. Billed as an exposé of this Vatican plot, their work concludes that the body of Jesus could have only made the impression by being alive, not dead, at the time the impression was made. They raise interesting points overlooked by other writers, including just why healing agents such as aloe and myrrh were used on a body already dead. They introduce the idea that a death and rebirth ceremony was actually a rite of a select group, and that Lazarus's seeming death and rebirth was a rehearsal.

While the Vatican's role is novel to such a plot (or possibly a plot to a novel), such a scenario has been suggested before *The Jesus Conspiracy*. Hugh Schonfield proposed a similar situation in *The Passover Plot,* in which even

Judas was part of the survive-the-Crucifixion plot. Jesus is arrested, beaten, and nailed to the cross and then somehow expected to survive the torture to be revived in his "tomb." But then the plot goes wrong. The spear of Longinus, thrust into the side of Jesus, pierces both his lungs and heart, and at the moment the plot appears to come to fruition Jesus is killed by the spear.

If one accepts the conclusions of Joseph Marino, Sue Benford, Dr. Garza-Valdes, and Stephen Mattingly that the dating is faulted because of the burns, the patches, and the buildup of bacteria, then the question can be approached again from the basic premise. The man depicted on the Shroud was Jesus, and some phenomena, normal or paranormal, created the image.

Back to Basics

How was the image created? The theories generally espoused include a painting of the image onto the cloth, a contact method (i.e., the cloth touching the body), a vapor-made image, and a "scorch" method.

Painting the cloth was a theory eliminated by scientific testing. While it has been hard to reach a consensus about any topic related to the Shroud, both STURP and the scientists at Los Alamos National Scientific Laboratories in New Mexico agreed that the Shroud had not been painted. The next theory was the contact method. Scientists and researchers believe that the contact method would not allow for an image to include the sides of the nose, the recesses of the eyes, the ribs, and parts of the neck shown on the cloth. The major point is that in any contact method, the back of the cloth would have been more saturated, therefore darker, than the front. Because this is not present on the Shroud, most agree that the contact method too must be eliminated. The vapor-diffusion method too does not hold up for the same reason the contact method fails. There is no way to account for all of the detail and explain why there is no diffusion effect of a rising "gas."

Several scientists put forward the "scorch" theory, which says that the image was caused by low-energy X-rays emitted by the body under the cloth. The explanation for just how and why the body of the man in the Shroud gave off such X-rays is limited, because this phenomenon has not yet been encountered anywhere else.[32] John Heller searched for Egyptian Copt burials and found that in all other cases where such a burial shroud was used, none exhibited an image.

After an estimated 150,000 to 200,000 man-hours spent researching the Shroud, scientists have not reached a conclusion shared by all. In place of a list of theories, the possible explanation indicates either a normal or a paranormal event.

With the normal theories seemingly ruled out, then a paranormal cause of the image on the Shroud becomes a possibility.

Christians believe, and it is the foundation of Christianity, that Jesus did not remain dead on the third day. He was resurrected, miraculously brought back to life. His lifeless body, bearing evidence of being beaten and scourged, nailed to the Cross, and finally pierced by a spear, was laid in a tomb. A large stone sealed the entrance. Then in a moment, the resurrection took place, which is the basis and focal point for the Christian faith.

The Gospels and tradition record a brief earthquake that shook the temple itself.[33] A flash of incandescent light scared away the Roman soldiers guarding the tomb. At the instant when the flash occurred, Jesus was resurrected. Jesus passed through the linen cloth, front and back. From the standpoint of believers, no explanation was required. From the standpoint of a believing scientist, instantaneously the cellulose of the linen degraded to leave a residue of sweat and blood. Only the image, and the residue of blood, remained. The image then is a quasiphotograph of the process of separation of the body through the cloth. This phenomenon, the flash theory, has never been encountered elsewhere.

This is nothing short of proof of the Resurrection.

Of the twenty-six remaining STURP scientists, thirteen have decided that only a paranormal explanation can account for that image appearing on the burial linen. They accept what is now called the "flash" theory.

This explanation is a difficult stance for scientists to take. First, there is no way of proving or disproving it, despite all the scientific knowledge available at this time. A second difficulty for the thirteen scientists who believe the body had to miraculously pass through the cloth, is that they are coming to the same conclusion of the Roman Catholic Church, which could lead to academic ridicule.

The controversy is far from over. In October 2000 the archbishop of Turin closed the last exhibition of the Shroud. In July 2002 the Shroud was quietly taken from the cathedral, and new repairs were started on it. The five-hundred-year-old patches were removed, as was the holland cloth (the cloth sewn onto the back of the Shroud to protect it). Immediately there was criticism, but the archbishop of Turin, Cardinal Severino

Poletto, ensured that everything would be done with the goal of preservation in mind. A full-length image scan was performed, which presumably will be available for additional research in the future. Photographs would document before, after, and the steps along the way. The cloth itself would no longer be folded, as the constant folding over the centuries was taking a toll.

Cardinal Poletto announced that the next exhibition would not take place until the next Holy Year, which is the year 2025.

The challenges too are far from over for both science and the church. Before 2025, it is almost certain that new scientific discoveries will provide new reasons for examination. The research into DNA and cloning presents the most intriguing and controversial possibilities. At this point there is no scientific technique available to clone a person from what can be referred to as the DNA of God. But the blood that remains on the Shroud provided scientists the opportunity to "clone" or replicate that blood. Today the blood can be tested to confirm, as it has, that the person on the Shroud was a man. While DNA advances are welcome to some of the Shroud researchers, there is no doubt that the church would fear that DNA evidence could mount a challenge to the tenets of the faith.

Recently, Cardinal Saldarini, the custodian of the Shroud, was presented with an article on the current ability of DNA technology. His reaction was to call back all samples of the Shroud.

2

THE SACRED FACE: THE VEIL OF VERONICA AND THE SUDARIUM OF OVIEDO

At a press conference in 1999 in Rome, Father Heinrich Pfeiffer, a German Jesuit and a professor of Christian art history, announced that he had found the famed Veil of Veronica in a monastery in Manoppello, Italy. The veil is, according to tradition, the cloth that a woman named Veronica used to wipe the face of Jesus Christ, who was carrying the Cross to Calvary and the Crucifixion. It was news to the world and especially news to the pope, who had thought it was already discovered and safely housed in Rome.

Pfeiffer had not been quick to jump to conclusions and had been conducting studies on the veil for thirteen years before coming forward in a press conference. The tests included several that were conducted on the Shroud of Turin. The dimensions of the cloth measure 6.7 by 9.4 inches. The cloth is so thin that it appears transparent. It is hard to gaze at the veil without admitting that it at least appears to have a paranormal quality. The image, already faint, can disappear completely, depending on just how the light hits the cloth. In medieval times it was considered miraculous that the image appeared and disappeared when light was shone on it from different directions.

The Shroud of Turin, the Veil of Veronica, and a cloth preserved in Oviedo in Spain called the sudarium constitute the three separate linens from the burial of Jesus. The Gospel of John gives the best description of the multiple cloths that were used to wrap the body of Jesus in the tomb. John 20:5 describes himself entering the tomb—"he saw the linen cloths lying." And then Peter saw the same thing: "He saw the linen cloths lying, and the napkin that had been about his head, not lying with the linen cloths, but apart wrapped up into one place."[1] Veronica's veil had most likely never seen the tomb, as it was taken away by her. So we have a third relic of Jesus in linen, the facial cloth known as the sudarium.

It was Jewish custom to clean the face with such a cloth, which is larger than a modern handkerchief. It was customary to remove it after the cleansing, although in the case of disfigurement the cloth might serve to cover the face permanently. John had also described Lazarus as wearing such a burial cloth when he was awakened from the dead.

Independent research indicates that properties of the veil are also shared with the Shroud of Turin. The first and most important study concluded that the veil, like the Shroud, was not a painting. In 1977 Donato Vittorio, a professor of the University of Bari, examined the veil using ultraviolet light and reported that the fibers do not have any type of added pigment. Through a microscope it became evident that the cloth was not painted and that the threads themselves are not colored.

What amazes those who have seen the face on the veil firsthand is that the image of a bruised and scarred man's face is exactly the same on both sides of the paper-thin cloth. No one will yet hazard a guess or provide an explanation of just how the image manages to appear on both sides of the veil. Digital enlargements confirm that the image is indeed identical on both sides; they are exactly the same. Further research shows that the dimensions of the face on the Shroud and the face on the veil are the same.

It also exhibits reddish brown marks that reveal blood on the face of a bearded, long-haired man. The faces are the same shapes, both have shoulder-length hair, and the beards on both the veil and the Shroud match. Skeptical historians claim this face is the exact copy of the Shroud because it was copied from the Shroud, although so far there is no evidence on how the image was created, even if it were simply a copy.

The veil has never received the attention the Shroud has, and until recently there has been no study of the relic. This has not kept the critics silent. To most the story of Veronica is just that, a story, and the veil as a real relic is equally fraudulent. Keith Ward, a professor of divinity at Oxford, claims, "Almost everybody accepts that it is a legend." Others scoff at the "coincidence" that the woman who offered her towel cloth to the suffering Savior had the name Veronica, which translates from Greek into "True Icon" (or image). For this reason there has been little study of the veil. For another reason there may not be much new study in the future. There is little hope that the Vatican would allow the required testing for establishing a date for the veil. Carbon dating the veil, for one, will most likely never be allowed due to the fragile nature of the cloth.

The sudarium too has seen a relatively small amount of research. There is a major difference between the Shroud and the veil and the sudarium. The sudarium is not an image. Like the Shroud, the linen does contain blood and lymph stains. Tests have shown these to be the blood type AB, the same blood type found on the Shroud. Evidence of pulmonary edema fluid is present on the sudarium, and this indicates death from asphyxiation, which is common to crucifixion victims. This corroborates the evidence that both blood and water came from the side of Jesus after he was pierced with the spear. The sudarium has not received as much attention as the Shroud, although there is powerful evidence of its authenticity. Max Frei, the Swiss criminologist who tested the Shroud for pollen, tested the sudarium. He found pollen that was found in Egypt and Spain but that was not found on the Shroud. No pollen from Turkey was found on the sudarium, although it was found on the Shroud. This verifies what is known of the route of the sudarium on the way to its final destination in Spain.

A palynologist from Israel's Antiquities Authority also studied the pollen and added that one match shows a thorn tumbleweed bush (*Gundelia tournefortii*) present. A palynologist is a scientist who examines minute microfossils, especially pollen grains and spores. The work is exacting and is helpful in numerous sciences, including reconstructing climate patterns and gathering data helpful to the petroleum industry. Called *kardi* or *kankar* in Arabic, this thorn tumbleweed is exclusive to the Holy Lands and is mentioned in the Talmud. Arabs, not Jews, use the leaves and stems for culinary purposes. The Romans may have fashioned the Crown of Thorns out of the bush, according to Professor Alan Whanger of Duke University in North Carolina.

In addition to finding this unique pollen on the sudarium, dirt was also discovered on it that contained crystals of travertine argonite. This rare form of calcite discovered by the Hercules Aerospace Lab in Salt Lake City, Utah, is indigenous to Jerusalem. A forger would most likely been unaware of this and thereby unable to reproduce such evidence.

Because the sudarium does not show a face, only a pattern of bloodstains, it does not yield the same type of image as the Shroud and the veil. But the pattern of the stains does conform to the bloodstains on the Shroud. Dr. Whanger, who studied the sudarium and the Shroud, presented a paper in May 1989 at the Shroud Congress in Bologna detailing one hundred points of coincidence between the blood on the Shroud and the sudarium.

The sudarium and the Shroud share such distinct phenomena as the same type of cloth, the AB bloodstains, and the pollen. While the Shroud's carbon dating indicated a medieval origin, the sudarium has an unbroken provenance from at least the seventh century. To some this alone does not constitute proof of the authenticity of either. At the same time, if both were produced by the same forger, it does invalidate the carbon 14 dating.

The Provenance of the Veil

There is agreement that the veil itself has been venerated from medieval times, and possibly earlier. The various tales of the veil do not always agree on the provenance of the cloth. Acknowledgment of its existence begins as early as that of the Shroud.

The tradition of Veronica is mentioned in early church writings. Eusebius wrote of her in Book 7 of *The History of the Church.* The early centuries of Christianity were a time of persecution and turmoil for the church. Writings during that period were purged by both Romans and Christians, often for opposite reasons. Eusebius, who lived between 260 and 340, did the Christian world a great service by compiling this early history, which otherwise, like many of his sources, would have been lost. He had learned and then worked at Caesarea in a school of Christian studies organized by Pamphilus.[2] The school provided Eusebius with a massive library whose texts no longer exist. Eusebius mentions over one hundred books and forty-nine authors that served as his sources. The school would come under attack as Christianity did, and his master, Pamphilus, was arrested and executed. Eusebius too would be arrested and briefly detained, but he survived the ordeal.

Unlike the great Greek writers of his time, his writing style was plodding and cumbersome. His straightforward, undramatic approach lends more credibility to this early historian. He was "by far the most important and reliable historian of the ancient church" according to Guy Schonfield.[3] He was true to his sources and consistent in acknowledging them.

He credits Bishop Dionysus of Alexandria for help on the portion of his work on the Veronica story, although the author visited her home firsthand. He recalls her as a woman who was cured of hemorrhage by the Savior and became such a believer that she erected a statue of him in her home while she was still alive. Eusebius says the home is in Caesarea Philippi, once called Paneas by the Phoenicians and the Greeks.[4] His source named her Bernice and gave the same accounting of her appearance during the brutal walk of Jesus with the Cross to Calvary recounted in Mark.

This naming of the pious woman is important. In the absence of scientific evidence on the veil, the name variation has been an embarrassment that many believe casts doubt on the entire story as well as the object itself.

Berenice, or Bernice, as the name has survived, is a Macedonian version of the name Pherenike. This Greek term means the "carrier of victory," as Phere means "carrier," and Nike, recalling the goddess of victory, simply means "victory." It was not an uncommon name. Bere-Nike was simply the Macedonian pronunciation. It may have simply been an ancient or medieval copyist who made the Latin translation to a more understandable Vera (true) Icona (image) as a clever device or simply a mistake.

Such devices are not unheard of in the Bible. Abrahm, meaning "exalted father," was a leader of his family, or clan, until he assumed the role of leader of the Jewish people. Then his name became Abraham, "father of the multitude." His wife was Sarai, meaning "contentious." After Abraham became the leader of his people she became Sarah, "princess." [5]

Changing the name to reflect the deed would not be the first time such a device was employed in religious texts.

Eusebius is not the only record of Veronica's act of kindness to Jesus. This story is told in the Acts of Pilate. It is an apocryphal text and relates how a compassionate woman was rewarded with the image of his face on the cloth. As mentioned in the first chapter, the Crucifixion was a cruel ordeal, often limited to enemies of the state. The savage beating of 120 lashes of the whip could easily kill a man. The forensic evidence of the Gospel story in which the Scourging is recounted also mentions that blood and water came from the wound made with the spear. This is an important indication of the state of Jesus after this beating. The "water" is fluid that begins to fill the lungs (or lung) as a result of a severe physical trauma. Such a condition may have meant his breathing was already hindered as Jesus began his walk up to Cavalry. The damage done by the beating was exacerbated by the Crown of Thorns. Blood was already streaming from the wounds on his head, obscuring his vision.

As a taller-than-average man, and possibly with a stronger constitution from working as a carpenter, Jesus may have started with a robust constitution, but he soon faltered. Shortly after being forced to carry the Cross, he fell to his knees. Urged on by beatings and shouts, he then encountered his mother, possibly adding to the distress. He stopped and may have been unable to continue, a situation remedied by the Roman soldiers enlisting the aid of a certain Simon of Cyrene, who helped to bear the weight. Even without the Cross Jesus staggered, and blood from his head covered his face. It was at this point that a woman pushed through the crowd and offered her handkerchief to Jesus to wipe his face.

The person who performed this act of kindness would later bring the evidence of the miracle to Rome. The Acts of Pilate was written in three parts, and the first two are redundant with Luke's Gospel. The third part may have been added later. It is certain that the text was not authored by Pilate, and while it is often also referred to as the Gospel of Nicodemus, he too is not considered the author. Since Eusebius was acquainted with the story, although not this particular text, and he seems to have had access to much of the body of Christian writing, it is believed to have been compiled after A.D. 325. Another Christian writer, Epiphanius, refers to the Acta Pilati in 376 as a Greek text. It is very possible that somewhere between 325 and 376 that a newer transcription was made, and the Greek translation of an Asia Minor record dubbed Berenice "Veronica."

While there are variations on the tale, Veronica's (or Berenice's) act of kindness is remembered in the Sixth Station of the Cross, which is recalled in thousands of churches. This too is evidence that this aspect of the Crucifixion was considered real. It is impossible, however, to date with any certainty when the Veronica chapter became part of the ritual.

The Stations of the Cross, also called the Way of the Cross, was developed by pilgrims who from the earliest dates enacted the ritual of following the route of the Crucifixion. There was no prescribed route, and actually there were several variations even after Constantine's time, when following the Way of the Cross became a goal of pilgrims. For the majority of Christians who could not visit the Holy Lands, the Way of the Cross was instituted in churches and occasionally even outside churches. At each "station," a name given to the practice by an English writer at a much later date, a particular feature of the suffering on the way to Cavalry was meditated upon.

For most of the last two thousand years even the number of stations was not set. In different churches there would be anywhere from five to fourteen places of meditation. In Germany the practice was called the Way of Seven Falls, and the meeting of Jesus with Veronica was one of the seven. Including Veronica in these places of meditation demonstrates that she was recognized by the church.

There is also more than one tale of how the veil was brought to Rome. The Acts of Pilate have the pious woman Veronica bringing it herself to present to the church. Entering the Eternal City, she hears that the Emperor Tiberius was very ill at the time. Veronica brought the cloth to the emperor and cured him by allowing him to touch the sacred cloth. She then turned it over to Pope Clement, the fourth pope. Healing through the use of what the church calls a "sacramental" (any object deemed worthy of use during a sacred rite) would exist in the church for over a thousand years.

Some believe that a certain woman mentioned in the Gospels as being healed simply by touching the cloak of Jesus was Veronica. Because of the strength of her faith she now had the power to heal. Jesus was known to have performed forty healing miracles, and the apostles too could heal simply by their touch. Christianity would not be alone in suggesting an approach to healing at odds with modern thinking or modern cures. Basic to all religion is the ability to confront the powers of the unknown or at least to ask their relief. The Egyptians believed all illness was the result of disturbing or disrespecting the numerous gods. Jews, believing in one God, believed that all illness was caused by Yahweh. Therefore praying to him could alleviate the suffering, although folk medicine was employed just in case. The Roman emperors, who cultivated being worshipped as gods, were supposed to be able to heal by their touch. Tacitus, the Roman historian, reports that Vespasian encountered such belief even in the Egyptian city of Alexandria. A blind man hurled himself at the emperor's feet, begging to be healed. A petitioner with a withered arm asked Vespasian to step on it, to effect a cure.[6] Such miracles, or at least their expectation, were believed in and sought after for hundreds of years.

In the fifth century St. Augustine taught that demons were responsible for all disease, and a long list of saints were assigned to provide cures. Saint Blaise took care of throat ailments, and St. Bernadine specialized in lungs. St. Appollonea was responsible for dental care, while St. Erasmus was called upon for assistance with stomach ailments. Relics of the saints were often employed to help focus prayers.

Sins too would bring the sinner punishment, and the bigger the sin, the greater the punishment. When the plague struck Europe it was, according to the Spanish clergy, because of the rise of opera. English bishops blamed it on theater. Some clerics thought it was God's irritation with the pointed shoes that were then fashionable.[7]

Healing was not limited to the church or its representatives. Edward the Confessor wrote that the kings of England blessed rings to cure epilepsy. Anyone suffering from scrofula was especially helped by the king's touch. The disease became known as the "king's evil." Philip of Valois reportedly touched 1,500 people in one sitting.[8]

It is not surprising, therefore, that relics or sacramentals were used to initiate a cure, especially one of such importance as a relic of Jesus. Relic cloths of Saints Theresa, Francis Cabrini, Maximillian Kolbe, and Italy's Padre Pio are all venerated as prayer cloths with special powers. Chapter 19 of the Acts of the Apostles in the Gospels records clothes were touched to Peter and Paul and then brought back to cure the sick. Sacramentals were not limited to cloths: holy water, holy oils, medals, pictures, prayer beads, blessed palms, and even chalk blessed on Epiphany hold value. An image of the King of heaven to cure the earthly emperor of Rome is dramatic.

The story of Veronica bringing the veil to cure Tiberius is unlikely, as there was no Roman Catholic Church at the time to which to present the gift (the veil). Tiberius was feared and hated during his reign and took pride in not having visited a doctor for most of his life. When he finally fell into a coma, Rome and Caligula celebrated, only to find out he had recovered. The celebrations resumed after he was left for dead, his own servants failing to bring him food.[9]

After they had traveled throughout the Roman Empire, Peter and Paul arrived in Rome two years after the death of Tiberius. While there may have already been Christians in the city, there was no one to found the church. The history of the Roman Catholic Church dates from Peter's arrival.

Because the church had not yet been established, it would have been impossible for the veil to have been given to the church during the reign of Tiberius. As for having given it to Clement, it is possible, although unlikely. Clement was not consecrated as pope until A.D. 88. Assuming Berenice was twenty when Jesus was crucified, she would be seventy or older during Clement's reign as pope.

The research of Father Heinrich Pfeffier offers a better suggestion on just how the veil was brought to Rome. He believes the image was given to the mother of Jesus. Mary took the miraculous cloth and later gave it to the apostle John. Referring to himself as the beloved apostle in his Gospel, rather than use his name, John was asked by Jesus to take care of his mother. John, along with the mother of Jesus, brought the cloth to the city of Ephesus, where they both would live.

John may have then been responsible for it being brought to Camulia in Cappadocia, now modern Turkey. Like the trail of the Shroud, it was then brought to Constantinople. There it was called the Image of Camulia, and it is mentioned by several Byzantine writers. The presence of the veil was noted in a poem by Teofilatto Simocatta (also known as Theophylact Simocrates), who gave it credit for assisting the Byzantine troops in the battle against the Persians near the Arzamon River in 586. He described it as "not painted, not woven." The writings of the monk Giorgio Cedreno from the eleventh to the twelfth century refer to the veil as "acheiropoietos," meaning that it was not made by human hands.

In 705 the veil was taken to Rome. Most likely it was stolen, and there is evidence that fear of a Byzantine reprisal kept news of its arrival, like the veil itself, under wraps.

Fifty years later Rome was being besieged by the Lombards. It was the fate of Pope Stephen II, who had been consecrated as pope the year before, to protect the city. It is said that he devoted himself to prayer and led a procession with the Holy Face, as the Veil of Veronica was then called, in his hands. The protective nature that the Holy Face is believed to exhibit saved the Holy City. Although a late agreement with Pepin that had this leader of the Franks head off the Lombard leader Aistulf in the Alps didn't hurt.

Gratitude for the divine intervention was shown. A chapel where the veil could be housed was constructed, and there is little mention of the veil from the eighth century until the first Holy Year jubilee in 1300, when it was exhibited again. Pope Innocent III was the first pope not to have to worry about the Byzantine emperor. The city of Constantinople had been defeated during the Crusades. During Innocent III's rule the veil was again venerated as Veronica's Veil.[10] At this time, the veil is again described by several writers. The most famous is the Italian poet Dante Alighieri, who mentions it in his *Divine Comedy*.[11] The Jesuit Father John van Boland, writing in the seventeenth century, said it was a "unanimous opinion of all sacred historians" that the veil in Rome was the "veritable cloth offered to the Redeemer on His way to Calvary."[12]

Somewhere around this time it was moved to the St. Peter's Basilica in the Vatican, where it remained until 1608. The last public exhibition may have been in 1575, a year that the church deemed a Holy Year. At one point 30,000 pilgrims crowded the Piazza of St. Peter for a chance to see the veil. Today four gigantic pillars support the cupola of St. Peter's Basilica. Inside one of these pillars is the chapel of Veronica. A sixteen-foot statue of her stands at the entrance. At the base of her statue are two doors, one leading to an interior vault where the relic is kept. The vault is entered only after opening three locks. The keys to these locks are held by the canons of St. Peter's.

Despite these precautions, the veil, a most precious relic, was eventually stolen. In 1608 the chapel was restored, which entailed destroying the old chapel. Around the same time the church was combating the Reformation, and part of the criticism against the church involved the reproducing of images. There were at that time numerous copies of the veil, but then Pope Paul V prohibited making any more exact copies. Up until his prohibition all the copies were made exactly like the veil; Jesus had his eyes open. After the prohibition, newer copies had his eyes closed. Not everyone was amused by the minor change.

The church was then purging itself of unauthentic relics so Urban VIII ordered all copies of the veil destroyed. It is said a priest removed the veil to protect it from destruction. According to the account of Donato da Bomba, a Capuchin monk, it was then stolen from his care.

In 1618 a Vatican archivist was compiling a list of all sacred objects held in St. Peter's. On his list is the reliquary that contained the veil. The glass is described as broken, and there is no further mention of the veil itself. By this time the veil was already gone. It should be noted that Father Pfeiffer's veil had small bits of glass stuck in the bottom of the cloth.

This most important relic had been taken by Marzia Leonelli, the wife of an imprisoned soldier. Her husband, Pancrazio Petrucci, was in prison in Chieti, and she needed money to secure his release. The veil was fortunately sold to a nobleman, Donato Antonio de Fabritiis, for 400 scudi. He kept it for thirty years before donating it to the Capuchin friars of Manoppello.

Today, with only 5,600 residents, Manoppello is still a very small town. It is about 150 miles from Rome in the Abruzzi region of the Apennine Mountains, lying on the banks of the Alba River. Its main business is farming, and the name of the village itself is derived from *manoppio,* the Italian word for wheat sheaf. It has several churches and shrines as well as the Capuchin monastery, which serves as a hotel for visitors to this remote area. Cut off by mountainous roads and out of the way for most tourists visiting Italy, the village is as insular in attitude as it is geographically. The villagers did not think much of the discovery. They had been safeguarding the treasure in the Sanctuary of the Sacred Face for four hundred years. On the second Sunday of every May the Feast of the Face is celebrated.

The Vatican has remained silent about the veil being in Manoppello, because the veil should be in St. Peter's Basilica, where there is a statue of Veronica and a plaque testifying that it is housed in the altar. It is possible that there is more than one veil, as the record shows copies being made and given as gifts hundreds of years before. So far, there is no plan to do a comparison of existing copies. In 2003 the Vatican Web site (www.vatican.va) began making the Treasures of the Vatican Library available to those who cannot travel to the Eternal City. Though not yet available in English, the section titled "The Face of Christ" will have nineteen versions of the face, as depicted on the veil. No notice has been given about research into just which veil may have been Veronica's.

The History of the Sudarium

Today the sudarium is protected in a cathedral in Oviedo, Spain. Its history has fewer gaps than other precious relics. It begins with the cloth being placed in a chest in Jerusalem, where it survived for six centuries. The chest is the size of a burial box, and it also resembles the box that is the Ark of the Covenant. In response to the threat of Persian invasion, it was taken to Alexandria, Egypt, and possibly through Carthage. The few texts that cover its history agree that it was taken to "Africa," although not on just where in Africa. If traveling from Alexandria to Spain, Carthage would have been the most important port on the North African coast, and there is little reason to doubt the claim that it did at least have a "layover" in that seaport. From there the chest traveled by ship to Spain. Legends surrounding the chest that held the sudarium and other relics are most likely exaggerated. It is said a wolf guarded the ark on its way to Oviedo just ahead of the Moors. For this reason the name of the port where it landed was changed from Subsalas to Luarca (Wolf of the Ark). Luarca still exists today on the northern coast of Spain, about fifty miles away from the inland city of Oviedo. The more reliable records mention that the veil was then taken to Seville. It is later recorded as having been brought to Toledo. It may have spent half a century in that city and then all the texts agree that in 711 it was put into protective sanctuary. The ark that contained the sudarium was opened in A.D. 1075 when the king, Alfonso VI, ordered an inventory of sacred items. It was listed as the "Holy Sudarium of Our Lord Jesus Christ."

Legend, rather than surviving documents, recall that when priests opened the ark they were struck blind. This recalls the fate of the unpure who dared to touch the Ark of the Covenant.[13] Finally, when King Alfonso opened it, he was with El Cid, the national hero of Spain, so they were spared any ill effects.

The records that tell the history of the sudarium include that of the Bishop of Oviedo, Pelayo. He had been named for a hero-king of Asturias who had turned the tide against the Moors in that ancient kingdom.

Writers on Christian relics during the twelfth century are often suspect, just because of the time in which they were writing, which was the height of relic collecting. Pelayo could also be suspect, as such a find would glorify his home in Oviedo. It was not only the capital of the ancient kingdom of Asturias, but it would also become a popular detour for pilgrims visiting the Santiago Compostela.

Pelayo's record, however, was predated by a record known as the *Codex Valenciennes*. The two vary only in minor detail. Three other texts also vary slightly, with one substituting Cartagena in Spain for a mid-Mediterranean stopping point, rather than the North African port of Carthage.

In addition to the Gospel of St. John there exists further documentation of the facial cloth. Mention is made in the *Life of St. Nino of Georgia* and in the writings of Ishodad of Merv. St. Nino brought Christianity to Georgia in the fourth century. Her sayings were compiled in a fifth-century text. In addition to her evangelical work she devoted time to tracking relics of the Crucifixion. She had heard that the wife of Pilate had taken the cloth to Pontus on the Black Sea. Ishodad was a bishop in Turkmenistan in 850 who wrote commentaries on all of the books of the New Testament. He recorded that St. Peter used the sudarium to heal people. A third mention is in a text attributed to an unnamed pilgrim to Jerusalem in 570 who claims to have seen the cloth.

The sudarium then, despite its relative obscurity in comparison to the Shroud, has fewer breaks in historical continuity than the Shroud itself. While the Shroud does get the vast majority of attention, future scientific techniques and less invasive testing may assist the process of verifying the authenticity of these *other* cloths. And they may, in turn, serve in the process of further authenticating the Shroud.

3

THE TRUE CROSS AND THE RELICS
OF THE CRUCIFIXION

In 1968 building contractors working in the Jerusalem suburb of Giv'at ha-Mivtar uncovered a Jewish tomb dating to the first century. As usual, work stopped immediately, a hazard to speedy construction in a city having such a rich archaeological heritage. Interred in the tomb, according to the inscription, was a certain Yohanan. Forensic archaeologists soon determined that Yohanan was male, five foot five inches tall, and between the ages of twenty-four and twenty-eight. Unearthing burial places is almost a regular occurrence in a land torn by war for thousands of years, especially since Jerusalem as well as the countryside are growing and expanding in modern times. But there was one very important aspect of this discovery: Yohanan was the victim of crucifixion.

He, of course, was not the only one crucified, as thousands had met the same fate. They were rebels, traitors, or in some cases those who would be made an example of by leaving the body at a crossroads, at a city gate, or at the top of a hill. The Jewish custom of having the body buried by sundown was not always possible under Roman repression. Even when the body was removed, the cross remained.

How then could the cross that bore Jesus be determined from the hundreds and thousands of others?

Christianity's First Archaeologist

In the fourth century the mother of Constantine, the new emperor of the Roman Empire, went to Jerusalem in search of the True Cross. Her name was Helena, and in part because of her success she is St. Helena today. While pilgrimages were commonplace in that era—people making such journeys even to pagan shrines—Helena's was a royal expedition. She had a huge entourage and was well funded by her son's treasury. The mission had two purposes: the primary goal was to find the places where Jesus had been. Secondarily, but of great importance to her son, she was also spreading goodwill, to make it easier for Constantine to consolidate his rule. In both cases she succeeded.

Helena, legend has it, was a daughter of a minor king of the Britons, Coel. Folk tradition remembers him as Old King Cole, and he led a rebellion against the anti-Christian persecution that was rampant when Asclepiodotus was Emperor Diocletion's appointed leader in Britain. Cole, a duke at the time, killed the Roman puppet and took the royal crown. After a brief peace, Rome sent Constantius to rule. Cole did not want to face him in battle but promised the normal tribute would be paid if the persecution ended. His truce did not last long, as Cole developed an illness that killed him within days. Quickly, Constantius seized the crown, and to validate his power married Helena. Her status, despite being a daughter of the king, was that of an innkeeper. This did not stop Constantius the elder from desiring her hand in marriage.

Their son would be Constantine. Eleven years after his birth, Constantius died in the English city of York. The kingdom went to his son, and Helena, as regent and mother, headed to Rome. Both his father and mother had prepared Constantine to rule the Roman Empire, and after Constantine defeated his rival, Maxentius, Helena too could then rule as the mother of the king.

She made her way to Jerusalem. Though her journey would not initiate the practice of venerating and collecting relics, this practice would expand exponentially by the time Helena was home. In A.D. 326 she found the True Cross, actually the three crosses of the Crucifixion, in a cistern in the Holy City.

There she gathered the wise men of the Jews to question them on the whereabouts of the True Cross. There was nothing gentle about her persuasion. First she threatened them with being burned. The group gave up one of their own, named Judas, who they said had inherited documents from his father that pointed the way to Golgotha. He was reluctant, so Helena had him thrown into a well, where he would either starve or confess. After seven days without food, Judas not only gave in, but he also claimed he would accept Jesus as his Savior. He told her a temple to Venus (also known as Aphrodite) had been built over the site.

The Roman pagans had erected the temple so that if Christians came to pray to Jesus they had to bend a knee to the Roman goddess. Helena had that destroyed, and Judas began the digging himself. At a depth of twenty yards, three crosses were found.

These, of course, fit the description of the three crosses at Calvary, those for Jesus and the two thieves. Helena's dilemma was which cross was the Cross of Jesus? They brought the three crosses to street level just as the body of a young man was passing by in a funeral procession. They held one cross over him, and nothing happened. They held a second cross over him, and nothing happened. The third cross was then held over the dead body, and the young man immediately rose from the dead.

It should be noted that there is more than one version of the story. A second version has a prominent woman of the city being cured. A third version has the sign, or scroll, that Pilate placed on Jesus' Cross as an indication of the True Cross. The sign read "King of the Jews." Judas then was baptized and shortly after was made bishop of Jerusalem. He went on to help Helena find the nails of the Crucifixion.[1]

While the story as told in *The Golden Legend* of Jacobus de Voragine and even Eusebius has its share of skeptics, recent investigation into the archaeology of Jerusalem confirms at least part of the story. The crosses of Golgotha were left in place after the deaths of Jesus and the two thieves. There they stood until a few years later, as an urban expansion project incorporated Golgotha within the city walls. The crosses were removed and thrown into a cistern. Twenty years later the city was plundered as a result of the brutal repression of the Jewish rebellion. The Christians of the time did not fight for or against the Romans, a fact not appreciated by the Jews. The Christians left the city for Pella and remained there until the rebellion was quashed.

When they returned from Pella, Jerusalem again had a Christian community, although it was not welcome to the Roman occupation. The Christians worshipped at several sites where Jesus had been, but the mound that was once Golgotha was now considered sacred. It was for this reason that in A.D. 135 a temple to Venus was erected.

While the story of discovery of the True Cross may have been colored, the basic story appears factual. There was one piece of evidence that would completely tip the scale toward factual. Within the cistern where the crosses were found was the sign that had hung on the Cross of Jesus.

The Sign on the Cross

It was common practice, especially in setting an example, to let the witnesses to an execution understand just why the victim was killed by the state. The sign could announce that the man was a thief, a rebel, or in rare cases a magician or sorcerer. In the case of Jesus the point was very important to make.

The Gospels say that Pilate ordered a sign for the Cross of Jesus to read "King of the Jews." This was a point of irritation to the Sanhedren (the Council of Elders), who wanted it to say that Jesus claimed to be King of the Jews. To modern readers of the Bible, the distinction between the two might be lost. When the high priest interrogated Jesus, he was asked if he was the "Christ the Son of God." The answer was "Thou hast said it."[2] If Jesus had said yes, his crime would have been against Rome. Tiberius believed himself to be the Son of God. Then Jesus was brought before Pilate who asked, "Art thou the king of the Jews?" and Jesus answered, "Thou sayest it."[3] Had the answer been the affirmative, the crime might have been more theological. It appeared neither side wanted responsibility, although both saw him as a radical and a troublemaker.

In any case Pilate had his way, and a scroll was prepared naming Jesus King of the Jews. It was written in three languages—Latin, Hebrew, and Greek—implying that those who would view his death, and be the recipients of the message, would be many.

The unique scroll also ensured the authenticity of the True Cross. The scroll was unearthed along with the three crosses. The scroll was broken, and soon so were the crosses. The largest piece of the scroll, as well as large pieces of the Cross, would be brought back to Jerusalem by Helena and later taken to Rome.

Constantine and the Church

There can be no downplaying the role that Helena's son, Constantine, served in developing Christianity from a popular sect to a powerful world religion. While not displaying any special devotion to Christianity, he did, however, see the value of organizing the growing population of the church into his own political camp. After three centuries of squabbling within the church, it was still divided into smaller sects that often professed conflicting beliefs. In 325 it was through Constantine that the Council of Nicaea came to make the church what it is today. That is, a catholic church, where it is the same from Ireland to Asia Minor and under the leadership of un-questioned authority. To accomplish that, an end to the conflicting truths had to be made. Constantine would reorganize the church. What he lacked in terms of sincerity, his mother made up for. While Constantine would consolidate church law, Helena would restore the sacred.

The True Cross

Many sacred objects began appearing in the West in the fourth century after St. Helena's archaeological dig in Jerusalem. Relic collecting became widespread, and within fifty years pieces of the Cross were spread across Europe. But the largest piece had stayed behind in Jerusalem, giving Bishop Cyril enormous leverage with religious and world leaders alike. Thousands flocked to see the sacred site where Helena and her son had a church erected. The Church of the Holy Sepulcher attracted crowds so great that within years another pilgrim, Egeria, would write that people were pressed so thickly into the sanctuary that the doors could not be opened.

While the bishop alone had the power to gift fragments of the Cross, other pilgrims would attempt anything to get their own splinter. People were forbidden to kiss the Cross after more than one pious individual was caught trying to take a bite out of it.

In 614 what was left of the Cross was taken by the Persian general Shahrbaraz. His army forced their way into the city, killing sixty thousand and enslaving thirty-five thousand more. He gave the Cross as a gift to Queen Meryem of Persia, who was Christian herself. It remained in Nin-eveh until 627, when Emperor Heraclius II defeated the Persians. For the next four hundred years most of what remained of the Cross was in Jerusalem.

During that time the world was rocked by a religious event whose geopolitical aftershocks are still front-page news today.

In A.D. 622 a traveling merchant from the Middle East named Muhammad, who had been preaching of the supremacy of the one God, Allah, moved to Medina. He taught that everyone owed submission, the Arabic word for which is *Islam,* to this one God. He consolidated his fol-lowers in Medina, and from that year on, year one in the Islamic calendar, he began a quest to take back his world from the worship of pagan idols. In 630 Muhammad captured Mecca, which had originally rejected his teach-ings. It had been a pilgrimage site for pagan Arabs who worshipped a sacred black stone called the Kaaba. After Muhammad captured Mecca, the Kaaba would then be an Islamic shrine, just as Chartres in France would go from being Druid to Christian.

After Muhammad's death Islam split into two major factions, Sunni and Shiite. The Sunni branch and one specific family of that branch known as the Umayyad dynasty would extend Islam from the home base in Mecca to the straits of Gibraltar and eastward to India. Rival dynasties would challenge the Umayyad. The lightning speed with which the Arab world expanded soon created challenges, mostly from within. Factions developed among the different dynasties, destroying unity. To the West, however, the armies of Islam represented one threat.

In general, Islam may have been tolerant of other religions, and Muslims were rarely accused of damaging the sacred objects of other religions. But Christianity still felt the threat that sacred Christian objects might be captured or damaged. So from the seventh century, in an attempt to ensure that such objects would be kept in Christian hands, Christians began moving these objects westward. After several centuries of Islamic expansion, the European world was able to exploit the lack of unity among Arab dynasties as a strategy for halting the onslaught of Islamic expansion.

To the Arabs, the English, the Germans, the French, and others were all Franks, and the Franks were soon on a Crusade. They halted the Islamic excursions into France, and following victory, they began the *reconquista,* the taking back of the Iberian peninsula. Norman adventurers from France went to Italy and Sicily to halt Islamic advances. But Constantinople had held its own.

Soon Europe was united in the glory of recapturing Jerusalem. Unfortunately in the process the Franks would destroy numerous towns, villages, and cities. They even did what Islam was unable to do, that is, conquer and destroy the city of Constantinople. When they reached Jerusalem, even that city was not spared the rampage of the Crusaders, who massacred indiscriminately Muslims, Jews, and fellow Christians. The savagery of the Christian conquest and the amount of looting of religious artifacts and art may not have been equalled until the Nazi war machine would roll over Europe nine hundred years later.

The conquest of Jerusalem was followed by the Frankish armies settling in for a long occupation. There they launched military campaigns designed to defeat the Arab nations. They now possessed the True Cross, or at least the largest remaining part of the Cross, and rode with it into battle.

In 1105 the Patriarch Evremar, at the request of King Baldwin, had a contingent of 150 men ride from Jerusalem to Ramleh to carry the Cross just before that battle.[4] In 1115 the troops were blessed with the True Cross at Tel Danith just before that victorious battle.[5] In 1119 it was brought out to bless the troops in the battle of Hab.[6] In 1123 a large Egyptian force reached Jaffa. Despite the fears of the bishop of Jerusalem, the Christian troops marched out of that city with the Cross to oppose them. The Egyptians fled.[7] It was carried as troops lay siege to the city of Ascalon in 1153.[8]

Then tragedy struck. On Friday, July 3, 1187, the Christian army rode out to engage Saladin. But the climate was sweltering, there was no water, and along the way they suffered sniper attacks from Muslim skirmishers who knew the rocky terrain much better. When they reached a plateau above the village of Hittim, the Knights Templar ordered a halt to the march. They spent the night in misery, listening to the Arab army singing and praying. Soldiers were dispatched to wander in the dark, looking for water. Then, on the morning of July 4, the legendary Saladin attacked. He had created a net so tight, one chronicler said, a cat could not have slipped through. The day ended with the Christians defeated, the bishop of Acre dead, and the True Cross in the hands of the enemy.

Some believe it was burned, as the army of Saladin had set fire to the brush to keep the Christians in their trap. Thirty-eight years later negotiations to end the war that would be called the Fifth Crusade took place. A stumbling block was that the Christians wanted the Cross back and the Muslims refused. When finally an agreement was made to turn the Cross over, it could not be found. The Frankish army sailed away in shame.[9]

While the largest piece of the Cross was no longer in the hands of the church, many smaller pieces had been spread across Europe. Cathedrals in Rome, Venice, Paris, Brussels, Ghent, Limbourg, and Mount Athos in Greece all possessed at least a small piece of the Cross. The Cistercian monks at la Boissiere in France possessed a large piece. Another large piece found its way to Scotland. Because of the honor, the palace of Holyrood was built and named for the relic. The Sainte-Chapelle in the Royal Palace in Paris, a depository for the greatest collections of important relics, holds a piece of the Cross. The largest piece of the Cross, outside of Rome, is in the Sainte Gudule convent in Brussels.

Just how valuable is a piece of the Cross? While the church would hardly place a value in dollar terms on such a relic, modern man has less qualms. In 1993 a Paris auction saw two splinter-size pieces of the "True Cross" in a pendant exchange hands for $18,000.[10]

But the Cross was not the only object of the Crucifixion to warrant attention. The scroll that hung over the head of Jesus, the Crown of Thorns, the nails, the sponge given to Jesus to drink, his coat and loincloth, all became sought after.

The Crown of Thorns

The Crown of Thorns was known to have been venerated in Jerusalem after the adventures of St. Helena. It was moved to Constantinople in the eleventh century but taken as part of the Crusader booty in 1204. One of the greatest of the Crusading kings was Baldwin II. He was also one of the greatest plunderers, and Constantinople was the source of many of the sacred items he brought back to Western Europe.

When Baldwin II took the Crown of Thorns home, it appears that he needed it more as a source of funds than as an object of veneration. While relics were not to be sold, Baldwin II needed money to pay his debts to the city of Venice. When the French King Louis IX sought to bring the Crown of Thorns to Paris, he paid dearly. He met the Crown at the French border and turned over an unthinkable sum of 10,000 gold pieces. The ban on relic sales was countered by the free exchange of the Crown for this very large sum in gold. The Crown was accorded much more reverence by the French king. He placed it at the head of a solemn procession back to the capital city, where Parisians crowded the streets to greet this sacred relic.

The Sainte-Chapelle in Paris was then built to hold the relic. The chapel's construction itself was almost miraculous, considering it was built in less than three years. Inside, a vaulted roof is supported by thin columns and a web of stonework that give it a cavernlike appearance. Outside, it stands like a finger pointing to heaven. Today this sacred spot stands within the walls of the Palais du Justice on the Île-de-la-Cité. It is surrounded by the walls where thousands were sentenced to die in the Terror of the French Revolution. The reformers of the church ushered in a sad chapter in the history of relics. They encouraged destroying relics with hammers, and during the French Revolution many relics were burned. The Crown of Thorns survived because Napoleon himself entrusted it to the archbishop of Paris, who in turn gave the responsibility to protect it to the modern order of Christian knights.

Because of such threats, the responsibility to keep, protect, and preserve the relics of the Crucifixion is taken seriously.

In April 2002 the Holy Shroud Congress, one of several organizations built around that sacred relic, met in Paris. The highlight of their meeting was a veneration ceremony for the Crown of Thorns. The Knights of the Holy Sepulcher, the modern-day inheritors of the Templar role as guardians of the sacred relics, were all allowed to see the Crown, encased in a round crystal reliquary. Mass in Notre Dame Cathedral followed. The Templars are believed to protect the True Cross, the Crown of Thorns, the head of St. John the Baptist, the body of St. Euphemia of Chalcedon, which had healing powers, along with numerous other items. After their order was disbanded, the role of guardian did not go away. The Knights of the Holy Sepulcher were founded at the same time as the Templar military order, but they confined their role to protecting the relics of Christianity. After both Jerusalem and Acre fell to Islam, both orders were forced out. In 1330 Pope John XXII designated the Franciscan order as responsible for the Knights of the Holy Sepulcher, and they survive in both Jerusalem and Rome today.

When the Sainte-Chapelle was being built, the Crown of Thorns was housed just opposite the palace, in the cathedral of Notre Dame. Both lie on the city's island in the Seine River. This soaring cathedral, with intricate carvings sculptured into its facade, was and is the repository of many items sacred to Christianity. Notre Dame and Sainte-Chapelle have housed the Crown of Thorns and are still the sites of its veneration on certain feast days. Both have held a piece of the sponge, a part of the True Cross, and one of the nails of the Crucifixion. Notre Dame in Paris preserves a fragment of the True Cross, a portion of the sponge presented to the suffering Christ, a nail of the Crucifixion, and the Crown of Thorns, without the thorns.

The Nails of the Crucifixion

While some victims of crucifixion were tied with rope to their cross, Jesus, as well as the man unearthed at Giv'at ha-Mivtar, were nailed to their respective crosses. Each wrist would be pounded through with a nail and either one or two nails for the feet. The nails are unlike modern nails used in construction. Roman nails used in executions had large heads. These served to ensure the wrist or the foot could not simply slip through. They would more closely resemble railroad spikes of modern times. So it can be assumed that three or four of these large nails were used. To the delight of skeptics, a total of twenty-nine cities actually claim a nail from the Crucifixion of Jesus.

The Paris Cathedral of Notre Dame has one. Rome's Vatican has one of the largest collections of relics, and it includes still another nail. Venice, never to be outdone, claims three. The German city of Trier has one, along with a thorn, the seamless coat of Christ, and a fragment of the Cross. According to legend, one nail is said to have been thrown into the Adriatic to calm a storm. Another nail became part of what is called the Iron Crown at Lombardy, used in the coronation of Charlemagne. Helena, the mother of Constantine, would have one nail made into a bridle for the horse of her son. This was done to fulfill the prophecy of Zacharias that said "that which is on the bridle of the horse shall be holy to the Lord." [11] Not everyone may have agreed with Helena's interpretation that the nail was holy to the Lord, or that the prophet meant Constantine, but nevertheless, neither son nor mother were ever accused of thinking small.

The church uses the term "multiplicity" to describe the proliferation of sacred relics. There are several explanations why so-called multiplicity takes place. In the case of the nails the explanation becomes fairly logical. Helena herself admitted to melting down three nails to have nine forged. Stretching a point, St. Charles of Borromeo would touch nails that were not from the Crucifixion to a nail that was and claim all the nails were now relics. These explanations do not pacify all, and from Martin Luther down to modern critics it is often pointed out that the fragments of the True Cross put together could build Noah's Ark. Explaining the proliferation of heads of St. John the Baptist would not be as easy. Guibert of Nogent wrote during the Middle Ages a treatise titled *De pignoribus sanctorum* in which he showed a high level of discernment by noting that at least one of the churches claiming John's skull must have a fake. [12]

Such criticism surfaced well after the relic mania spread through medieval Europe. Seemingly everything touched by Jesus surfaced. The robe is in the church at Treves. The swaddling cloths of Jesus are preserved in Aachen, Germany, along with his loincloth and a piece of the sponge. The lance (and offspring), which will be covered separately, has been located in four cities.

The Sacred Blood

Even the tears and blood of Christ were somehow gathered. The Basilica of the Holy Blood in St. Basil's Chapel in Belgium is just one receptacle preserving the blood. Each year, on the fortieth day after Easter, the Holy Blood is taken out of the chapel. The city of Bruges already has a medieval look, but each year when thousands of citizens dress in costume to celebrate the return of the Crusaders, the city is truly a sight. Floats show numerous scenes from the Bible. People dress as everyone from Moses to Roman centurions carrying shields, lances, chains, and helmets. Thousands watch from grandstand seats as finally a solemn procession led by the bishop carries the reliquary with a single vial of blood. It is said that Joseph of Arimathea had washed the body of Jesus after the Crucifixion and preserved his blood. As the story is related, the count of Flanders brought the souvenir home during the First Crusade, in 1149.

Not to be outdone, just three years later an abbot of Voormezele, near Ieper, brought his own sample of the blood of Jesus. Today this rival town has six hundred actors putting on the Passion in gory glory[13] after a procession.

In France there is a small town, Neuvy, which served as a pilgrimage point for those who could not travel to Jerusalem. The Sacred Sepulcher of Neuvy was constructed to represent Jerusalem, and both a basilica and a cave representing the tomb are located in the town. In 1254 they received a gift of three drops of the sacred blood, and today these are held in a small reliquary upon a statue of a miniature angel. During the French Revolution a mob attacked the tomb and stole the container that held the sacred blood. But they had been duped; the real blood had been carefully hidden away and a reliquary holding fruit juice substituted. After the revolution the archbishop founded a commission, in 1805, to confirm the authenticity of the treasure. The blood is displayed for veneration three times each year.[14]

The Sponge and the Reed

While on the Cross, Jesus was given a sponge to drink that was said to be filled with vinegar. It was somehow lifted to him on a reed. Both the reed and the sponge are said to have been preserved. Objects of veneration in Jerusalem, they were then carried, as many relics had been, to Constantinople for safety. The sponge was said to be divided, and several cathedrals obtained pieces.

Many sacred items can be authenticated or at least studied, by science. But claims of authenticity about items such as the reed and the sponge, as well as the tears of Jesus or the milk of the Virgin, are generally ignored by science and considered to be only part of the relic mania.

. . .

Before the relic collectors could stretch the limits of credibility any further, it dawned on those deprived of their own relics that even the greatest taboo could be broken. The basis of the entire Christian faith is that Jesus, of course, ascended both body and soul into heaven. So there could be no relic associated with a body part of Jesus, as with the saints and martyrs of the church. But it was only a matter of time until someone could even get around that detail. Monks of Saint-Medard de Soissons claimed they had a baby tooth of Jesus. This was no small event at the time, as it raised a serious issue. If a tooth was left behind, was Jesus fully resurrected? While the argument seems trivial today, it was not allowed to be put to rest. John Calvin would raise the issue at the height of the Reformation.[15]

Charles the Bald, a ninth-century king of France, had no doubts and rewarded the order's monastery with numerous estates and even three mills.[16] A Marseilles cathedral and several other churches claimed to possess vials of the tears of Jesus. At Lucques in the Auverge the "holy naval" of Jesus turned up. Presumably it was a reference to the umbilical cord, which had been preserved.

The relic collectors ultimately abandoned any limits on taste and common sense, and even the foreskin of the baby Jesus was claimed by not one but thirteen dioceses. It had been preserved, according to the apocryphal Gospels, and despite the fact that these were not part of the accepted Gospels, during the manic phase of relic collecting, anything was fair game where a profit could be made. Charroux Abbey takes its name from a corruption of *chair rouge,* meaning red flesh.

The Eucharistic Miracle of Lanciano

In the eighth century in the tiny church of St. Legontian (a variation of the name St. Longinus), a monk of the order of St. Basil was undergoing a crisis of faith. His quandary was accepting that the Lord was actually present in the Eucharist, which is the miracle of the transubstantiation. When a priest says mass he is the agent through which the bread and water are changed into the flesh and blood of Christ. It had long been argued that such a miracle was just a representation. The unnamed monk had his doubts that this change actually occurred. In answer to his doubt the transformation literally took place. The host, the tiny wafer of bread, turned into flesh. The wine turned into blood. The transformed host and the blood, which soon formed pellets, were preserved in a reliquary.

The monastery passed to the Franciscans, and a document preserving the story of the miracle survived. Over the centuries several tests have been performed on the transformed host and blood. In 1574, in 1637, in 1770, and again in 1886 the Franciscans have allowed tests to be done. The latest was in 1970 when Dr. Odoardo Linoli, a professor in anatomy and pathological histology, and Professor Ruggero Bertelli of the University of Siena, teamed up. They confirmed that the flesh was real flesh and that the blood was real blood. A test called Uhlenhuth's zonal precipitation reaction proved that both the flesh and the blood were human. The flesh was actually identified as the muscular tissue of the heart. Tissue from both the left and right ventricles of the heart were detected, although less than normal, possibly the result of earlier testing.

The blood was tested through a thin-layer chromatography test. This test identifies the presence of blood even in badly preserved samples that may not test positive for hemoglobin. It confirmed that the blood preserved in the Lanciano monastery was real blood. It also tested to be AB, the same outcome of the testing done on the Shroud of Turin by Dr. Bollone. A test called the "elution absorption method" verified the blood group was the same in both the flesh and blood. The flesh and blood have been preserved for twelve hundred years and still show proteins in the same percentages as normal fresh blood. Only one test showed that the blood had aged, and that is a test where calcium is increased to get a mineral level. The reduced level of potassium, phosphorus, and sodium are often the result of the container housing the blood.

The flesh and blood of Lanciano are on display above the altar of the Church of St. Francis in that city. While the Lanciano miracle was the first recorded in such detail, scores of other miracles of the same nature have taken place. For the most part the scientific community regards these politely as matters strictly for the faithful.

The True Cross Today

Perhaps because the Cross is the most revered symbol in Christianity, it has inevitably been divided into innumerable pieces. Possibly the most sacred site housing an original relic of the Cross is the Church of the Holy Cross in Jerusalem. In Italy it is called the Santa Croce in Gerusalemme and is located on the Piazza di Santa Croce on Rome's Esquiline Hill. This church was consecrated in 325 to house the relics of the Passion brought home by Helena. The church was actually built on a former estate of the emperor's mother.

The church has undergone numerous repairs and renovations, and in 1930 the "passion relics" were taken from a subterranean sanctuary and given a new chapel. Here visitors can visit the fragment of the Cross of Jesus, as well as a piece of the thieves' crosses. Thorns from the Crown of Thorns, a nail reputed to be one of the originals, and a piece of the Titulus (the sign, or scroll, placed on Jesus' cross), along with a re-creation of the full inscription are all here as well.

The church is the scene of several celebrations in the course of the year. The relics are exposed and carried in procession on the fourth Sunday of Lent and on Good Friday. The Discovery of the Cross is celebrated on May 3 each year and the Exaltation of the Cross on September 14.

4

THE SPEAR OF DESTINY

The scene is Golgotha, the Place of the Skull, and three crosses bear two thieves and the man who would be the King of the Jews. All are condemned to death. The hour is getting late, and according to the Gospels, the condemned cannot stay on their crosses. Annas, an aged adviser to the Sanhedrin, and Caiaphas, the high priest, orders the legs of the crucified be broken. The Roman soldiers come to break the legs of the condemned to hasten their death. One, then the other, have their legs brutally broken by the soldiers, who use clubs. Then just before they get to Jesus, he cries out to God in a loud voice and dies.

Mark, Matthew, and Luke are almost in agreement that a centurion noted both the last words of Jesus and his death. Mark and Matthew have him saying, "Indeed this man was the Son of God" (Mark 15:39) (Matthew 27:54), while Luke has the centurion declare "Indeed this was a just man" (Luke 23:47). John goes much further. While he doesn't declare it was a centurion, he says when the soldier reached Jesus he saw he appeared dead and thrust his spear into his side.

Longinus and the Spear

From there the legend grew. The centurion's name is Longinus, and he was horrified to see the soldiers clubbing the other victims to break their legs. He rushed up to the Cross of Jesus and pierced his side with his spear. Blood and water issued from the side of Jesus. In an instant the eyesight of Longinus, which had been failing, was completely restored.

Longinus becomes one of the first to convert. He seeks instruction from the disciples of Jesus at Caesarea and then spends the rest of his life in Cappadocia, converting pagans to the Savior. At some point the governor of that area has him arrested and orders him to sacrifice to the pagan idols. He refuses and instead smashes the idols with his axe. The demons emerging from the idols take possession of the governor. Longinus tells the Roman governor that only through Longinus's death will the governor be cured. Longinus is ordered to be executed. The governor then has his own sight and sanity restored and becomes a Christian.[1]

The church canonized Longinus as a saint, and his feast day is on the Ides of March, the fifteenth day of that month.

The spear that Longinus used to bring about the death of Jesus filled a very important prophecy of the Old Testament regarding the true Savior. Isaiah had said "a bone of Him shall not be broken," which adds validity to Jesus as the Savior. Ezekiel had said "they shall look upon him whom they have pierced." By fulfilling the prophecy, the spear served an important role in confirming that Jesus was God. It also is the weapon that killed Jesus, a powerful talisman.

Such a powerful icon then might give the owner incredible power. For that reason the spear is credited with a long history of bringing such strength to leaders, from ancient times to Adolf Hitler. Trevor Ravenscroft's *The Spear of Destiny* traces the spear throughout a terrible history of murder and destruction.

The Spear and History

After the actions of Longinus the spear ends up in the hands of the commander of the Theban Legion, Mauritius. Though the legion fights for Rome, it is made up of Christian soldiers, notably a pagan sect known as Arian Christians. After a battle they are called upon by Maximian to take part in a pagan celebration, but Mauritius begs off. Maximian insists and threatens the legion with death if they refuse. To preserve his men from taking part in the pagan festival, their commander kneels and offers his own head to be sacrificed. Instead, Maximian orders all Theban Legion Christians to be killed. In all, an apocalyptic 6,666 men are killed professing their Arian-style Christianity.

Next we find the spear in the hands of Constantine at the Milvian Bridge. He is not actually fighting for or against Christians but is claiming a sign in the sky is that of the True Cross. He uses this sign to unite his Mithraic soldiers with the mass of Christianity, which by that time was growing. Through the Cross in the sky and the Spear of Destiny in his hand, Constantine seizes victory and the leadership of Rome.

Then Theodosius in 385 carries the spear to defeat the Goths. Theodosius was born in Spain in 346, and he would be one of the last emperors to be given the appellation "the Great." At age thirty-five he was in Greece when a severe illness brought him to seek baptism into Christianity. He then became the church's most effective weapon, rooting out paganism, including Arianism, from one end of the empire to the other. An edict banned all other religions. He made little attempt to convert others, so all who stood in his way were in danger. In Thessalonica he had seven thousand put to death, an act that caused St. Ambrose to not allow him into church. By 394 Theodosius entered Rome as the new master of a Roman Empire. His greatest victory, that of stopping the onslaught of the Goths, was short-lived. He died on January 17, 395, and the Vandals, Goths, and Huns all threatened the West shortly afterward.

A brief thirty-five years later the spear is in Rome when the city is plundered by Alaric. The Roman Empire, once considered as invincible as its invincible god Mithra, was near collapse. In 410 the Eternal City of Rome showed it too was mortal, as it was overrun quickly by the Visigoths. They were not there to stay. For three days the destruction, slaughter, and outrage that took place in Rome would have the Christian writer St. Jerome comment that "the human race is included in the ruins."[2] Jewels, gold, silver, and even the silks of the senators were taken for ransoming or by outright looting. Then the Visigoths left. Alaric, who may have taken the sacred spear, would be dead within days and buried under the Busento River, which was diverted to protect his burial.

The Spear of Destiny was no longer in the hands of the Romans. The empire that had held Europe together would be split in two, and the West overrun by successive hordes of raiders that threw the world into what would be called the Dark Ages. As Rome retrenched, the inhabitants of England, Gaul, and the Iberian peninsula were left to hold back Angles, Saxons, Goths, and Visigoths.

The Visigoths would advance through southern France into Spain and create their own kingdom, which would survive for three centuries. The sacred spear was now in the hands of the Gothic invaders. Ownership passed to the grandson of Alaric, Theodoric I. This Theodoric used the spear to halt the advance of the Huns at Troyes in 451.

One hundred years later the Visigoths would seek out the help of the emperor Justinian. While there is no record of other treasures taken from Rome being recovered by the Romans, the spear is soon in the hands of this emperor, implying that there might have been a trade. Justinian sent troops into the lands of King Athanagild to put down a rebellion against that king. The Romans stayed and later would fight with the Visigoths over lands in what would be called Septimania.

Justinian followed the example of Theodosius and purged Greece of its classical schools and libraries. He is remembered most for codifying law.

In the Hands of the Franks

The next owner of the spear is Charles Martel, known to his people as Charles Martellus (Charles the Hammer). The year 732 saw Martel lead the Frankish troops into combat to halt the rapid rise and territorial expansion of Islam. The Battle of Poitiers would be the turning point against Islamic expansion. In the years that followed he freed Aquitaine from Islam and sent several expeditions into Provence. The Arabs were not defeated, but they would never again penetrate quite so far into Western Europe. The *reconquista,* the reconquest of the Iberian Peninsula, would take centuries.

Charles Martel would consolidate the Frankish role on both sides of the Rhine River and be responsible for sending Saxon missionaries west into France and England.

His grandson would be Charlemagne, Charles the Great. He is the architect of the Holy Roman Empire, which has been criticized as being neither Holy, Roman, nor an empire. It did stretch from beyond the Pyrennes in the West to the Elbe in the East, although warlike factions continually arose within the state and were beaten back. He did much to restore greatness to Christianity, often by wheeling and dealing with a succession of popes who were allowed to expand the church's land, in turn allowing Charlemagne their blessing in expanding his domain. He was sincere in his Christianity. He made his own pilgrimage to St. Peter's Basilica in Rome, where he reverently kissed every step of the staircase that rose to the atrium. Together with Pope Hadrian he visited the remains of St. Peter, one of Christianity's favorite pilgrimage sites.

Pope Leo, the new pope, reacted to Charlemagne's concept of himself as "appointed by Christ to be the Leader of the Christian people" by letting the world know of his own power. On Christmas Day 800, Charlemagne was attending mass in St. Peter's when Pope Leo placed a crown of gold on his head. Charlemagne was too smart to act surprised, but through that act the pope maintained that it was his right as representative of God on earth to anoint kings. Thus the pope maintained his own authority. And

Charlemagne was no longer simply king of the Franks, he was now the new David.

The Holy Roman Empire of Charlemagne

His own palace at Aix-la-Chapelle, now Aachen, Germany, was a vast complex of buildings where the Roman baths had been restored and pools were built that could accommodate hundreds. But the emperor respected not only the secular but also the religious, so he had several buildings created to house his collection of relics. An octagonal structure still stands, a baptistery built to resemble the Holy Sepulcher in Jerusalem. Charlemagne's capital city became an important center of the Christian world and provides great insight into what the world of A.D. 800 was like.

The empire of Charlemagne is said to have been neither holy nor Roman, but there was no question who ruled. God was depicted as a distant and severe Lord—a king of his own castle who inspires fear more than love. For that reason the cult of the saints provides a welcome intermediary between man and God. And what better way to appeal to a saint than to have a part of the saint. The emperor capitalized on the market for religious relics. They were greatly treasured, and Aachen had a treasury of relics rivaled only by Rome. Charlemagne could boast that his monks protected pieces of the robe of Jesus and his sandals, the milk of the Virgin, the hair of St. John the Baptist, the beard of St. Peter, the stones that crushed St. Stephen, and the bones of numerous saints. Upon hearing of the death of two Christian clergy in Cordova, the Frankish king would send men to recover their bodies.[3]

What was called "translation" by the church in the ninth century would be called armed robbery in modern times. For example, a certain Rodoin was sent to Rome to steal the skull of St. Gregory from St. Peter's crypt. Rodoin subdued the guards and threatened them until he got not only the skull but also the guard's oath that the pope would not find out.[4] Tradition has it that Charlemagne, who had carried the spear in forty battles, dropped the spear only once. Once, however, was enough, as he died immediately after it fell from his hands.

The Spear and the Holy Germanic Empire

Germanic leaders would be in possession of the spear for a thousand years to come. In the early tenth century it was in the hands of the Saxons and was owned by Heinrich I the Fowler, who used it to battle the Magyars. His son Otto used the spear in his victory in the battle of Leck, where the Mongol advance was halted. When Hitler would serve a five-year prison sentence for his role in a premature rebellion, he was imprisoned in the Landsburg Fortress. He was treated with honor and during his captivity could look outside and gaze on the River Leck, where Otto I was victorious.

From the time of Otto and the dynasty of Saxon kings to the rule of their Germanic Hohenstauffen descendents, there is little record of the spear. Athelstan, who ruled England between 925 and 938, was said to be one owner. Athelstan was crowned king of Wessex, or West Saxony, in 925. Known for his military effectiveness, he was able to defeat the Danes and Norsemen that held the rest of England. By 934 he was already beyond the Forth, but before he could return south he had to defeat a formidable coalition of Scots, Britons, and Vikings from Dublin. After his victory at Brunanburh he could call himself King of All England. The widespread kingdom would not stay united after his death, but it did serve as a model for a "Great Britain."

His sisters were sought in marriage by the continental Germanic rulers, which explains how the spear returned to Germany. Sister Eadgita married another German Otto, who became Otto the Great.

Frederick Barbarossa was another Germanic ruler who united warring tribes in his own domain and headed south even to Rome. The man who Hitler regarded as the greatest hero even brought the pope to defeat. Still, he would then kneel before the pope for recognition, the spear that killed Jesus in his hand. Hitler would name both his assault on Russia and a mountain hideaway after this hero. Barbarossa may have depended on the spear as a talisman. But his demise came when he was leading the advance guard of his army through Asia Minor in 1190. Like the poorest of his soldiers, he endured the hot weather and the torturous travel over the plains of Seleucia in Sicily. They came to a river that offered to save them a voyage over mountains, and Frederick thought to shorten the trip. Warned against entering the swirling river, he didn't heed the advice and tried to lead his troops himself. He dropped his sacred spear, and within minutes the current became too much for the emperor. Dragged out of the water by other nobles, he collapsed and died on the riverbank.

Ownership of the spear passed to Frederick II Hohenstauffen, a mystical king with legendary occult powers who could speak Arabic with the opposing Saracens and in imitation of their leaders kept his own harem. It was claimed that not only did he favor Saracen learning over Christian teaching, but that he was also so much against his own church that he might be the anti-Christ.

The spear would pass from the Hohenstauffen to the Habsburgs. When Napoleon attempted his eastern expansion and was victorious at the battle of Austerlitz in 1805, he attempted to get hold of the spear but was not successful. It had been smuggled to a place outside the city just before the battle. One hundred years later it was given to the Hofburg Museum in Vienna, where it remains today.

Hitler and the Spear

If Ravenscroft's tale is correct, it was in the Vienna museum that a young Adolf Hitler would first see the lance. He was put into a trance by the sacred object and understood it was in his power to change the destiny of Germany. From that point on he worked to become chancellor. In 1938 he annexed Austria and had the spear brought from Austria to Nuremberg.

Hitler's occult influences are nothing short of remarkable, despite the effort of historians to play them down. Hitler had served with distinction in World War I, earning the Iron Cross, First Class. He was a victim of a mustard gas attack that left him blinded and possibly mentally disturbed. His ailment was diagnosed as "psychopathic hysteria," and he was placed under the care of a psychiatrist. His doctor Edmund Forster may have induced visions in the young soldier to cure his blindness, and it is possible such visions affected him later. When he recovered he was placed as an undercover espionage agent to root out Communist agents in the German military. His membership in the secret Political Department of the Army District Command would link him to Ernst Rohm and others who were part of a secret society called Thule. Named for a mythical Germanic homeland, Thule acted in its own interests, which included creating a new Germany.

Thule started shortly after World War I when Germany was torn between the right-wing militarists and the Socialists. Despite its true purpose, Thule presented itself as being only a literary society. In 1918 it had 250 members in Munich, where Kurt Eisner, a Jewish intellectual, had declared a Socialist Republic. In Bavaria it had 1,500 members. It also had the backing of some of Germany's wealthiest citizens, who would play their own behind-the-scenes roles. Prince von Thurn und Taxis was one of these.

Well connected and related to the crowned heads of Europe by blood, he among others was directly threatened by the spread of Communist ideas from Russia.

Thule would use the swastika and dagger as its symbols. In February 1919, Eisner would become one of the early victims of Thule's assassins. The killer was a count and a Thulist, and the backlash was immediate. On April 30, just two months later, the Red Army, a Communist faction, would execute a number of Thulists. This served to escalate the situation, and within days a group called the Free Corps marched twenty thousand strong under the swastika banner of Thule.

With the power of the army's intelligence organization, which resembled the American CIA, Thule and an underground sister organization, called Germanorden, committed numerous terrorist acts and assassinations to bend Germany to its will. Hitler's entrance into the German Workers' Party was brought about by the Army Command, which transformed the party into a political tool. By the time Hitler took over the group it was no longer Socialist. Members of Thule, Germanorden, and another secret group, Vril, would play very important roles behind the scenes. Soon Hitler was no longer an agent. The student had become the master.

There is no certainty of the extent to which Hitler himself believed in the occult, but he certainly understood its power over others. Germanorden had a series of rituals, complete with knights in armor and a program of secrecy.[5] Though they may have recruited Freemasons, they were anti-Freemason, anti-Socialist, and anti-Jew. When Hitler's power was secure, he would institute purges against many of those whose ability to control others through the occult could rival his own.

In the purges that followed, many of Hitler's longtime associates, like Rohm, were killed or committed suicide. Rohm was an occultist, a homosexual, and the leader of the SA (predecessor of the SS). Any of these facts might have, in the eyes of Hitler, justified his death, although eliminating Rohm then made Himmler the second most powerful man in Germany. Rohm was given the choice of committing suicide or being arrested. He chose arrest and was shot in prison. Hitler's psychiatrist chose suicide.

Himmler and his SS consolidated power and became the Knights of Germany. The Thule members were behind the SA, which brought about Hitler's rule. But they were now no longer needed to stake a claim to Germany's mythical heroic past. Himmler was the new Aryan superman, and he employed the Sig runes as the emblem of his SS and a way of ensuring control over the occult forces of Germany. Hitler ordered that Sig runes were now to be part of any typewriter keyboard manufactured in Germany.[6] Power was not consolidated and complete. First, Germany had been taken, now the world itself was the goal.

Hitler had lived for years in Vienna and learned the tales of German mythology at the Hofburg Museum. After Austria was among the first to be brought under the Nazi yoke, Hitler would visit the city again. Though a tour of the city was planned, the Nazi leader wanted no part of it. Instead he and Himmler rushed to claim the spear. Germany's design on Austria was that it was rightfully owned by the Germans. Party members were promised the businesses whose owners were dispossessed and the government posts that were vacated. But many Nazis headed into Vienna just to take everything that could be stolen.

In 1794 much of what had been in Charlemagne's collection had been brought to Vienna and the Hofburg Museum for safekeeping from Napoleon. While the Hofburg survived, the Hapsburgs as a dynasty did not. In 1806 the Holy Roman Empire was dissolved, and Germany, still a group of states rather than a nation, was separated from Austria. Austria kept the collection, and Germany wanted it back. The Charlemagne collection included reliquaries of saints, swords, scepters, orbs and coronation regalia, jewel-encrusted gloves, the king's prayer book, and the spear.[7]

After a handful of territorial expansions, the Western world started to awake to the reality of Hitler's design. In 1939 war was declared after Germany invaded Poland. The spear and other treasures acquired by the Nazis were moved into hiding when the war turned against Germany. The spear was moved to the Church of St. Catherine's, where it was placed in a vault.

The Hitler war machine also entailed well-organized looting of Europe's greatest treasures.

The Sainte-Chapelle in Paris and the cathedral built by Charlemagne in Aachen (Aix-la-Chapelle) housed two of Europe's finest collections of sacred artifacts. Aachen is Germany's most western city, on the border with Belgium. It had once been the center of Charlemagne's Holy Roman Empire. Both the Paris and Aachen collections would be threatened during World War II, as religious art was stolen by Nazi invaders and often destroyed intentionally or unintentionally. The collection of Charlemagne, put together one thousand years before, had been taken from Aachen and along with religious art including cathedral windows of Cologne, moved farther east into Germany. It would remain there for several years. Then the tide of war changed. The Allies had landed first in Italy and then in France and made a sweep toward Germany. The Russians turned the tide in the East, and soon Germany was surrounded on three sides.

The Spear Recovered

As General Patton's army moved into the heart of Germany, the army commanders were acutely aware that art taken from all over Western Europe had been hidden by the Nazis in over one hundred secret repositories.

The small city of Siegen was known to contain one of the greatest treasure hordes, and all efforts were made by the army to rescue these treasures. The United States had set up the Monuments Commission (actually called the American Commission for the Protection and Salvage of Artistic and Historic Monuments in War Areas), which would accompany the army in liberating and capturing cities. In Siegen the artwork had been placed in a mine. Before the Monuments people arrived, German prisoners captured by the Allies were placed in the same mine. A locked door protected a room containing six hundred important paintings, one hundred sculptures, six cases of gold and silver artifacts, and shrines from Aachen, along with Charlemagne's relics collection. From cathedral doors to the robe of the Blessed Virgin all survived,[8] but the spear was in a separate repository.

It would remain safe until the Allies entered Germany. The Allied forces led by General Patton took over a towering fortress that the American Seventh Army made their headquarters. Army intelligence then began an important search to recover plundered treasures. Army soldiers were searching houses, looking for hidden Nazis. On April 30, 1945, at 2:10 P.M. a vault was reached. The doors were massive, and using dynamite seemed to be the only way to break into the bunker. At the last minute a German was found who had the combination to open the door.

Inside, on an ornate altar looted from St. Mary's in Krakow, Poland, was the Spear of Destiny. Eighty minutes later Hitler, reminiscent of his hero Frederick Barbarossa, died. Arguably his death was less heroic, as he took his own life.

General Patton was one of the few that had understood and was fascinated by the object now in his possession. He had made a study of the search for the Holy Grail. He had read Eschenbach's *Parzival* and even searched for a supposed castle of the Eschenbach character Klingsor in Sicily. Patton requested that local historians brief him on the history of the spear and how it came into the control of the Germans. Though numerous American congressmen would soon travel to Germany and visit the massive art and other loot recovered by the Allies, few mirrored Patton's understanding.

He instinctively understood the terrible power that was held by those who controlled the spear, which was now in the hands of the Americans. Patton, who had seen the German concentration camps and was aware firsthand of the destruction the Nazis had done to the world, had seen the horrible things done by the last owners. Still, he explained to his aides, they were on the brink of a worse terror than the world had ever seen. Within months, the Americans dropped the first atomic bombs on Japan.[9]

Creating a Myth

Ravenscroft's history of the spear is dramatic and tells an almost incredible history of the world. But the question remains: is it true? One author, Charles Lawrie, believes Ravenscroft cleverly grafted fiction onto factual history. Lawrie regards Dr. Walter Johannes Stein's work researching the Holy Grail as among the greatest efforts in recent times. In a chapter written by Lawrie that is included in *The Household of the Grail*, he refers to Stein as Dr. Stone, alluding to the stone that fell to earth as the Grail. Stein had researched the spear and said "the actual history of the Spear is a novel in itself."[10]

This may have inspired Ravenscroft to write the novel and leave the true history behind if it conflicted with telling the story. There are embarrassing gaps between the time Otto and Frederick Barbarossa own the lance and when it is "discovered" in Antioch by Crusaders. There is also a paucity of documentation.

There was only tradition and possibly one source for the Ravenscroft compilation until Laura Hibbard Loomis published "The Holy Relics of Charlemagne and King Athelstan" in *Speculum: A Journal of Medieval Studies*, vol. 25, no. 4, in October 1950.

Ravenscroft had been born in England and studied history for twelve years with Dr. Stein. Stein had been aware of Hitler's occult leanings, as well as his use of drugs. That combination and Hitler's possible schizophrenia influenced the megalomaniac in making decisions. Churchill brought Stein to England to advise him on Hitler's possible actions. Though Churchill was aware of the occult influences and activity within the Nazi higher-ups, he ordered that nothing be written on the subject. Only little by little, years after the war, did the true extent of Nazi occultism become known.

From Ravenscroft's studies with Dr. Stein he put together a fascinating study of the spear and Nazi Germany. While everything in the twentieth-century part of the story may be factual, early in the tale Ravenscroft makes an unusual admission. Hitler, as a young student, was the researcher who began to trace the ownership of the spear throughout history. Once he was in power, he and Himmler had the Nazi Occult Bureau further research the gaps in ownership. Then, "Dr. Walter Stein, by means of a unique method of historical research involving 'Mind Expansion' " further bridged these gaps.[11] Since Dr. Stein died in 1957, we cannot be certain if he or his student was behind the "mind expansion" role (creating "facts" or using unconfirmed legends to dramatize true history) in writing this history.

Just how accurate the results of such a technique might be is further clouded by an embarrassing wealth of spears. The Ravenscroft Spear of Destiny is the spear held in Vienna and is called the Hofburg Spear. It differs from the others, as a Crucifixion nail is attached to it by a wire. A second spear exists in Krakow, Poland, and it can be traced back to the rule of Otto III, who had it copied, without the nail attached, as a gift. A third is in the Vatican, and the church makes no claims to its legitimacy.

Another Version

The *Catholic Encyclopedia* states that the first mention of the lance is by the pilgrim St. Antoninus of Piacenza, who traveled to Jerusalem in A.D. 570 and saw it in the Basilica of Mount Sion. Around this same time was developed the legend of Longinus, the visually impaired centurion healed by a drop of blood. The name Longinus is used in the Gospel of Nicodemus, a medieval text that was grafted onto a much earlier Acta Pilati. The Acts of Pilate was not written by Nicodemus but was compiled after A.D. 325. It not only repeats the Gospel of Luke but also goes on to recount many of the traditional incidents surrounding the Crucifixion not recorded elsewhere until later. The Acts of Pilate is not necessarily historically accurate, although it preserves such traditions. Because it also preserves the Veronica tradition and the name that is apparently contrived from True Icon (Vera Icon), it is said Longinus is a name contrived from *lance* (*logche*). While the Gospel of St. John has the Roman spearman piercing Jesus after his death, Nicodemus has Jesus being stabbed prior to his death.

Forensic science believes that the same blood and "water" reaction is a real consequence of a spear piercing first a lung, then the side or even the heart. The "water" would be fluid built up in the lungs, a very likely response to the cruel treatment.

In recent years speculative works like *The Passover Plot* and *Jesus the Magician* have added new mystery to the Crucifixion. The Christian version is that Jesus knew his destiny from the very beginning. His destiny was to redeem man by his death and Resurrection. If this is true, then why was his body treated with healing and purgative remedies when brought to the tomb?

Could Jesus have had a plan to save himself? The "plot" may have involved a careful plan that included providing him with an opiate-based drug that could make him appear to be dead. The biggest problem confronting such a plot is that normally the bones of those crucified would be broken before the victim was removed from the cross. If the bones of Jesus were broken, he could not be an earthly king. The solution: have a Roman come to the plotters' aid. Longinus, who would later be made a saint, wounded Jesus. The body was hurriedly rushed to the tomb, where the myrrh was administered to counter the effect of the drugs administered. The aloe was a healing agent used to treat Jesus' many wounds. One modern writer's version is that Jesus was aware of the plot to kill him and the counterplot to fake his death, but he himself wished to fulfill the prophecy.

Could a handful of insiders, including Longinus, have plotted anyway? It is possible. The reason Longinus was sainted, however, is not because he was complicit in such a plot, or even because he helped ensure that Jesus would reach the grave with his bones intact in order to fulfill Old Testament prophecy. He was canonized for his faith and later piety. His spear did play a role very much like that of the Cross, as an instrument of God's will, rather than as an evil associated with Christ's execution.

To the faithful, as terrible as items such as the Cross, the spear, and even the column upon which Jesus was scourged were, they are also to be treasured. There is more than one way of looking at the lance. It was after all the weapon that killed the man who would be King of the Jews as well as the Son of God on earth. In that sense it must contain a most unearthly power.

But is the Hofburg Museum lance the one that killed Jesus?

There may be as many as five candidates. Since it is known that the Krakow lance was a copy, that one can be eliminated. The first historical lance would be the lance found by Helena when she unearthed the True Cross.

While Ravenscroft says this lance went on to be part of the Milvian Bridge episode, that must be regarded as creative fiction, or speculative nonfiction at best. Helena left the lance in the Holy City, where it was seen by Antoninus in Jerusalem in 570. This is most likely the same lance that was in Jerusalem in 615 when the armies of the Persian king Chosroes took the Holy City. The *Chronicon Paschale* tells that the point of the lance was broken off and given to Nicetas, who brings it to Constantinople where it is placed in the Church of St. Sophia.

The second lance is the Vatican lance. The Vatican lance was given to Pope Innocent VIII in 1492 from the Sultan Bajazet, who had captured Constantinople. It was not actually a gift, as the sultan was trying to get favor from the pope, who held his brother captive. This relic remains in Rome and is stored under the dome of St. Peter's. The sultan was part of a Turkish invasion that captured Constantinople, and since the first lance, discovered by Helena, was known to be in Constantinople, it is very likely these two are one and the same. In the fourteenth century the writer and traveler Sir John Mandeville claims to have seen two lance points—one was in Paris and the other was in Constantinople. Pope Benedict XIV studied a drawing of the Paris spear tip and concluded that the two were actually once one and that it had simply been broken. The Vatican lance and the Jerusalem lance then are one and the same.

The third lance was discovered in Antioch in 1098 during the First Crusade. The discovery was said to have been made with the miraculous guidance of St. Andrew. A writer on Christian artifacts, M. de Mely claimed in his 1904 publication *Exuviae Sacrae Constantinopolitanae* that this relic ended up in Etschmiadzin in Armenia. Etschmiadzin is the sacred center of Armenian Christianity. It was named for the "Descent of the Begotten One" in the Armenian language and refers to the apparition of Jesus to St. Gregory, the apostle of Armenia. Very important relics, including the arm of that saint, are zealously guarded in the fortresslike monastery that has survived invasion and occupation by the Persians, Russians, and separation from the Roman Catholic Church.

The fourth lance is the lance coveted by Hitler. The Hofburg lance is called by some the lance of St. Maurice. It was known to have been used in the 1273 coronation of the "Emperor of the West" and was used as an emblem of investiture even earlier. When it first came to Nuremberg in 1424, it was said to have been the lance of Constantine, and this is the one lance that meets the description by Ravenscroft. It contains a nail of the Crucifixion, which some believe dates it into the first millennium after Christ, although there is no certainty to its date, as modern dating techniques have conclusively shown.[12]

The Spear and a Future Destiny

Ravenscroft and his blend of fact and invention have certainly added to the myth of the spear and its effect on history. But is it myth? The Habsburg family and their relations through intermarriage, the House of Lorraine, have been at the center of plans to revive the Holy Roman Empire for two hundred years.[13] Thwarted by the French Revolution, they again attempted to create a Holy League, a unified Catholic Spain in the nineteenth century. France, Italy, Austria, and Spain would again be the center of this European powerhouse. Franco-German wars and the growth of Russia hindered their plans. A third attempt at a pan-Europa movement after World War II directed by Dr. Otto von Habsburg[14] has played a role in igniting the forces toward a single currency and a nearly borderless Europe. Is there a new Holy Roman Empire in the future? Will a Habsburg dynasty rule under the Cross of Lorraine and the Spear of Destiny?

5

THE SKULL OF ST. JOHN THE BAPTIST

In December 2000 it was announced in Jordan that the skull of St. John the Baptist was uncovered near a cave in Jordan's Wadi Kharrar. The cave, which had been carved into the rock, dated to the first century A.D. according to the project director Mohammed Waheeb. In Arabic, Wadi Kharrar means "valley of trickling water," which describes this area just a few hundred feet from the Jordan River. While the announcement was made, and before any testing could be done, its premature release was following other news. A residence of John the Baptist had been uncovered near the east bank of the Jordan River, underneath a fourth-century Byzantine church. Waheeb and a handful of Jordanian archaeologists had uncovered several holy sites in the area, including three other churches. The skull was buried alone and found near the cave.

Wadi Kharrar was known as "Bethany beyond the Jordan" in ancient times. And for early Christians it had been a site of pilgrimage. Traditionally this is where John baptized his converts. Luke 3:3 simply referred to it as the "region about Jordan," while John 1:28 referred to it as Bethany beyond the Jordan. Other sources called the area Bethabara, the border between the tetrachy of Herod and the kingdom of Nabatea. While the area of the uncovered cave was close to where John preached, it was not the only spot where he supposedly was buried.

This did not dissuade both the country of Jordan and the Vatican from declaring the spot to be very important. Pope John Paul II would visit the area, and the Vatican announced it was among five Jubilee sites, including the Memorial to Moses on Mount Nebo, the modern Mukawaer where John was beheaded, the birthplace of the prophet Elias, and a shrine of the Blessed Virgin at Anjara. According to one Jordanian church leader, the entire Jordan River is sacred. Unfortunately much of it is dangerous territory due to land mines.[1] With the Vatican seal of approval, Jordan's tourism minister announced plans to attract tourists even though, as he declared, "It won't be a Disneyland." And since there are fewer signposts than banana plantations, it could be a long time before visitors arrive. The Ministry of Tourism funds the archaeological work, and much of the money comes from U.S. sources. This border area between a once hostile Jordan-Israel neglected to build any form of infrastructure. When a peace treaty was signed, Mohammed Waheeb and his crew braved the minefields to begin excavations.

Even though the Bethany beyond the Jordan may have been the true place of John's ministry, a skull unearthed at that spot still has a great deal of competition proving its authenticity.

It was said that St. John the Baptist was beheaded and buried under the fortress at Machaerus. It was also said that his body without the head was recovered by the apostles and taken away.[2] One possible place it was taken is the town of Sebaste in Samaria, which was much farther away. While it is doubtful he was buried in Samaria, from the fourth century his tomb there has still been honored. But not by all, and at one point it was desecrated and his bones partially burned. A portion of his bones were rescued in 395 and brought first to Jerusalem, then to Alexandria and placed in a basilica built over the site of Serapis.

Despite the removal of part of his bones, Sebaste remained important, and pilgrims were rewarded with miracles that were recorded by St. Jerome.

John's head is the most revered part of his remains, and it was said to be buried both at the prison fortress of Machaerus and at Herod's Jerusalem palace. Mark 6:28 describes the head being delivered to Salome, who gave it to her mother. The mother, Herodias, took the head and after piercing the tongue with a needle ordered it buried in an unclean place. The wife of Herod's steward, secretly a devotee of John's, took the head and put it in a clay vessel and buried it on the Mount of Olives where Herod owned land.

During the reign of Constantine relics were moved and removed everywhere. A skull said to be John's head was taken to Emesa in Phoenicia where it stayed possibly until the fifth century.

Before the Crusades, another head of St. John was supposedly in Constantinople. Since there is no record of the first head leaving Damascus, there were now at least two heads. Constantinople had been accumulating the relics of Christianity since the mother of Constantine traveled there. The sacred relics were protected and preserved in that city from that time, and great churches were built to house them. The city would enjoy peace and a higher degree of culture than anywhere in Europe, but this only attracted the envy of other trading cities. The Fourth Crusade was diverted by the doge of Venice, Enrico Dandolo. The doge had the army of French Crusaders attack the Christian city of Constantinople. After three days of butchery that left very few survivors, the Crusaders turned to looting. The sacred Santa Sophia was ruined as soldiers on horseback entered the cathedral to steal anything they could find. The altar was broken, the icons of the Byzantine church smashed, and tapestries and mosaics stolen. A prostitute was placed in the patriarch's seat to sing and egg on the Crusaders to further the destruction. Other churches and monasteries fared no better.

It was said that over one hundred churches were destroyed and their sacred and precious relics stolen. The True Cross, the Crown of Thorns, and the heads and bones of other saints were plundered. It was at this time the Shroud of Turin disappeared. It was also at this time that the head of St. John the Baptist preserved in Constantinople was brought to Amiens in France, where it is preserved today.

One year after the announcement of "the" skull of St. John the Baptist, another expedition in the Qumran area announced it had found his bones. Professor Richard Freund at the University of Hartford in Connecticut said there was some evidence that the bones they had unearthed were those of John the Baptist. The skeleton had been found five feet underground in a prominent burial chamber in the easternmost portion of the cemetery. The skeleton was found facing east, making it the first among the buried to receive the sun. Freund pointed out that the Essenes felt a great deal of reverence for the sun. The body was found complete, although not intact. The skull was not attached, which did not help in providing what would be important evidence of it being a beheaded man. Freund also mentioned that it was common practice to inter the skull of a beheaded man with the rest of his bones.

Professor Freund's critics were as quick to make their own opinion heard. Hanan Eshel of the archaeology department at Bar Ilan University declared Freund's theory to be "nonsense." He pointed out that it was way too early to try to decide whose skeleton it was, but he added that Muslim burials in the Qumran area were also oriented east. A December 2002 article in England's *Evening Telegraph* on the controversial discovery indicated that dating and DNA tests were scheduled[3] to help determine its authenticity.

The Voice in the Desert

There is more to John the Baptist than what is discussed in the Christian literature. This may in part account for the importance as well as the multiplicity of John's head.

There are many who believe that John the Baptist was the most important holy man in the first century. He was the holy man preaching in the desert who attracted thousands from far and wide. He is the holy man who introduced baptism, a new rite that would be instrumental in bringing in the non-Jews to the new covenant. He was to some the Son of God. When Jesus asked in Matthew 16:13 "Whom do men say that the son of man is?" the answer in Matthew 16:14 is "Some say John the Baptist."

Most feast days of the saints are on the date of their death. But John the Baptist's feast day of June 24 is on his birthday. Other than Jesus, he is the only important person of the Christian faith whose feast day is his birthday. (The date of Jesus' martyrdom is remembered also, as Good Friday.) Clearly there is more to John than meets the eye.

Matthew began the story of the ministry of Jesus with the meeting between Jesus and John in chapter three. As Jesus was baptized, a dove descended from heaven, which was the spirit of God. The dove is also a symbol of enlightenment.

Mark began his Gospel in chapter one with the same meeting. Luke begins his Gospel with the announcement of the forthcoming birth of John, who is to be a cousin of Jesus. The Gospel of John the Evangelist also starts with John baptizing Jesus. It is clear that John was an important figure at one time.

He was a lone voice crying in the desert, and while he is claimed as a focal point by many, just what sect John belonged to is elusive. The Essene group is often considered a candidate, although John's rite of a one-time initiatory baptism was not to be confused with a regular ritual cleansing common among that sect. Essenes believed they were the Temple and did not need to be in Jerusalem. They were a closed group, allowing only members with a verifiable lineage. As Jesus' lineage shows he descended from David, Essenes also had to be members of one of Israel's twelve tribes. They numbered four thousand, and there were two hundred living at Qumran where the Dead Sea Scrolls would be found. They instituted a regular meal of bread and wine, which Jesus would imitate at the Last Supper. But neither Jesus nor John were members. Jesus was not strict enough, and he repudiated the harsh judgment of the Essenes, their uncompromising attitude toward the law, and their overall omnipresent discipline. The men of the Essene sect had very little to do with the women and would certainly neither travel nor dine with a member of the opposite sex, as Jesus did regularly. On the other hand, John may have been too strict even for this sect. He lived and preached in the desert, reputedly eating only honey and locusts.

There are several characteristics of the Essenes that are in common with aspects of both Jesus and John. The Essenes had a regular ritual supper that some believe was the basis for the Last Supper. They wore all-white garments, which to them represented purity. All four Gospels refer to the presence of men in shining white garments at the tomb of Jesus when it is discovered empty. Most assume these are angels, but *angels,* which is based on the Greek *angelos,* means messenger and not necessarily a divine messenger. The Essenes had a Teacher of Righteousness, who some claim was John, although there is no evidence. Most importantly there are words Jesus used in his teachings that can be found in Essence texts that were found in the Qumran area fifty years before and have recently been allowed to be translated.

In all, there is evidence that Jesus and John were exposed to Essene thought, but both stopped short of membership in the sect. John was also not a Zealot. That group was known for violent anti-Rome activity. Today they would be portrayed as terrorists.

John was a threat nonetheless. He irritated Herod by publicly condemning Herod's second marriage to Herodias as illegal. He had abandoned his lawful wife, who was the daughter of neighboring King Aretas. It would prove to be a serious mistake for a number of reasons. Why such a lone voice crying in the desert would appear to be a threat to Herod is never fully explained unless John's following was much greater than any of the four Gospels let on.

Herod, son of Herod the Great, had married Herodias, who already had a daughter, Salome. His first wife was still living, and his new wife had been married to his brother Phillip. This was against the Jewish law, and apparently John was vocal on the matter, denouncing Herod for his breach of faith. Herod soon had John arrested, possibly because the crowds that came to hear John preach were easily aroused, and the area Herod governed was already a hotbed of rebellion. John was not mistreated in prison at first. Herod was not sure what to do with the holy man, but near isolation kept him from inciting public opinion against him. Possibly this was Herod's fear, as such an anti-Herod contingent might play into the hands of the Arabian Aretas. Herod's divorce from a Nabatean princess, his first wife, had been seen as both an affront to the Nabatean people and a sign of disrespect to their king, Aretas.

John was allowed the visits of his own disciples, who traveled and exchanged news between the holy man and the followers of Jesus. The preferential treatment, however, was not to last forever. On more than one occasion Herod had appealed to John, offering to give him back his freedom in exchange for keeping his mouth shut. It would become obvious that besides the threat of bad public opinion and the threat of war with Aretas, there was another thorn in Herod's side thanks to John—Herod's wife. She was making threats of her own to Herod to silence the irritating voice of John.

While John was in Herod's Machaerus prison, the tetrarch threw a party for his new daughter, Salome. In appreciation of her dancing before him, he promised that he would give to her anything she would ask—even "half of my kingdom." [4] No doubt influenced by her mother, Salome asked for the head of John the Baptist . . . on a dish. Herod soon regretted his promise, as he had no intention of killing John out of fear of the repercussions. Nevertheless, the promise had been made, so John was beheaded. Though the feared uprising on behalf of John's followers did not happen, bad luck did fall on Herod and his family as a result of the sacrilege.

Daughter Salome would perish by falling into the ice of the frozen water of the Sikoris River. Crushed by the flowing ice, her head and body were separated, but not before, as legend tells it, her legs danced frantically under the ice.

The Arabian king Aretas went to war with Herod. His army quickly overwhelmed Herod's, and the peace was brought by the removal of Herod as tetrarch by Rome. Exiled to Gaul, then Spain, Herod and his wife perished in an earthquake.

Meet the New Boss

It was a dramatic step for Jesus, who is described in Mark as seeing the multitude of John's followers as sheep without a shepherd. Jesus had already recruited his inner core among John's disciples. It will be seen that there were some that resented Jesus as the head of their sect. Both John and Jesus were prophets and remain prophets in Koranic teaching. John, called the Precursor in Christian theology, was more than that to the breakaway sects. According to the four Gospels, John was not a rival but simply making ready the way for Jesus. In the Gospels the baptism of Jesus was the pivotal role in his ministry, and Jesus then took center stage. To others, it was the death of John that allowed Jesus to fill the primary role.

While the ministry of Jesus did expand at this time, so did the danger. The war with Aretas allowed an anti-Rome uprising to take place in Samaria. This made the threat of Jesus to the authorities greater and the danger to Jesus greater as well.

For those who attached greater importance to John than the Gospels does, it appeared that a plot had taken place. The evidence is that this rival to Jesus was now reduced in importance by the church. The various cults that center on John go beyond making him the Prophet or the Teacher of Righteousness, important to Islam and the Essenes, respectively. To some, such as the Aramean population of the Middle East, he was a god in his own right, a sun god. The Arameans, who stretched from north of Jerusalem to Asia Minor, were not all a Jewish population. They also had a sun god, Hadad, who was like Zeus or Apollo.

The Sun God

Those who adhered to the cult of the sun god Hadad had a huge temple built to him about nine hundred years before the ministries of John and Jesus. In the temple were ancient carvings of another era. A basalt bas-relief shows a winged sphinx, possibly an influence of both Mesopotamian and Egyptian religions. It also depicts the head of a bearded man with a double crown. But before the temple of Hadad could somehow transfer devotion to the bearded head of John, the Romans intervened.

On the site sacred to the Syro-Phoenecian god Hadad, the Romans brought their own very similar god, Jupiter, and rededicated the temple. After Rome gave way to early Christianity, a church was built here and dedicated to John the Baptist. He looked like the bearded Jupiter and the bearded Hadad, and to some who worshipped in the church it is possible he was. Despite whatever amalgamation of faiths were blended in the holy site, the church contained the head that was said to be that of John the Baptist.

Later, when Islam grew to become the dominant religion, it was decided to change the Christian site of John into a mosque. And not just any mosque. Under a tolerant Islamic leadership the magnificent Umayyad

Mosque was built. Consent was given by the city's Christians, who in exchange were allowed to build a grand St. John church of their own. It took ten years to build the mosque, which became a centerpiece of the modern city of Damascus. It contains an expansive courtyard decorated with sacred mosaics. The courtyard contains a huge fountain of ablutions and several domes. The builders allowed a prominent spot for the skull of John, who was important to the Muslim faith as well, as he was a very important prophet. This grand mosque is very important today as an Arabic pilgrimage site. It is one of the few mosques with three minarets. One of those minarets is dedicated to Jesus.

Pope John Paul II was the first leader of the Roman Catholic Church to enter a mosque and visit the shrine of John the Baptist (and Prophet). It was a goodwill visit to promote tolerance between Syria's Christians and Muslims. In a curious display of just how religion adopts and accepts the unorthodox, Muslim women pray to St. John if they cannot get pregnant.

After the fall of Constantinople, Europe was flooded with the most important relics that had been preserved in that city. The skull of John the Baptist was brought back among the thousands of other relics.

St. John in Amiens

Amiens is a town about ninety miles from Paris in Picardy. Crusading knights and holy men of Picardy are credited with bringing home at least their share of Christian booty from the Crusades. In this case it was the canon, Wallon de Sarton, who carried home the head of the saint. Already ancient at the time of the Crusades, Amiens had a church dedicated to the first bishop of Gaul, Saint Fermin, from the early fourth century. This early church burned during the Fourth Crusade, and it was decided that the head of St. John merited a cathedral. In fact, France's largest cathedral in terms of area was built for John's head and dedicated to the Blessed Virgin. It is called the Cathedral of Notre Dame, and it is France's tallest. It can be seen from anywhere in the otherwise drab textile city. From inside, soaring piers and pointed arches draw attention toward heaven. The floor was once a maze that pilgrims had to crawl through. In the sixteenth century choir stalls were added, with four hundred biblical scenes carved into the oak. The most holy relic, however, was the head of St. John. Today the skull of John is in an area of the cathedral called the treasury. For a small fifteen-franc donation one can visit the treasury in the basement crypt of the church. Better still, on June 24 of each year the skull is brought out on a pillow and exhibited.

St. John in Aquitaine

It made little difference to the people of Amiens that the head of St. John was already being venerated in France (and Damascus). In 1016 monks in Aquitaine claimed they had discovered this most holy relic. The head had just been sitting in a basilica in a stone reliquary in the town of Angely. No one could fully explain just how the head came to be in Aquitaine, as it was also claimed to be back in the Holy Land at the same time. An odd liturgical text claimed later that it was brought from Alexandria to France by sea shortly after John's execution. The head was taken on a tour across Europe before being returned to Angely.[5]

It became customary in medieval times to share saintly relics, and it is possible Amiens is responsible for the proliferation of John's skull artifacts. The church of St. Sylvester in Rome, a church in Ville du Pay in France, the Sainte-Chapelle in Paris, and the abbey in Tyron all claim a part of the head. John's jaw is said to be in St. Chaumont in Lyonnais. His finger is in Malta. Most of the hand is in Montenegro, having traveled far and wide throughout Europe.

It was given by the Knights of Malta, who venerated St. John as much as their rival order the Knights Templar, to the Russian czar after Napoleon took their island. Napoleon was content with stealing the jewels of the reliquary that held the hand, although he had no use for the hand itself. The czar provided the Maltese knights with a base for years. After Czar Paul was executed it went to St. Petersburg. There the very anti-religious bias of the Russian Revolution threatened the relic, so it was again moved, to Serbia. During World War II it was taken to a monastery at Ostrog in Montenegro. It was not heard of again until the fall of the Soviet Union in the early 1990s.

St. John and the Knights Templar

The strangest case of the worship of John's head might be by the Templars themselves. During the time between their arrest and their trials, hundreds were subjected to Inquisition-style torture. They admitted to almost anything while enduring having their feet roasted and being stretched on a rack, and several admitted they worshipped a bearded head. The name of this head was Baphomet, which some claimed was a devil.

Hugh Schonfield, the author of the *Passover Plot*, used a code-breaking device called the Atbash Cipher to translate the mysterious name Baphomet to the Greek word Sophia. Sophia was the female principle of wisdom. Wisdom was present even at the creation. The Catholic Douay Rheims version of the Bible has "the spirit of God" moving over the waters in Genesis 1:2. Other versions translate this Holy Spirit as the principle of wisdom.

This principle of enlightenment is often symbolized by a descending dove, the same dove that appeared over Christ's head during his baptism. There is another connotation to wisdom, however, as Sophia is considered to be the Bride of God. The authors of *Holy Blood, Holy Grail* put forth the thesis that Mary Magdalene played a much greater role in the life of Jesus, and the name Magdala may be translated as "place of the doves." There is no explanation about the connection between Mary Magdalene and John the Baptist, as only one "bringer of Enlightenment" sports a beard. However, the proliferation of churches in medieval Europe either dedicated to Mary Magdalene or John the Baptist hints that there was some connection of much more significance than is known today.

Jean Markale in *The Templar Treasure at Gisors* points out that not all Templars were subject to interrogation by torture and lists several Templars who witnessed the head of John at various temples.[6] Hugues de Pairaud claimed it had two feet in front and two in back, a variation on the Manx flag sun god symbol.

Symbolism aside, to critics the many heads of St. John represent what is wrong about venerating saints through relics. Science so far has been unable to help. Is the skull of Christianity's most important prophet in an Arab mosque or an Amiens crypt? Or has it just recently been removed from Wadi Kharrar in the desert near the Jordan River? Science has no way of providing an answer with any certainty. DNA testing and carbon dating may be able to date the skull and bones and also match racial characteristics. If the skull is determined to be of a Muslim as the east-west burial suggests, it could eliminate the Wadi Kharrar head. If the skull is determined to be that of a Jewish man, it would not necessarily be St. John.

6

THE BLESSED VIRGIN MARY

On March 19, 2002, a fiberglass statue of the Blessed Virgin Mary owned by Patty Powell began shedding tears. It was the Feast of St. Joseph, the husband of Mary in the Gospels, but otherwise the phenomenon was inexplicable. Ten days later it started again and cried for three days, between Good Friday, when Mary's son Jesus was crucified, until Easter Sunday, when he was resurrected. The owner was not sure what to do, but when it began shedding tears again on Corpus Christi in June, she contacted her parish priest. He told her it was miraculous but that it was private and she should keep it to herself.

To the Roman Catholic Church itself, trying valiantly to keep pace with the twenty-first century, it might seem that Mary is almost an embarrassment. From apparition to apparition, from crying statues to mysterious appearances on church walls, it is an embarrassment of riches that must be explained away or dealt with. To the faithful the many apparitions of Mary, from Fatima to Medjugorje, Mexico, to Australia, are to be considered as blessings, warnings, or simply miracles.

In Rockingham, Western Australia, Patty Powell considered her statue a miracle. She had purchased it in Thailand in 1994 for just under $100 (U.S.). For years it was simply a point of reverence. Then suddenly and strangely it would shed tears. When Mary started crying again on the Assumption, Patty contacted the local newspaper. The church normally will reserve taking an opinion on such a miracle. In Patty's case the archbishop of Perth, Barry Hickey, was quick to voice his opinion. He could not determine the statue to be a hoax.

Within weeks, the statue performed its first "cure." A cancer victim with only months to live saw his white blood cell count improve immediately after his visit to the statue. By September 2002 thousands were making their way to Perth to see the miraculous statue.

Numerous scientists were called upon to verify the miraculous statue. Rob Hart of the medical imaging department of Curtin University, whose specialty is X-rays, started as a skeptic but could not find a channel within the statue. While he said that didn't rule out the possibility of a hidden reserve, there was no basis to show evidence that fluid could be stored within. Douglas Clarke, a chemist at Murdoch University, believed that some form of trickery was involved, but he could not find the source. He believed the tears were vegetable oil with a rose-oil mix or olive oil and jasmine. Brett Lindsay, a fiberglass expert, said it is possible that a statue could leach a liquid if there was a defect in the workmanship. However the liquid would contain styrene, which was not evident in Ms. Powell's statue. A biomedical chemist, Gary Whitaker, examined the statue under a microscope. Enlarging the eyes on the statue forty times, he observed that the liquid appeared during his examination, even though the statue was lying down. He could detect no holes in the eye area that could produce this effect.

The statue was also given credit for another miracle. Father Finbarr Walsh said a dying priest was anointed with the oily tears, and within two hours he was revived and cheerful. The last news was that a team of "miracle investigators" from the University of Western Australia was going to be allowed to give the statue a CAT scan. Up until recently Ms. Powell had believed that the tests for fakery were being overdone but has still consented.[1]

So many miracles surround the Blessed Virgin Mary that they are nearly commonplace. In recent years at any given time there are over 150 investigations and reports of crying statues and other phenomena. Pope John Paul II said that "the tears of the Madonna belong to the order of signs. She is a mother crying when she sees her children threatened by a spiritual or physical evil."

The mother of God, Mary, has come to take on a role that to many is at least as important as her son, Jesus. She has three very important feast days. The first is the Annunciation. While we know very little about her family or her ancestors' genealogy, it was actually Mary whom the church believes gave birth to Jesus. The Annunciation is the feast celebrating the day when an archangel of God, Gabriel, came down to earth to deliver the message that Mary would bear Jesus. Both Mary and her sister Elizabeth would conceive and bear the two most important religious men on the planet.

To Elizabeth, it was a surprise, as she was very old. Like many important women in the Bible, she was also barren. To Mary, it was a potential embarrassment, as she had to explain it to her husband-to-be. Joseph, initially upset, was told in a dream it was to be the Savior, so he went ahead with his marriage.

The second feast is the Immaculate Conception. Many Catholics regard this feast as the conception of Jesus. But the feast of the Immaculate Conception actually celebrates Mary. She alone would be born without "original sin." All Catholics believe that, thanks to Adam and Eve giving into the serpent's temptation in the Garden of Eden, everyone is born with a sin and must be redeemed. As Mary grew in importance in the religion, it was decided she had to have been born without this sin to give birth to the Son of God.

During his lifetime her son was full of surprises. Born by divine intervention, Jesus was a quick learner. For example, at age twelve his earthly parents once couldn't find him and believed he was lost. When they found him, he was teaching the elders in the temple. When he began his ministry, his family, Mary included, questioned his sanity. He is accepted later, however, and at the wedding feast of Cana, for a reason not easy to understand, Mary asks him to do something, as the affair is running short of wine. It is possibly the first and only time he performs a miracle for a seemingly trivial matter.

By the time Jesus is crucified, Mary is a follower and at his side. She too is in danger, as are the followers of Jesus and other family members. She may have left the area with Joseph of Arimathea and later met with John the Evangelist, whom Jesus asked to take care of her.

The Gospels make no further mention of Mary, and she is basically ignored in the books of the New Testament. The tradition evolved that she has been bodily assumed into heaven after her death. When and where are both uncertain. Mary's Assumption is her third feast day. The date of her Assumption is somewhere between three and fifteen years after the death of Jesus. St. John of Damascus said that she died in the presence of the apostles, but when her tomb was opened, at the request of Thomas, she was gone. This story appears to have been put together to fit both the nature of St. Thomas and the story of the Assumption. Given the importance of Mary today, the wide range of dates and the conflicting stories is at least surprising. The place of her Assumption too is far from being certain.

There is a tomb of Mary in Jerusalem, but it was unknown until the sixth century. There is also a house of Mary in Ephesus where the tradition of her Assumption may have started. There are claims to tombs in Bethlehem, in England, and in eastern Asia as well.

The celebration of the feast of the Assumption of Mary into heaven may have begun without the recognition of the church. The *Catholic Encyclopedia* believes the date may have simply been the date of a dedication of a church to Mary, and later that date was accepted. By the year 700 the Feast of Mary's Assumption had become one of Rome's largest annual events. The church finally made the belief in Mary's Assumption into heaven a part of official church dogma in 1950.

To understand the role of Mary in a non-Catholic sense requires looking back at the history and development of religion. At some time in ancient history the entire world believed in the power of a goddess. In some civilizations the goddess was more powerful than a male god. Invasions by Aryan and Semite peoples out of Asia brought a patriarchal culture and a backlash against the goddesses and women themselves. Greece kept its goddesses, but women were blamed for the evils of the world, thanks to Pandora, once the "All-Giver," who now gave the world bad things like disease and strife. Eve too would ruin the idyllic life in Paradise that came to an end when she gave in to temptation and then induced Adam into sin. Jesus brought a new message to the patriarchal world and welcomed women into his circle of insiders and into his fold as followers. The early Christian church not only accepted women but also allowed them to actively participate in the church. Mary was understood by pagans who had clung to their sites of worship and to their female gods. The earliest depictions of Mary in Rome are in the catacombs and date to A.D. 150. Mary is dressed plainly and holds the baby Jesus, which might imply that she is simply an earthly woman. In Ephesus, however, in the second century, Mary is depicted with outstretched arms, wearing a crown, bathed in heavenly light.[2] She was even depicted with a crescent moon, just like Artemis.

As a human mother or a glorious goddess, Mary filled a role that was sorely missed.

Ephesus was a very important city up until when it was overwhelmed by Gothic barbarians one hundred years later. At that time hundreds of thousands then fled west to Rome, where they played a great role in the theology of the church. At Nicaea, the first great council of the church in

Constantine's era, bishops of Asia Minor outnumbered Roman bishops. The Ephesians did more to establish doctrine and seriously elevated Mary within the church. They may have even played a role in teaching the church how to win friends and converts. The church would encourage its missionaries to continue to allow worship at pagan sites but attempted to reorient the focus of the worshippers' beliefs. Mary made that much easier to accomplish.

Soon Mary replaced the goddess but not without inheriting her titles. Mary became Regina Coeli, the Queen of Heaven. She became Stella Maris, the Star of the Sea. She replaced Eve as the Mother. In Alexandria, Bishop Athanasius had visions of Mary being the queen of heaven. In Cyprus, Bishop Epiphanius wrote the *Refutation of All Heresies* and pointed out that St. John's vision in the Apocalypse (Rev. 12:1–2) had a reference to a crowned woman in heaven giving birth to a child.

The church was not unified in accepting Mary, so in A.D. 431 a council was held at Ephesus to debate her status. It was actually held in a church that Constantine's mother, Helena, ordered to be built for Mary, and it was called the Church of the Most Holy Virgin. The pro-Marian bishops won. Mary's Holy Days became official, and the Hail Mary, the most commonly repeated prayer in Catholicism, was composed.

From then on there was no stopping her importance in converting pagans to the faith. Shrines to goddesses great and minor existed all over Europe. Bringing Europe into the Christian fold was accomplished by replacing the pagan goddesses with Mary. Pope Gregory understood that false conversion would not last and that pagan belief would take a long time to be eradicated. He wisely chose accretion and wrote to an abbot "that the temples of the idols . . . should on no account be destroyed." Instead he instructed that through holy water and relics, the temples of old simply be purified. "Let some other solemnity be substituted . . . such as a day of dedication or the Festivals of the holy martyrs whose relics are enshrined there."[3]

While there is no shortage of examples of reorienting pagan sites, the spectacular and mysterious cathedral at Chartres, the Cathedral of Notre Dame, may serve as one of the best. One hour southwest of Paris, this Druid worship center maintained a tradition of goddess worship into Gallo-Roman times, when a female deity under different names still reigned. The spread of Christianity was better served, believed the church, by occupying the sites of pre-Christian worship and converting them before the faithful. The worship of the goddess gave way to Christianity's most sacred woman, Mary, the mother of God.

At an unknown date a wooden church was built over the Druid site. But fire destroyed the original church and three reconstructions before the spread of Gothic stone cathedrals began. In 867 Charles the Bald, a Germanic Frank, gifted the chemise of the Virgin Mary to tiny Chartres. Already on the pilgrimage map, the importance of Chartres brought the faithful from all over Europe.

The site of this great monument in France, it is claimed, has significance way beyond the obvious. Many secrets of the initiated, both Christian or otherwise, are preserved in stone and glass. The stained glass windows tell of the preservation of the Ark of the Covenant and the Holy Grail. They depict the son Jesus crowning Mary as queen. Such a depiction would have shocked the Jerusalem church, but by the twelfth century, there was no marginalization of the importance of Mary. She had replaced Eve, as well as Isis, Venus, and Ishtar.

For the faithful who sacrificed to make the pilgrimage to Chartres, there was more to see than the huge physical presence of one of the world's greatest monuments. One of the many statues is what is called a pillar-Madonna. Here at the choir of the cathedral stands a miracle-working statue that has drawn the hopeful for the last five centuries, when its power was first recognized.

The miracles of Mary began as early as A.D. 40, when she appeared to St. James near Caesar-Augusta in Spain. She told him to build a chapel on the banks of the Ebro River. Sixteen feet long and eight feet wide, it is considered to be the first chapel to Mary. By the time of the Crusades, the rebuilt church to Mary would be a huge domed basilica the same dimensions as the goddess temple at Ephesus.[4] Near Madrid a chapel was built to Mary after a statue of her was given to the people by the apostle James. Eusebius built a sanctuary to her that became famous for another miraculous statue.[5] Images of her painted reputedly by St. Luke began appearing in Athens, Lebanon, and Constantinople. In January 590 the pope led a three-day procession with one such miraculous statue to stop the plague. As it reached St. Peter's a vision of St. Michael sheathing his sword told all the punishment of God was complete, the piety of the faithful would stop the plague. During the reign of King Dagobert a Dark Ages *Mary Celeste* appeared on the Liane River. Without passengers, sailors, oars, or masts, the ship carried only a statue of the Virgin. It was placed in the chapel at Boulouge and became the source of miracles.[6] Charlemagne acquired a portrait of Mary that was painted by St. Luke. It is now in the Polish shrine of Czestochowa.

Such miraculous images and statues appeared everywhere.

Mary in the New World

In the Americas the Spanish missionaries were the first to attempt to convert the native populations to the European faith. Mexico's indigenous religion already had numerous similarities with Christianity. This may have assisted the conversion.

In December 1531, only ten short years after Cortez defeated the Aztecs, the missionaries were already at work. A new convert, Juan Diego, saw a bright light on a hill called Tepeyac. At the top of the hill a young girl, radiant, said she was Mary, the mother of God. She wished that a church be built to her on the site. Juan went through great difficulty to get an audience with Bishop Zumarraga. When he told his bishop, the bishop did not accept the story and finally dismissed him, saying that he might believe if there was a sign that he could see. Juan returned to the hill and again saw the Blessed Virgin. On the instruction of Mary he gathered flowers to bring to the bishop. He wrapped them in his white cloak. When he returned to the bishop to show him the out-of-season flowers, the varieties of roses alone was a miracle, but the bishop was in awe when he saw Juan's cloth. It now held an image of the Blessed Virgin.

Bishop Zumarraga kept the sacred image in his own private chapel until the church could be built and dedicated. When it was complete, it was renamed Guadeloupe.

The church was built, and over four hundred years later the site is the destination for ten million pilgrims each year. It is estimated that on the Feast of Our Lady of Guadeloupe in early December, two million pilgrims come to Mexico City to visit the shrine. The Guadeloupe image is everywhere. Even in outdoor stalls of the marketplace in Mexico City, merchants erect altars where the image is most prominent. Millions of Mexicans wear a medal struck in the image, and it appears in advertising and on bullfighters' capes. It may be safe to conclude that it has brought millions to the Catholic faith.

Not everyone is convinced, however, of the authencity of this story, since it may be a reworking of a previous story. The name Guadeloupe was taken from a river in Spain, where in 1326 a miraculous appearance of a statue of the Virgin took place after the Virgin appeared to another peasant, a cowherd by the name of Gil Cordero. The story is somewhat less than romantic, as the cowherd finds a dead cow and decides to take the skin. He pulls out his knife, preparing to skin the corpse, when suddenly the cow rose back to life. At the same time Gil heard a voice claiming to be the mother of God. She instructed the cowherd to tell the clergy of what he had seen and to come to this spot, where they would find an image of her. Gil, of course, had a hard time convincing anyone of what he heard and saw. But he was so persistent that he ended up with a contingent of townspeople, who moved boulders and dug through rocks until they found the statue that was promised. No miracle was involved in creating the statue; it had been buried long ago to avoid being taken during the Muslim invasion. A church was built, and it quickly attracted pilgrims. Soon many who had visited the church of Our Lady of Guadeloupe were claiming miraculous cures took place during their visits. The possibility that the missionaries in Mexico had brought the story to the New World, where it "inspired" a new miracle, is more than a remote possibility.

A second reason to be skeptical is the site itself. The hill in Mexico where the image was discovered was already sacred. It was a place where the Mexican goddess Tonantzin was worshipped. She is called the "Little Lady" and the "Corn Woman" and is also identified with the moon. Anthropologists see the transfer of worship as a Christian modus operandi of absorbing the pagan culture into the Christian faith. The Spanish site had been the locale for worship of what is called the Black Virgin. All over Europe there have been images and statues of this darkened version of the Blessed Virgin. In some cases the church just explains them away as having become black through exposure to candle smoke over the years. Another explanation is that they are leftovers from pagan goddess worship. The mother-and-son theme was not unknown before Christianity, and in fact it was an important theme in Isis-Osiris, and Ishtar-Tammuz. The Virgin-and-child image of Guadeloupe in Spain is much more typical of a pre-Christian form.

The image itself has been the subject of investigation, both in 1556 and in recent times. Joe Nickell, in *Looking for a Miracle,* points out that the image of Our Lady of Guadeloupe is very similar to a Spanish depiction that had been painted one hundred years before Mexico was even discovered. Numerous copies were made of that early painting, and there is no doubt one could have been carried to the New World. Second, and more damaging, is that there is abundant evidence of paint on the cloak. There are even areas where Nickell says it appears the image had been sketched out and even corrected before paint was applied. The other side of the argument is that the cloth itself, called a *tilma,* is made from a fragile cactus called the maguey plant. It is so thin that it rarely lasts for twenty years, never mind centuries, and is unsuitable for absorbing paint. Artists report that they can find no evidence of brushstrokes, and a University of Florida biophysicist, Dr. Philip Callahan, says no such sketch is underneath the blue and pink pigment. He was particularly impressed that the picture from close-up appeared white, while from farther away olive.[7]

Dr. Leonicio Garza-Valdes, whose work on the Shroud of Turin presented a strong challenge to the carbon dating issue, took an opposing stance on the *tilma* of Guadaloupe. He claimed that by studying photographs taken in 1999 and using various filters, he determined there were actually three paintings, one over the other. He in fact declares that the facial features of the Virgin show a degree of change from the first to the third painting. In the first painting he declares that the face is more "Indian" in nature.

Dr. Jose Asta Tonsman of the Mexican Center of Guadalupian Studies has been studying the image for twenty years and has declared the picture to be miraculous. He started his work shortly after getting his doctorate from Cornell while working for IBM. He scanned at very high resolutions a photograph of the original image. Through digital technology he has magnified the irises of the Virgin's eyes 2,500 times. Then, using optical procedures, including filtering to eliminate "noise," the Peruvian engineer was able to identify people reflected in the eyes of the Virgin. He claims this recorded the scene of the moment when Juan Diego opened his cloak to the bishop and a small audience back in 1531.

His study may have been the most exacting, although it was not the first. From 1956, when the ophthalmologists Dr. Javier Torrocella Bueno and Dr. Rafael Torrija Lavoignet independently discovered the presence of the Samson-Purkinje effect, until now, over twenty physicians and ophthalmologists have reviewed the image. The Samson-Purkinje effect is a triple reflection characteristic of all live human eyes. Images reflected in human, not painted eyes, are located exactly where they should be, with the minor distortion that would correspond with the curvature of the cornea.

Dr. Tonsman believes that the reflection in the eyes is there for a reason—to help authenticate the image well into the future, when technology such as his own could challenge or confirm the miracle.

Miracle or not, native conversions took place at the rate of one million a year after the discovery of the image.

A Modern Marian Miracle

Searchers for the miraculous do not need to search in Fatima, Lourdes, Medjugorje, or even Mexico City to find paranormal apparitions of the Blessed Virgin. And Patty Powell of Western Australia is not the only one to be so closely involved with a modern miracle. In 1992 Father Jim Bruse, a parish priest in a Virginia suburb, ordered a statue of the Blessed Virgin for his mother. He brought the statue to her house to bless it, just before Thanksgiving. The statue began exuding tears from the moment the house was blessed. At first he thought he might have been the cause, since he had spread holy water through the house during the blessing. But even afterward the statue kept weeping. The amount of water from the statue was enough to fill up a jar. When he went back to his church, other statues around him too exhibited tears. He became even closer to the miracle as he started showing signs of the stigmata. It should be noted that only one other parish priest has exhibited stigmata out of three hundred other recorded cases. With numerous statues weeping in addition to stained glass windows and even a cement statue, parish attendance rose to the point where parking was a premium. A CBS television show caught a weeping Madonna statue on film, and the *Washington Post* as well as *U.S. News and World Report* ran stories on the event.

Bishop John Keating of the Arlington Diocese was not amused. His reaction was to take the statues and order Father Jim to undergo a psychological examination. The doctor who would examine Father Jim in the priest's office talked with him for two and a half hours. At the end of the examination the psychologist commented that a statue in the office was shedding tears. A meeting with the bishop and several other priests was set up. When Father Jim entered the room, every statue in the room began weeping. Bishop Keating was now convinced.[8]

Father Jim was transferred.

7

CHRISTIANITY'S MOST SACRED WOMEN

Mary Magdalene: Saint and Sinner

St. Hugh, born in 1135, was still alive and, of course, not yet a saint when he visited the arm of Mary Magdalene Fecamp in Normandy. He had become the prior of Witham in England, which was founded by Henry II. A church investigation of King Henry's involvement for killing St. Thomas à Becket, the archbishop of Canterbury, found him not responsible. Yet he was told to go on a Crusade for his penance. The king was too busy. Instead he set up the first house of the Carthusian monks in England. Hugh, the good man that he was, was made prior of the church.

He fought for the poor and stood up against the forest laws of the king, which allowed no hunting by commoners. He even rebuilt Lincoln Cathedral, which had been destroyed in an earthquake.

Since every monastery worth its salt held a relic, Hugh, with his typical tenaciousness, decided it was time to get one.

He crossed the channel to France to visit the remains of Mary Magdalene. He carried with him a silver casket that already contained the relics of numerous saints. At the monastery at Fecamp in northern France, he would view the arm of Mary Magdalene. As he leaned over the relic of the saint, those present thought the holy man was reaching over to kiss the bones. But they recoiled in horror when he used his teeth to bite off two fingers from her hand. He later explained it was easier than breaking them off. Though chastised for his behavior, he and his career somehow survived. He was canonized by 1220, and his own bones were placed in a magnificent gold shrine. During the Reformation they were stolen.

· · ·

Mary Magdalene had suffered more at the hands of the church than just having her bones scattered. Possibly the most maligned saint among Christianity's women, Mary Magdalene was simultaneously considered to be a rich woman, a prostitute, a temple priestess, possessed by demons, and saved by Jesus. Churches and cathedrals, as well as hospitals and homes for unwed mothers, have been dedicated and named for her. A recent body of literature goes as far as suggesting she was even the wife of the Savior.

How was it that a woman could be loved as both sinner and saint? Understanding how modern Christianity developed from pagan roots helps to separate the historic Mary from the contrived replacement of the goddess. The Blessed Virgin Mary as a historic person was the mother of Jesus. As a focal point in the process of converting pagan Europe and Asia, she filled the role of the virgin goddess as well. She was both the Virgin and the Mother.

Mary Magdalene, also an historic person, served the church in replacing the goddess in another context. But it is her tradition and myth that brought her to this point. If one reads the Gospels literally and carefully, she is not the same as Christian tradition depicts her. She was not a prostitute, love interest, or wife of anyone, but was simply a companion in the circle of Jesus.

It was during the feudal period that she became very important. Part of the reason may have been that Mary, the mother of Jesus, had ascended to heaven. There could be no relics of Mary that would not contradict the teaching of the church. Mary Magdalene was seen as being very close to Jesus and had remained on earth, allowing the seekers of her relics to find them.

Mary Magdalene may have enjoyed the attention of Jesus, who broke convention by traveling and breaking bread with women. She was the first to reach his tomb and witness the first sign that Jesus was resurrected. Yet she received little respect. In one apocryphal Gospel, Peter wanted her excluded from the group. After her life she was equated without basis to the prostitute in the Gospels. It was during the feudal period that the attributes of Mary Magdalene took on a new role, and she was seen in a better light. Churches throughout France were dedicated to her. But her new-found popularity did not always bring welcome attention. During this period at the hands of another fellow saint, she would suffer that great affront from St. Hugh of Lincoln.

Mary Magdalene in the Gospels

It is evident that Mary Magdalene is important in the Gospels. She apparently traveled with Jesus, as did other women. The role of women was marginalized in the Gospels, which may be in part the result of the editing process done on the Gospels when Constantine put his stamp of approval on the church in Rome. One of her key appearances took place at the house of Lazarus late in the ministry of Jesus, although the Gospels are not in agreement about this. Matthew (25:7) has Jesus going to the home of Simon the leper in Bethania, where "there came to him a woman" who anoints him with a precious ointment. The apostles criticized the waste of the expensive ointment. It could have been sold and the money given to the poor. Jesus replies that wherever his Gospel is preached so should the fact of his anointment. The name of the woman is not mentioned. Immediately afterward Judas betrays Jesus. It is almost as if by this act, some dissent had crept into the band of twelve.

Mark (14:4), possibly the basis for Matthew's Gospel, also has the unnamed woman anointing Jesus and asking, "Why was this waste of ointment made?" He has the apostles murmuring against her and Jesus saying, "Let her alone, why do you molest her?" Again the Judas betrayal is immediate (Mark 14:10), and it might even be considered a consequence. Luke mentions Mary at a much earlier point in his retelling of the life of Jesus. She apparently travels with the group, an unacceptable behavior among unmarried women of the times. Luke, however, avoids the anointing story. John provides the most detail and the most drama. Jesus hears that Lazarus is sick and waits to come to Bethania. When he gets there two days later, he summons Mary Magdalene to go with him to the tomb. Jesus himself cries (John 11:35) on his way to the tomb and is "groaning" in distress when he gets there. Nevertheless he commands the stone be moved away and summons Lazarus from the dead. John then has Mary anointing Jesus with the expensive jar of spikenard (John 12:3) and Judas himself as the initiator of the complaint about the waste of the precious ointment.

Mary Magdalene is apparently well known to the apostles a few days later when Jesus is lying in a similar tomb. Mary arrives first and finds there is no need to roll away the stone, as in the case of Lazarus. It is already moved and the tomb is empty. Jesus then appears to her, before any of his disciples.

While that is the last mention of this obviously important woman in the accepted Gospels, through the so-called gnostic Gospels, early Christian writings that were plundered and burned by both Roman and Christian censors, Mary survives.

In 1945 an Egyptian digging near Nag Hammadi unearthed a horde of early Christian writings. They had survived two thousand years and, more importantly, the ravages of numerous book burnings. They included much of the accepted writings of Clement of Alexandria and Origen. And they included the Gospel of Thomas, which apparently had numerous sayings of Jesus. In one, the Gospel of Mary, Peter and Mary Magdalene are very much at odds, and Peter resents the fact that the "Savior loved [her] more than the rest of the women." Later it has Peter complaining that Jesus imparted secrets to her in private that he did not share with the men.[1] The Gospel of Philip, also not accepted by the church, had Mary as the constant companion of Jesus. Possibly worse in the eyes of the church is that Jesus is depicted as openly showing affection toward Mary.

While an exact history is difficult because of the contradictions among the various writings, there is no doubt that she was part of the inner circle. There is also little doubt that this inner circle would have serious reasons for not staying in Jerusalem. Where did they go?

Out of Jerusalem

A fourth-century writer, Etheria of Galicia, recorded Mary's early visit to Palestine in which she came across the tomb called the Lazarium. In Arabic it was called the Aizirieh.[2] In the fifth century the church doctor St. Jerome wrote of his mother's visit to Jerusalem, where she too had seen the tomb of the resurrected man. Shortly afterward, however, tradition claimed that Mary Magdalene had gone to Ephesus, and Lazarus, regarded as her brother, followed. There he became bishop. Gregory of Tours, writing a hundred years later, mentioned her tomb in Ephesus. A sepulcher had been built at the mouth of a grotto where she had lived. During the Roman persecutions of early Christians, seven men were walled up in the cave. Mary miraculously interceded, and two hundred years later the seven awoke, alive. Thus Mary Magdalene was connected with the Cave of the Seven Sleepers, and pilgrims often visited the tomb in hopes of a healing miracle.

As Constantinople grew in importance during the Byzantine period, relics of the saints were taken from around Asia Minor and brought to that city. The Byzantine emperor Leo VI is given credit for "translating" the bones of both Lazarus and Mary from Ephesus. In 1205 his city would be sacked during the Crusades, and the relics of the brother and sister saints were lost.

A Different Tradition

There is one problem with the Jerusalem-to-Constantinople trail of Mary's bones. A completely separate story has her going directly from Jerusalem by sea to France.

This tradition has the inner circle of Jesus' group leaving Jerusalem on a ship owned by Joseph of Arimathea. He would certainly have had a motive for leaving Jerusalem, as he had stuck his neck out to get the body of Jesus, only to have it disappear from the tomb at the moment of the Resurrection. Joseph's freedom and possibly his life were in jeopardy. Because he was considered to be a tin merchant with ships capable of reaching Atlantic ports, he thereby had the means to help Mary Magdalene and others escape persecution.

In one version Joseph transports Mary Magdalene and a handful of the faithful to France. Her small party became famous for their first-century adventures, and the area of the Camargue where they worked miracles became known as Les Saintes-Maries-de-la-Mer. While Mary preached, Martha took it upon herself to battle a terrible dragon called the Tarasque. She defeated the dragon, and the feat is celebrated even today in a colorful annual pageant. This group also included Sarah, the dark-skinned servant girl, who was claimed by the Gypsies as their own. The Gypsies flock to the town every year for the two-day (May 24 and 25) celebration. After an all-night candle procession the streets come alive with flamenco, bullfights, and horse races, creating a festive climate that draws both Gypsies and tourists from all over.

It is not the only version that has Mary coming to France. One of the oldest written traditions is the account of Mary Magdalene by Rabanus, the archbishop of Mainz, written in the ninth century. Around the time of the Crusades, respect for Mary Magdalene began to grow. The thirteenth-century biographer of the saints, Jacobus de Voragine, tells of a Mary completely different from what the Gospels would let us believe, but he confirms much of the "three Marys" tradition. She was highborn, owned properties, and had amassed great wealth. And she followed Jesus of her own accord, not as a desperate sinner or a prostitute. She was present at the Crucifixion and was the first to visit the tomb and recognize the risen Christ. Fourteen years after the death of Jesus she left Palestine with a small party that included Martha; her brother, Lazarus; Mary Salome; Mary Jacobe; and Sarah, the servant girl. They landed in France near the port that is now called Marseilles. She performed miracles and preached the word of Jesus until her death. Her body was then laid to rest in an oratory constructed by St. Maximinus at a place called Villa Lata. Later it would be called St. Maximin.

She was at rest until 769, when a monk then broke into her sarcophagus and stole her remains.

Charlemagne had just built a church at Vezelay in Burgundy, and for his new church he wanted a suitable trophy saint. Mary did not disappoint. One miracle tells of how a blind pilgrim to Vezelay was cured simply by wishing he could be worthy to see her church. Another tells of a man who begged forgiveness for a list of his sins he left in her altar. The next day all the sins listed were erased from the paper. In the ninth century her relics were moved from the church to an abbey. This abbey, built by the pious Count Girart de Roussillon at Vezelay, was not always in the best repute, and a wealth of correspondence recalls its quarrels with other monasteries and the Crown. In the eleventh century the Cluniac abbot Geoffrey took over, and shortly afterward Mary's relics were uncovered. He went on his own "crusade" to build Mary Magdalene's status. He would point out in sermons that she was a model of zealous devotion who had stayed at the Crucifixion long after the apostles ran away. They were said to be known to be there but were somewhat forgotten. All that changed when the abbot convinced the pope to write a bull announcing her remains to be at Vezelay. Pope Stephen IX had confirmed her as sole patron and ratified the abbey's possession of her relics.[3] Pilgrims from as far away as England came to offer precious gifts. They sought to be healed, forgiven, and even freed from being slaves or prisoners, a reward for making the pilgrimage. It was said she even resuscitated a dead knight who had fallen in battle.

Today the great basilica of Mary Magdalene rises from a rock in the valley. By the mid-eleventh century the Abbey Church of Saint Mary Magdalene at Vezelay was an important pilgrimage site.

But not everyone was convinced it was her body that was in Burgundy, despite additional papal bulls of Urban III and Clement III. During Geoffrey's rule as abbot, no one had been allowed to see the bones. When Geoffrey, plagued by questions, decided to open the tomb, the abbey was plunged in darkness.[4]

In 1146 at Eastertime, Pope Eugenius III came to Vezelay, where he announced the Second Crusade. This was a high point for that shrine, indicating both its importance and prestige. Another hundred years would pass without the relics of Mary ever being viewed. In 1265 Clement IV finally sent a monk to investigate. In front of two bishops her tomb was opened, without serious consequence. The body of a woman with a large amount of hair still preserved was in the tomb.

Two years later the "most Christian" French king, Louis IX, came to visit her remains on Easter Sunday. The relics were given a new coffin, and many bones from the body were handed out to various dignitaries. The king took bones from the arm, the jaw, and three teeth, and in exchange he provided the abbey with relics from his own collection.[5]

From there it was all downhill. Another body of Mary Magdalene was discovered back in the crypt of St. Maximin in Provence in 1279. This was five hundred years after the body had been first "translated" or stolen from St. Maximin. By now, both Autun and Marseilles claimed the relics of Lazarus, who many called her brother. The body in Maximin was almost completely intact, missing only a leg bone. A witness to the opening of the sarcophagus claimed a fennel plant grew out of the mouth, providing a fresh fragrance to the tomb.

The popularity of Vezelay faded slightly as there was now a rival site in France. It would be sacked by Huguenots, French Protestants, in 1567 and again during the French Revolution. Today the medieval town still draws thousands of tourists and faithful alike. Most famous is the tympanum of the basilica, where the apostles and Jesus are depicted during the event known as the Pentecost. Visitors can still go below the basilica into the crypt to view the bones of this most important early saint.

The Jesus Family

Since the unearthing of the Nag Hammadi Gospels and the publication of *Holy Blood, Holy Grail*, there has been much speculation on the relationship of Mary Magdalene and Jesus. Could they have been husband and wife?

The Gospels do accept Jesus as preaching about the value of marriage, and nowhere in any accepted text is there a hint that he regarded celibacy or abstinence as being of any particular value. Certainly at least two of the apostles were married and had children. Why then are the Gospels silent about the marital status of Jesus?

It is possible that the mention of a wife and children would have condemned them to death. The Gospels not only claim that Jesus fulfills the Old Testament prophecy of a savior and king but also depict the king as an heir to the Davidic bloodline. Before and after Jesus there were revolts that had Rome massacring thousands. The purge that took place at Masada, a generation after Jesus, is nothing short of genocidal. A purge of other members of the family of Jesus is recorded fact. A direct heir to Jesus would certainly be marked for death. But simply because they are not mentioned does not mean there were no heirs.

The church writer Eusebius comments on heirs to the family of Jesus surviving into the time of Trajan (A.D. 98–117), and in A.D. 318 Pope Sylvester met personally with several.[6] By this time leaders of the Nazorean church and the leader of the Roman-based church were at odds. Others, like James, had not survived for long after the death of Jesus. Eusebius quotes an earlier writer, Hegesippus, whose works are lost, as saying: "Vespasian issued an order that, to insure that no member of the royal house should be left among the Jews, all descendants of David should be ferreted out."[7] Later, Domitian did the same, specifically targeting Jesus' family members—"And there still survived of the Lord's family, the grandsons of Jude, who was said to be his brother humanly speaking."[8]

The five books of Hegesippus are very important, as they are one of the earliest non-Gospel records of the church. They were written in the second century, possibly A.D. 130, a time when the church was not yet allied to a philosophy that had to cater to politics. It was also not written to please the Judaic faction of the still new Christianity. The split between Judeo-Christianity and Gentile Christianity was in the past. In other words, it was a true history, unadulterated and unedited. Hegesippus set out simply to construct a list of bishops that were in charge of different cities where a church was founded by the apostles. Along the way his comments regarding the family of Jesus are revealing. According to Hegesippus, Jesus had brothers and sisters, cousins and uncles, and at least his brothers had generations of heirs. What Hegesippus does not mention is a married Jesus.

Much of the Gospels and early Christian writings employ code known to have one meaning to the initiate and serving others as a moral parable. Early Christians were referred to as little fishes and the baptismal font as a fishing pond. As Jesus instructed Peter that he would be fishing for men, this image was packed with meaning. To others it would just be a reference to the fact that several apostles were from a fishing town and made their living as fishermen. Jesus, however, is not referred to as the "Fisher" or "Fish," although that symbol is said to have been derived from the Greek letters for "Jesus Christ, Son of God and Savior." He is referred to as the Bridegroom and the Shepherd, although he is neither in the Gospels. The meaning of other passages and parables and their meanings for Jews, Gentiles, and Samaritans have been debated for two thousand years.

Hegesippus had no such coded references.

While there is certainly motivation for not mentioning the family of Jesus in the Gospels, it is not "proof" that Jesus was or was not married. Proponents of the married-Jesus theory have only negatives to call evidence. Surely being a single Jewish male, especially one regarded as a "rabbi," would imply marriage by the late age of thirty. And if Jesus was not, that would invite comment. Yet John the Baptist was not considered to be either married or not married, and there is no comment on that being remarkable.

It is possible that in the process of fictionalizing Gospel characters, Holy Grail literature did much to create new tradition. Medieval writers may have built on a burgeoning industry of Grail literature, which developed later and took license with the existing early history of Jesus. Grail stories do have a Fisher King, wounded, and who because of such an injury can no longer lead. Just how much of a reference this is to a wounded but not dead Jesus is a subject for debate. Jacobus de Voragine wrote that Mary Magdalene had been engaged to marry John the Baptist. The marriage was first delayed because of John's ministry. Then John's ministry became the cause of his death. Mary, in her grief, took to promiscuity, and it was Jesus who interceded and rescued her from that life. We do not know his sources, but he lists her mother's name as Eucharis, a term of respect often given to the goddess Aphrodite.[9]

The concept of Mary having escaped Jerusalem and sailing to France were in place long before the Crusades, which brought great popularity to the body of work based on the Holy Grail. St. Bernard, who increased the prestige of the Cistercian order of monks and the Knights Templar, would have much to say about the women of the church, both Mary the mother of Jesus and Mary Magdalene. While this could have influenced the inclusion of certain themes in the Grail texts, the tradition was already in place.

During the period of the Crusades a great passion for building cathedrals and churches swept across Europe. The two who lent their names to the greatest number of churches are John the Baptist and Mary Magdalene. Her relics are spread far and wide within France.

At the church of St. Victor in Marseilles, she wears the fleur-de-lis, the emblem of that country, which originated with the Merovingian dynasty. The abbey of St. Victor was founded in the fifth century when the Merovingians entered the territory. The present church was begun in the eleventh century. It is one of the numerous Mediterranean churches where images of the Virgin are depicted in black, which indicates a connection is being made between the pre-Madonna goddess of Isis. As bright colors were used to depict the male sun gods, dark colors depicted the goddess, who represented the moon. The Black Madonna, Isis, had been a widow who gave birth to her son after her bridegroom was dead. The mystery of a Mary-John union or a Mary-Jesus union would simply continue the mythical Isis story.[10]

The Merovingians did not survive the usurping Carolingians, but for centuries to come, French royalty went out of their way to marry into the Merovingian line. The crown of Charlemagne had the title "Rex Salomon," indicating a descent from the Davidic bloodline. Louis XI is said to have regarded the Magdalene as the source of the imperial bloodline.[11] A degree of skepticism must be preserved in the study of such "genealogy," as French kings claimed to rule by divine right and French royalty had themselves written into the body of Grail literature as patrons and had their artists paint their images as being present at historic religious events. Early Merovingians claimed to being descended from Troy, from Scythia, from a being that was half-human, half-sea creature, and from the scattered remnants of the family of Jesus.[12]

What is reliable truth is that Mary's roles, based in fact or fiction, would have a strong influence on church history. To the Catholic Church, Mary was the penitent sinner, praying in a grotto. When Martin Luther denied the need for confession, Mary was used as an example to counter his claims. Both Zwingli and Calvin specifically targeted the Magdalene for attack and called her worshippers a cult.[13]

Her greatest message then may be that she has survived criticism ranging from St. Peter to Protestant reformers, survived historians whose goals were often simultaneously that of both devotion and distortion, and survived even the faithful who scattered her bones among Europe's churches and cathedrals. She remains a saint to all of them.

Today her shrines at Villa Lata and at Vezelay are considered her two most important worship sites and the repository of her relics. In the province of Toulouse, where she is the patroness, mass is offered to her daily.

St. Anne: The Grandmother of Jesus

The church today is reluctant to call a divine intervention a "miracle." The term invites skeptics who demand "proof," which is not forthcoming. As a result the church has played down miracles by referring to them as occurrences and in other subtle ways. After a fire in the 1960s at Chicago's Brighton Park Shrine of St. Anne, it was decided to remove the numerous crutches and canes left behind by the many believers who had been on the receiving end of such an occurrence. The occurrences did not stop, and new momentos began to accumulate.

In the early 1980s an infant was born with two clubfeet. Several visits to the doctor led to the inevitable diagnosis for the child—surgery. The mother of the child was told by her aunt, a nun, that the Holy Spirit would help if she asked St. Anne. She prayed to the saint and, as instructed, applied St. Anne oil, which had been blessed by the relic of St. Anne, to her child's feet. She kept her appointment with the surgeon, who told her the boy's feet were now fine. The child grew to adulthood without ever having problems with his feet again. His baby shoes are in the church today.[14]

Anne was the mother of the Blessed Virgin Mary. Very little about her is found in the Gospels, although there are numerous legends about her. She is mentioned in a gnostic text titled *The Protevangelium of Saint James*. Here she is mentioned as having a husband, Joachim. Her story starts with her, like many biblical women, somehow having trouble conceiving a child. Through prayer and the intercession of God, she does conceive, at a later age. This has caused comparisons with the Old Testament story of Samuel who was borne by Hannah. Samuel's mother had a hard time conceiving. Her name is also very similar to the alternative pronunciation of Anne, *Anna*.

The child of Anna is Mary. While Anne was not important to the Gospel writers, and few details of her life are known, tradition in literature and art depicts her as a dutiful and doting grandmother, represented holding her daughter's child. Tradition says that when the three Marys leave Palestine for France, they took along her bones for safekeeping. The sacred remains are brought to Apta Julia, modern-day Apt, and placed in a crypt. The first bishop of Apt, St. Auspicius, buried the body in a subterranean chapel even deeper in the ground because of the threat of barbarian invasion.

When Charlemagne turned back the Saracen tide, he went on a binge of relic collecting. At Apt, he had a local noble, Baron Casanova, search for the bones of Anne. From the altar they dug into the chamber, and steps were found leading to the subterranean chamber. The blind and deaf son of Casanova, John, was fourteen at the time, and he raced into the passage. For the first time he spoke, declaring this to be the tomb of St. Anne. A wall was torn down and her casket was uncovered. Charlemagne told this story in a letter to Pope Adrian.

Separate tradition has her bones remaining in Nazareth until the year 710, when she carried away to Constantinople.

Her bones were then scattered far and wide and are still traveling in the twentieth century. Part of her head went to Bologna, Italy. Her right hand went to Vienna, Austria. And an arm went to the Benedictine monks. In Brittany, on the western coast of France, her story melded with more pagan traditions, and she became the queen of Brittany. Statues of her miraculously appeared in two Breton towns. In St. Anne de-la-Palue one was pulled by fishermen from the sea, and at St. Anne d'Auruy one was unearthed from the ground. The Christian-pagan tradition melded together well, and she became the patron saint of fishermen and is most revered in that part of France.

The Bretons of France, like the Basques, were among the first fishermen to discover the bountiful fishing grounds of Canada. In 1658, Breton fishermen in the St. Lawrence River were on the verge of being wrecked in a storm. They promised St. Anne they would build and dedicate a church to her if she would save them. Through her intercession, they were saved, and they kept their promise. Today St. Anne de Beaupre, twenty miles outside Quebec, is one of Canada's finest shrines. The cathedral there has seven relics, including the wrist of the grandmother of Jesus.

During the erection of the first church, a crippled worker, Louis Guimont, insisted on bearing a burden of stones to build the church. He was immediately cured. One healing miracle after another took place, attracting pilgrims from all over Canada. Lines of crutches of those miraculously cured by St. Anne started to appear, so many in fact that today the church can no longer accept them. Anne was named the patroness of Canada, and her cathedral near Quebec remains a popular pilgrimage destination.

It would also spawn other churches that would be dedicated to her. In 1900 a very small relic, a one-inch piece of bone, was given to the French Canadians in Chicago to build a shrine to St. Anne. The shrine is the Church of Our Lady of Fatima in Brighton Park, and it immediately became a pilgrimage spot of no small importance. The mother shrine of St. Anne in Apt in 1914 gifted a larger relic to the new shrine. Miracle stories would continue for the hundred years since the church was built.

At the shrine the waters of a fountain run past a statue containing her relic bones. Because of the curative properties of the water, pilgrims to this shrine bring cups and bottles to preserve or drink the sacred water. Of special significance is an annual novena, a nine-day prayer vigil that begins on the saint's feast day each July 26. A novena is a chance to ask the saint for a special favor.

A Chicago newspaper article tells of a crippled man who attempted to get to the novena. He missed the streetcar and, despite his condition, walked to the shrine. He arrived and was cured.

St. Thérèsa of Lisieux: Postmortem Missionary

Each year almost 100,000 pilgrims climb a hill in Normandy to visit the Basilica of St. Thérèsa of the Child Jesus. This pilgrimage destination ranks second in France only to Lourdes. The story of her very short life is often re-garded as a miracle in itself. Her postmortem fame is also nothing short of phenomenal. She died in 1897 and by 1925 was not only made a saint but also considered as a doctor of the church, an honor given to very few. Pope Pius XI declared her to be "the greatest saint of modern times."

Her life itself is ranked as a miracle. On the first night of her parents' wedding, her father declared he had no intention of consummating the marriage, but time took its toll on his resolve and later "nine flowers bloomed" in his garden. Thérèsa was last and dubbed the "Little Flower." Frail in her infancy, she struggled to survive. Four of her siblings died in childhood. Her mother only lived until Thérèsa was four. By age nine she had an altar in her room and was preoccupied with her faith. At nine she also had a near-death experience that served only to increase her desire to be accepted in a convent. Against convention, and perhaps instigated by her constant campaign, she was admitted at the age of fifteen to the Carmelite order.

From behind the closed gates of the convent she penned the *Story of a Soul,* an inspirational autobiography that touched the hearts of millions. She described herself as the Little Flower planted by God. From the age of twelve she would tell anyone who would listen that she intended to bring the message of faith to North America and ultimately to China. Her un-timely death did not stop her. Her role as a patron saint of missions led to the idea of carrying her relics around the world.

Her feast day is October 1, as custom says she entered heaven one day after her death on September 30. She was only twenty-five years old. Be-cause of her devotion to a replica of Veronica's Veil, she is also regarded as Thérèsa of the Child Jesus and the Holy Face.

Not everyone who leads a holy life is declared a saint. Often the process is long, as the church seeks definite signs. She was almost immediately considered Venerable for her extraordinary holiness and inspiration for others. Beatification, the next step, requires two miracles. For Thérèsa these occurred in 1923 when two spontaneous cures, both unexplained by treatment, occurred. One was a young seminarian diagnosed with pulmonary tuberculosis. His doctor was shocked when the fruit of the seminarian's prayers brought about his cure. His "destroyed and ravaged lungs had been replaced by new lungs." Another cure was of a nun who had suffered stomach ulcers for years. Her prayers were answered. Declared "blessed," Thérèsa was credited with two more miracles in another two years. One involved another case of pulmonary tuberculosis. The day after returning from St. Thérèsa's shrine the sick woman was declared cured by her doctor, who found her "literally transformed." Two other physicians confirmed the testimony of her doctor.[15]

Thérèsa was canonized in 1925.

It was not the end to the many miracles Thérèsa performed. The French singer Edith Piaf was blinded because of meningitis as a three-year-old. Her grandmother brought her to Thérèsa's grave when she was seven. Her sight was restored. She wore a tiny medallion of Thérèsa for the rest of her life.[16]

Because it was her desire to act as a missionary after her death, and because her presence as an inspirational saint is so powerful, it was decided to take the relics of Thérèsa on a world tour. Since then, her bones have visited several continents. They have crossed Russia, Siberia, and Kazakhstan by bus, covering eighteen thousand miles in the hinterlands of the former Soviet Union alone.

The first leg, excuse the pun, of her world tour began in South America. After touring that continent, she was flown from Buenos Aires to New York. Masses in her honor were said in St. Patrick's Cathedral in New York City and the Cathedral of the Sacred Heart in Newark before she headed to Maryland. There she resided in a Carmelite monastery in La Plata, Maryland and then in another monastery in Washington, D.C. From there she headed to Philadelphia, where Cardinal Anthony Bevilacqua wished to have her considered as one of the Top Catholics of the Century. Even though Thérèsa lived in the nineteenth century, she too received enough votes to merit that honor. While the technicality of having lived too early disqualified her from meriting that distinction, her popularity continues to grow. From Philadelphia the tour took her through many U.S. cities and towns, especially to the Carmelite monasteries. After an extensive cross-country tour, Honolulu and the Philippines were next. In the Philippines the tour made a remarkable visit to Muntinlupa Prison's death row. There Bishop Ramon Arguelles said mass to thirty-three men sentenced to death for crimes ranging from murder to drug trafficking. A hoped-for conversion took place after the condemned men were allowed to touch her reliquary. Another mass was said for the other four thousand convicts.

In Siberia, where twenty-four priests cover an area of millions of square miles, the autobiography of St. Thérèsa was printed and distributed to those who were refused access to Christian teachings for a century. The book became Siberia's best seller.

Two years after Thérèsa left France, her relics were near the end of the tour when they arrived in Wexford. Seventy thousand people came to witness a ceremonial unit of the Irish Army carry her four-hundred-pound gold and silver casket to Ireland's Bishop Brendan Comiskey for a special blessing.

St. Catherine of Siena

During her life and after her death, miracles were almost a constant for St. Catherine, the patron saint of Italy. As a result of her very unusual life, she is accorded honors given to very few saints. Her remains are preserved between those of two popes in the Church of Santa Maria Sopra Minerva in Rome, the title meaning the church "built over" the temple to Minerva. Large angels mount her coffin, and a prone statue of her lies behind the coffin, wearing the ring that she claimed betrothed her to Jesus. From the fourteenth century she has always attracted pilgrims, and even today a steady stream of her faithful pass through the church every day.[17]

Catherine di Benincasa was the twenty-fourth child born to a mother who would bear twenty-five children. She was the youngest to survive, as half would not. From her earliest days as a child she saw visions and was said to be able to levitate while in prayer. At age seven she visited her sister Bonaventura. Though her sister was regarded as being happily married, her husband was described as being rough and brutal. When Catherine left her sister's house, she saw a vision and pledged to remain celibate, a bride of Christ. She also decided to stop eating.

Soon afterward, Bonaventura died giving birth. Catherine's mother, Lapa, was concerned with the welfare of Bonaventura's lower-middle-class family and tried to get Catherine to marry her sister's widower. Catherine's refusal put her at odds with her mother, despite evidence that she had been the favorite until that time. Relations in the household grew tense, and Catherine is reported as feeling a sense of guilt after one of the family's many children died. Her weight was now half of the proper weight for someone her age, and her mother sent her to the local priest. In the fourteenth century, as would be true for centuries to come, the priest served the function not only of spiritual adviser but also of amateur psychologist. Catherine began teaching herself to vomit rather than keep food down.

Catherine's father finally relented and acquiesced to her desire to devote her life to Jesus. She lived in a small cell in the family home and survived on only the communion host and occasional salad. Her days and nights were filled with prayer and self-flagellation. She was admitted into the Order of St. Dominic as a tertiary at age seventeen, but she still lived at home in seclusion.

After the death of her father, when Catherine was twenty-one, she suffered an intense pain in her side, where Christ had been pierced by the centurion. She also began her ministry to the sick, the poor, and incarcerated prisoners. Her piety and selflessness attracted followers. In the plague years she devoted her time to the victims other caregivers feared to help.

She also claimed to enjoy an intimacy with the Son of God that had him bringing her a ring of gold and precious stones while she was in a vision. No one could see the ring, as was the case with her declaring that she suffered the wounds of stigmata.

Stigmata is the condition of suffering the wounds of Jesus on the Cross. The word was originally shared by both the Greek and Latin languages, and it meant a brand for cattle or human slaves. As early as the fourth century Christians reported marks that resembled the wounds of the Crucifixion, and they were called stigmata. Sometimes the palms, and the reverse sides of the hands, show a bloody nail wound. Sometimes the feet too bear the wounds of the nails. Others can have five wounds, including the wound from the spear. In rare cases wounds from the Crown of Thorns are indicated. While stigmata has generally been confined to ecstatics, all who bore the stigmata suffer from the pains.

The first individual known to have suffered from stigmata was said to have been St. Francis Assisi, who died in 1226. The Impression of the Stigmata of St. Francis is observed as a feast of the church on September 17. St. Francis lived only two years after the stigmata first appeared, and a short life poststigmata is common.

The church does not maintain a list of those who have exhibited the marks of the Crucifixion, although an unofficial tally numbers around three hundred.[18] Skeptics point to the fact that the early stigmatists generally had wounds in their palms, but after recent discovery of the anatomy of crucifixion, those marks were moved to the wrists. Others claim that the marks are real and simply combine a highly charged mental state with mystical experience. While acknowledging that fakes have attempted deception, and reluctant to be seen as encouraging self-destructive behavior, the church does accept that stigmata can be genuine.

St. Catherine was especially unusual, as the wounds of the stigmata were visible only to Catherine. Catherine prayed constantly that the Lord take her heart. Soon she received a vision in which he held her heart in his hands. She was left with a scar that she showed a friend who told her confessor she had witnessed it. Despite not being born into a wealthy family, her piety and devotion soon spread her fame, and she even came to the attention of the pope. She implored Gregory XI to leave France and end the "Babylonian Captivity" that had the pope residing in Avignon, France, rather than in Italy. When the clash within the papal states grew to be an outright conflict, the pope chose Catherine to act as his emissary to secure the neutrality of Pisa. She would also act as an ambassador between Florence and Avignon, and finally in 1377 the pope returned to Italy. As a reward for her efforts the once illiterate nun was able to write, or at least dictate, and soon she began composing her *Dialogue*.

Miracles almost seemed commonplace to her, and at one point when her city endured a famine, she was credited with multiplying the stored wheat in the home where she was staying until all could be fed.[19] At other times witnesses saw her face radiant with light.[20] While receiving communion in church she often went into a trance, and on one occasion her body was lifted from a prostrate position to kneeling with outstretched arms. She said that she also received the stigmata at this time, although the churchgoers only saw her body rise and no visible wounds.

After years of subsiding on nothing except the communion host, while exhibiting vitality and energy even during the abstinence from food, she passed away at the age of thirty-three. For three days her body was on view, and the faithful paid their respect. During that time not only did her body and even her extremities remain flexible, but the stigmata, which could never be seen before, was suddenly pronounced.

In her lifetime she was venerated as a saint, and it was no surprise that she was canonized in 1461, eighty-one years after her death. Once considered illiterate, she wrote on spiritual doctrines of the church, and the importance of her writings caused her to be named a doctor of the church, one of the highest honors, shared with only three other women.

Explaining the unexplainable is the province of science, and Catherine has more than her share of inexplicable attributes. More than one modern writer claims that over half of the Italian women that would be canonized as saints suffered from anorexia nervosa. When Catherine was alive the condition was hardly recognized. The first paper on the subject was published in 1695. If such a diagnosis were true, Catherine would exhibit the correct symptoms and even share the sad outcome.

Anorexia, which affects women more than men, usually has its onset in adolescence. The symptoms are not only a lack of eating and induced vomiting afterward but also an exhibition of disturbed aversive behavior when confronted. In modern days the appeal of supermodels and the thin "heroin chic" look is claimed as a reason. Women suffer from anorexia at the rate of one in two hundred, while dancers suffer at the rate of a remarkable 20 percent. Wanting to be thin was not the cause during medieval times, and it is more likely that achieving divinity through self-punishment was the cause. The reaction of Catherine to being pushed to marry an unwanted, threatening husband might raise an eyebrow from a modern psychologist, although her early devotion preceded that situation. The term "anorexia nervosa" was not even coined, and most likely understood, until recently. Now a new term, "holy anorexia," is used to describe the condition of women and at least one male saint.

A female suffering from this condition could slip into a trace, into levitation, or into a catatonic state, and display sudden lactation or bleeding and stigmata. Catherine's biographer and confessor described several instances where she was levitated, in front of witnesses.[21]

In death, Catherine's body was still miraculous. Three years after her death, her tomb was opened. Despite the damage that dampness had done to her clothing, her skin was not affected. The Dominican order decapitated her corpse. Her head was taken and placed in a reliquary and sent along with an arm to Siena. Three fingers were given to Venice. Her hand was given to the Dominican order in Rome. Her left foot was examined in 1597 and, with evidence of the stigmata still present, was sent to Venice. The finger that bore the mystical ring of Jesus was sent to Florence. The translation of her relics is actually commemorated each year in a procession every August 5.

8

THE BONES OF CONTENTION—
THE RELICS OF THE APOSTLES

During the height of what would be called "relic mania," every church and cathedral wished to have their own apostle or at least a relic of an apostle. This caused numerous unfounded claims of possession of relics of the apostles. And later, during the Reformation, it brought numerous and outspoken criticism on the collection of relics. Martin Luther reportedly asked, "How it came to pass that eighteen apostles are buried in Germany, when Christ chose only twelve?"

Separating fact from fiction is a near impossible task, two thousand years later. A historical provenance is helpful, as forensic science cannot identify a body without a suitable comparison. DNA testing has recently been used to verify the bones of suspected murdered Romanovs by comparing samples from the dead with a living heir. Prince Philip, Queen Elizabeth's husband and a descendant of Czarina Alexandra's sister, contributed his DNA for the test.[1] Without known heirs to cross-check against, tradition and history still play the greatest role in hoping to identify remains.

St. Peter

Before his death in 1939, Pope Pius XI had requested to be buried alongside some of the church's most important figures in St. Peter's Basilica. He wanted to be near the first pope of Rome. While no one was certain exactly where Peter's bones were located, it was believed that Peter's grave was within the basilica. The new pope Pius XII launched one of the largest recent excavations within the Vatican and in the process a remarkable archaeological detective story. The search for the grave of St. Peter had begun.

St. Peter's Basilica in the Vatican is possibly the world's greatest religious monument. The length of the church is nearly seven hundred feet. Its scale is large but well proportioned, so as not to overwhelm. It holds the *Pietà* of Michelangelo as just one of 450 statues, 500 columns, and 50 altars. The high altar of St. Peter's is one of Christianity's most beautiful works of religious architecture. What is not immediately evident, however, is even more intriguing.

Twenty feet underneath the high altar are graffiti-covered walls where boxes set in the walls are the repositories of the bones of early Christian saints and even older pagan burials. Here, in an area called the Grottos, where numerous dignitaries lie, there is a subterranean crypt. This crypt would be earmarked for expansion as part of the greatest excavation within Vatican City. It was decided to build a sort of a lower church, which actually involved lowering the floor. To accomplish this, workmen dug down to the floor of a basilica erected during Constantine's age. From the ancient church, built between 326 and 335, they entered an avenue of Roman tombs that stretched east toward Vatican Hill. Tombs from the second century were so numerous that the excavation soon revealed an entire city of the dead. All had been filled in with dirt when the basilica was built. This upped the stakes, as it required a massive engineering feat to remove the massive amount of earth while preserving the integrity of the construction above.

The mission within the necropolis under the ancient church itself was twofold: first to find the bones of St. Peter, and second to find a suitable tomb for the deceased pope. Searching westward through an avenue of the dead, the excavators found numerous inscriptions. One, painted on the wall of a mausoleum, read: "Peter, pray Jesus Christ for the holy Christian men buried near your body." The date of the graffito was determined to be A.D. 300. From there the diggers found an open court protected by a plastered wall. In the wall was an altarlike structure that they determined was directly under the high altar. Digging throughout this area they came across a trove of coins and finally a cache of bones—bones that would be determined to be those of St. Peter.

The church's archaeologists, however, were not yet ready to make a statement and would later get more than they bargained for. The pope felt differently. On December 23, 1950, Pope Pius XII had concluded that after ten years of work, the Jesuits who carried on the archaeological research were prepared to announce that they had found St. Peter's tomb. While they may have had the correct tomb, as there had been indications among the graffiti that it was St. Peter's, there was still uncertainty regarding the bones in the tomb.

The bones they found were said to be those of a sixty-year-old man who was robust and healthy up until his execution. To review their work, the Vatican then hired an anthropologist to examine the bones further. Verenando Correnti and his team discovered in their research that while some bones were those of a sixty-year-old man, others were problematic. There were also bones belonging to an even older man, a younger man, a woman, a chicken, a pig, and a horse.

The results were a huge disappointment. Soon afterward, an epigraphist, Margherita Guarducci, researching the inscriptions on the monument above the tomb, discovered that there had been more than one burial associated with the same monument. The second tomb was actually unearthed by workmen much earlier, but there is evidence that rivalry may have served as a motive for hiding the discovery. Monsignor Ludwig Kaas, the administrator of St. Peter's Basilica, may have had conflicts with the two Jesuit archaeologists who he oversaw and took it upon himself to interfere. The two, Antonio Ferrua and Englebert Kirschbaum, had done much of the work, while the Vatican architect Bruno Apollonj-Ghetti and the catacomb inspector Professor Enrico Josi oversaw the Jesuits. Kaas directly intervened and had the workmen remove the contents from the tomb. Kirschbaum found what he thought were St. Peter's bones. He personally passed them through a dirt tunnel to his workmen under the supervision of Pope Pius XII himself. These bones, however, may have been from a later tomb. Margherita Guarducci heard about these events by accident. Exactly what had happened to insert a degree of distrust among Kaas and the Jesuits is uncertain. It is possible that the original scope of the excavation was being overwhelmed by the numerous discoveries. A mosaic of Christ riding across the sky in a chariot—an amalgamation of early Christianity and late Roman Mithraism—was just one of the marvels encountered under the church. Kaas may have been afraid that such amazing revelations might overshadow the original intentions of the excavation. It is also possible that because World War II was raging on around them, he was concerned that word of the excavation would get out, and treasures of the church could be lost forever.

After the death of Pius XII, Guarducci told Pope Paul VI, who was a friend of her family, what had transpired. The bones that were secretly preserved by Monsignor Kaas were recovered and examined, and these were determined to be those of a healthy and robust sixty-year-old man. They also were determined to have been in a tomb where tiles dating to A.D. 69 had been found. It was again announced by a pope, on June 26, 1968, that they had discovered the bones of St. Peter.

St. Peter played an important role in the church from the very beginning. He was Simon, a married fisherman and a disciple of St. John the Baptist, when he was called by Jesus. He took his place as the head of the apostles and is often called the prince of that small group. He was among those present at the wedding feast in Cana, at the feeding of the multitude, at the Last Supper, the wait in Gethsemane, and the first of the men at the open tomb. Jesus named, or nicknamed Simon as Petrus, meaning the Rock.

Peter had shown a great deal of weakness in the Gospels. He was afraid to walk on water, as Jesus instructed. He was denied knowing the name of the man Jesus said would betray him, because as two church writers pointed out, he would have killed him on the spot.[2] He showed his anger at Jesus' arrest by cutting off the ear of the centurion Malchus in his haste. After the Crucifixion, among the crowd in the priest's courtyard, he denied three times even knowing Jesus. Yet, as Matthew 16:18 records, Peter was the Rock on which Jesus said he would build his church. He was present at the Pentecost, where because of the apparition of Jesus, he was said to have converted three thousand people in one day. After the death of Jesus, Peter was the center of the debate on allowing non-Jews into the new religion.

While some in the Jerusalem church took a hard line, Peter finally decided the message of Jesus was for all. He rallied the other apostles from their post-Crucifixion depression and sent them all over the globe. The tradition of the church is that St. Peter headed west after the execution of Jesus. Along with his wife they passed through Antioch, where he started an epistolic see, then to Corinth, and eventually Rome. They were there at the wrong time, however, as Emperor Nero was at the height of his anti-Christian frenzy. Nero, according to Eusebius, "gave himself up to unholy practices" that are so evil that the church writer found it hard "to describe the monster of depravity he became."[3] Other writers on the story of Nero did not share the restraint of Eusebius. It is said that when Nero's teacher came to him for his reward, he told him he would have the choice of what tree to be hung from. He ordered doctors to cut open his mother's stomach, so he could see where he came from. He burned Rome to see what the last days of Troy were like.[4]

This was the realm that Peter had to contend with. Simon Magus was a rival of the church and had Nero convinced that Simon was the son of

God, not Peter's Jesus. Early tales of the battle between St. Peter and Simon, a magician, have Peter endlessly outwitting Simon. Peter can quiet raging dogs, raise the dead, and cast out devils to the constant betterment of his rival. Nero, however, remained faithful to Simon. First Peter would witness his wife dragged away to her death. Then Peter himself would be arrested and condemned to be executed in A.D. 64. While crowds looked on Peter requested only that he be crucified upside down, as he was not worthy to meet death in the same way Jesus had.

The place of his execution had once been the Gardens of Agrippina. Her son, Caius Caligula, converted the garden to a circus, but one that had little to do with our conception of a modern circus. Nero used the circus as a spectacle to keep citizens enthralled watching slaves battle one another to death and Christians being murdered by wild animals and in mock battles.

Peter indeed would be the rock of the new Christian church, and he would be buried in its foundation.

At first it was said that he and Paul, executed on the same day, had their bones placed together in the catacombs. In A.D. 324 a church father had to have them weighed to determine which bones belonged to which saint. It was determined that Paul's were the larger bones. The bones of Peter were then placed in a marked tomb.

The basilica of St. Peter's has existed in some form since the second century. A shrine is said to have been built in A.D. 155 by the pope, Anicetus. He built an oratory over Peter's tomb, of which the only surviving record is from the Christian writer Gaius, who lived around the year A.D. 200. Then in 326 Pope Sylvester I requested that a basilica be built and consecrated. Constantine oversaw the construction. The position of the altar was to be directly over the tomb of Peter. To accomplish this, he had to build over the graves of hundreds of people whose relatives were still alive. He built a platform that served as an altar nine feet wide by six feet long. Underneath was a grate that lead to Peter's grave.

That structure lasted until 1452, when it was determined to be in such poor condition that Pope Nicholas V decided a new basilica should take its place. In this fifteenth-century expansion toward the modern St. Peter's, numerous artists were called upon to perform the work. Bramante created the design of a Greek cross. Antonio da Sangallo changed Bramante's plans to accommodate a Latin cross–shaped church. Michelangelo then stepped in to completely redo the previous designs. Before it was complete, Raphael and Bernini, who created the bronze altar canopy, would have their say. Bernini would also use wood from St. Peter's original chair as part of an ornate throne.

The platform built by Constantine was now thirty feet below the area called the high altar. At this time other dignitaries began ensuring their postmortem rest would be in a most sacred spot. Several popes, Queen Christina of Sweden, and a handful of Stuarts all have monuments to their greatness in St. Peter's.

All the work done, especially with the goal of preserving the sanctity of St. Peter's final resting place, would seem to ensure that the bones were certainly those of St. Peter. But there is little certainty, thanks to Rome's history. When Peter was killed in A.D. 64, Christians very obviously were not held in high regard. Often the bodies of Christians executed or killed in the Coliseum were simply thrown into a mass grave. St. Peter, as at least one of the two most important Christians in Rome, the other being St. Paul, may have received better treatment by his fellow Christians. If so, he had other enemies to contend with three centuries later. First the Goths, then the Vandals would sack Rome, carrying off a great deal of plunder. In the ninth century Saracen invaders attacked Rome and are specifically known to have defiled graves and tossed bones, searching for treasure. Since no inventory was kept or reviewed after the attack, it is unknown how much, if any, damage was done to Peter's tomb.

On June 27, 1968, the bones of St. Peter were placed in Plexiglas boxes. A simple nonpublic ceremony took place, and the bones were placed back into the repository beneath the altar. Since then it appears that the Vatican will attempt to keep better track of its precious site under the basilica. With the financial help of the state's power utility, renovations underground continue. Modern visitors can walk through a gate to the underground labyrinth and view the sacred burial grounds with better lighting, ventilation, and climate control to protect Rome's necropolis. When walking through the underground passageways, pilgrims are greeted with numerous *In Christo* inscriptions as well as other symbols of the faithful. The fish represents Jesus, the dove represents the soul, and an anchor represents hope.

St. Andrew

St. Andrew was the older brother of Peter. In his life and even after his death, he is said to have done a great deal of traveling, which accounts for the varied and widespread countries—Greece, Russia, and Scotland—that regard him as their patron saint. His bones are in several locations around the world, and in at least two instances they display a remarkable phenomenon: they produce a substance known as "manna."

Like his brother Peter, St. Andrew was a fisherman from Bethsaida in Galilee when they met Jesus. Though they recognized him as the Messiah, they continued at their occupations until the arrest of John the Baptist. Jesus met them again at the Sea of Galilee and said, "Come and follow me, I will make you fishers of men." The Gospels say little about Andrew during his ministry with Jesus. After the Crucifixion the apostles separated, and Andrew traveled first to Scythia. The apostles often received hostile treatment from those they tried to convert, and an angel came to Andrew, telling him that Matthew was in very dire circumstances. Matthew had traveled to Murgundia in Ethiopia, which then meant almost anywhere in Africa outside of the Nile area. There the inhabitants had blinded him, bound him in chains, and left him in prison, waiting to be executed. Andrew, guided by the angel, sailed to Ethiopia, freed his fellow apostle, and through prayer, helped Matthew regain his sight.

From Africa he went to Achaia, where he performed many miracles. In Nicaea he exorcised seven devils that had plagued the road leading into that town. He brought a great many people into the faith, and through his efforts many churches were built. At Patras he converted the wife of the Roman proconsul Aegeus. The proconsul commanded that Andrew sacrifice to the Roman gods, and Andrew refused. Threatened with death on a cross, Andrew told Aegeus he did not fear the cross. Threatened with flogging and other tortures, Andrew said, "Make them the worst you can think of!" Twenty-one men bound him to an X-shaped cross and flogged him. After three days on the cross, a crowd of twenty thousand had gathered, and Andrew was somehow still preaching. The crowd reached a fever pitch, and soon the proconsul was afraid he would have a revolt on his hands. He went to see Andrew on the cross, who calmly told him he wished to die. According to the church writer Augustine, a blinding light prevented the Roman henchmen from taking the still living Andrew off the cross. When the light stopped, Andrew was dead.

Maximilla, the wife of Aegeus, took the body and instructed that Andrew be given an honorable burial. Aegeus never made it to his home. Along the way he was seized by a devil and died in the street amid many witnesses.

In death, Andrew's fame was not extinguished. He would become the patron saint of fishermen and fish dealers. Barren women pray to him to be made fertile, which skeptics claim is because the pagan Greeks had a fertility symbol "andro," meaning "man," whom they just transferred to the saint. He is invoked especially by those inflicted with gout and to aid sufferers of a stiff neck.

For three hundred years Andrew's bones rested in Greece. There his bones produced a crystalline powder that the church calls "manna." It is not to be confused with the manna left on the trees when the Jews wandered in the desert. The term was borrowed from the Old Testament to describe a substance that is exuded from the bones of saints and defies explanation. The manna can be a powder or a liquid, and sometimes it is clear like water, while at other times it is thick and oily. Manna is often explained as being just the result of humidity, dampness, or another atmospheric condition. But some bones have been moved from one climate to another with no change in the result. In other cases a partial translation of a saint's relics leaves the same bones in both arid and damp climates at the same time. In both areas the effect remains the same.

St. Andrew, who died in the first century, was the first saint recorded to exhibit the strange phenomenon. His bones started by producing a powder and later an oily liquid. It was first noted in a document before he left Greece and then recorded afterward.

The Emperor Constantine the Great had Andrew moved to the center of the Byzantine church in Constantinople in 357. Cardinal Baronio noted at that time that the entire Christian world knew of the phenomenon of Andrew's bones. St. Andrew got to rest another three hundred years, but when Islamic conquests threatened the Greeks, a Greek monk was warned in a dream that St. Andrew's bones were no longer safe. He disinterred the saint and removed an arm bone, a tooth, a kneecap, and several fingers from Andrew and headed, as instructed, "to the ends of the earth." At that time Scotland was considered one of these ends. St. Rule, or St. Regulus as others called this Greek monk, landed on the east coast of Scotland. St. Rule actually landed in hostile Pictish territory, and there is little recorded about his reception. The Greek monk, however, must have been resourceful, as today St. Andrew's is a well-known destination outside of Edinburgh, and the Tower of St. Rule still stands.

Scotland honors St. Andrew as their own, and their flag was based on the X-shaped cross of Andrew. During the Reformation, however, Protestant mobs, revolting against the idolatry of the church, attacked St. Andrew's Cathedral and left it in ruins. A plaque marks where his bones had been stored.

In 1210 larger parts of his remains were taken from Constantinople and brought to Amalfi, in Italy. It is reported that a blind man visiting the tomb was allowed to have some of St. Andrew's manna rubbed on his eyes. His vision returned. St. Andrew's skull, which had been left behind by St. Rule, somehow managed to get to Rome in 1462, where it remained until 1964, when Pope Paul VI returned it to the people of Patras. Today it is contained in a reliquary in St. Andrew's Church. Never allowed to rest for long, a thief destroyed the protective reliquary while attempting to steal the skull, but it was recovered. In 1969 the same pope gave a shoulder blade to the Catholic Church in Scotland, and it is displayed in the Roman Catholic Cathedral in Edinburgh.

In Amalfi the remains of Andrew were lost for a time until 1603, when a mason working in the church found them under a marble slab with an inscription indicating they belonged to St. Andrew. They were interred again with a document and disinterred two hundred years later, in 1846. Since that time they have still been producing the strange substance. The manna is collected regularly, and on one day in 1933, fifteen vials were filled.[5]

St. Thomas

Every year, on the first Sunday in May, the people of Ortona, the largest seaport in the Abruzzi province in Italy, go all out for a feast they call the *Perdono*. Pilgrims come from all over Italy, a huge pageant is performed, and for those who have been less than perfect throughout the year, indulgences are offered. All this is the result of a celebration for the doubting St. Thomas, one of the twelve apostles.

Thomas is regarded in some texts as resembling Jesus and in others as actually being his twin. Thomas Didymus literally means "Thomas the twin," and this may have inspired certain Christians to improve on the story. In the fourth century a very influential teacher brought a different version of Christianity to Spain. This was Priscillian, who taught that Thomas was literally the twin of Jesus. This, combined with a distinctly heretical approach to the Christian faith, earned the teacher and some of his disciples the distinction of being the first heretics condemned to death by the church.

Attributed to Thomas is the so-called Gospel of Thomas, which was discovered around the time the Nag Hammadi library was unearthed. This Coptic text was found by an Egyptian, Muhammad Ali, who was riding his camel near a cliff not far from where the other texts were discovered. He came across a large jar which, as he tells the story, he was initially afraid contained a jinn. It contained no such genie and no gold but the Gospel of Thomas, which claimed to contain the original sayings of Jesus. Denounced as again being a heretical text, more likely a work of a follower of the gnostic Mani, the text does contain many statements found in the Gospels. It starts with the mysterious instructions that "whoever discovers the interpretation of these sayings will not taste death."[6]

Even while reading the Gospels seriously, one cannot miss the humorous cynicism of Thomas. The first mention of Thomas is when Lazarus is raised from the dead. Jesus is warned that if they return to Judea, they may be stoned. But Jesus is insistent that they return. After arguing with his companions, he says he will go alone if he has to. Finally sarcastic Thomas says, "Let us go too, and be killed along with Him."[7] The second mention is when Jesus instructs the apostles that he will be crucified, and after death will return, and that he expects the apostles to meet him. Of course it is Thomas who asks, "How are we to know the way there?"[8]

His most famous scene is meeting with Jesus post-Crucifixion. The other apostles had already seen Jesus, and Thomas didn't believe them. When eight days later he did see Jesus, he had to feel the wounds on the hands of Jesus and touch his side to check the spear wound. From then on he believed.

Thomas himself never made it to Italy during his lifetime. After meeting Jesus after the Crucifixion and insisting that Jesus show him the wounds incurred during his torturous death, Thomas headed east. He preached to the Parthians, Medes, Persians, Hyrcanians, and Bactrians. He traveled to India, where he performed many miracles and brought his faith to thousands. A long and fascinating story of the ministry of Thomas is the Acts of Thomas, written in the third or fourth century. To some it is considered heretical because it leans toward gnostic attitudes, which were out of favor with the church, including the necessity of all Christians to remain celibate.

The Acts of Thomas is one of two works on Thomas. The other is the Gospel of Thomas, unearthed among the Nag Hammadi texts in 1945. In it Thomas is said to have collected the sayings of Jesus in their purest form. Written in Coptic, most likely a copy of an original, it is said to be compiled in the first century and is possibly older than the accepted Gospels.

To the faithful in the Indian subcontinent, there is little doubt that Thomas the doubter reached their country, and there is much historical tradition to his travels.

One of his first acts on the way to India was in the employ of King Gundafor. He was asked by the king to build a palace, which would explain why today he is regarded as a patron of architects, builders, and masons.

Along the Malabar Coast there exists a large group of Christians who hold to the tradition of him preaching there and inspiring the construction of seven churches. These Christians of St. Thomas, as they call themselves, were alive and well fifteen centuries after Thomas, when the Portuguese, who colonized India, met up with them. In Mylapore today stands the Cathedral of St. Thomas.

How much of the Acts of Thomas is true? It records that his attitude of promoting celibacy would lead to his demise. He converted a daughter of the Indian king, who was just getting married. He convinced her that even in marriage she should remain a virgin. This no doubt enraged her noble husband, who complained to his new father-in-law. The king had had enough. He imprisoned Thomas and intended to inflict on him the cruelest tortures. First Thomas would be forced to walk on a red-hot grate of iron. Miraculously a spring emerged under the grate and cooled it immediately. Next the king had him thrown in a fiery furnace. The next morning the furnace was opened. It was cool, and Thomas was alive and well. The king had Thomas brought to him again. Commanding him to worship an idol, Thomas spoke to the idol in Hebrew, ordering the demon inside to destroy itself as soon as Thomas bent his knee. The idol melted like wax in front of Thomas and the king. A great wail came from the crowd, and the high priest jumped at Thomas, killing him with a sword.

The king and his priest fled as the crowd went wild. The new Christians then gave Thomas a decent burial in a tomb of ancient kings. The pagan sword that brought the demise of St. Thomas is also remembered. At the spot where Thomas was killed lies a stone engraved with a cross. From 1558 until 1704 the stone oozed blood every December 18. The miraculous appearance would last for four hours after mass was said. Then the stone would turn white and finally to its original black.[9]

In one of the earliest mentions of a saint's bones being moved, the emperor of Rome, Severus Alexander, acts on behalf of Christians in Edessa. He writes a letter to the king of India and requests that Thomas's bones be allowed to be taken to that city. While Severus was not known to have taken a pro-Christian stance, it may have been a political favor promoting goodwill in the Roman frontier. In A.D. 232 Thomas's body, or most of his bones at least, were brought to Edessa, the city of King Abgar who protected Christians. The act of taking bones was called, in ecclesiastic terminology, a "translation." In many cases *translated* and *stolen* meant the same thing, especially to those who no longer held the sacred items.

The Indian Christians of San Tome in that country say the bones were never removed. In 1522 the intrepid Knights of Christ from Portugal finally sailed around Africa and reached Indian coast. There the tomb was "discovered" by the Portuguese explorers, who were told his remains lie beneath.

In the thirteenth century the bones that had been taken to Edessa were again transferred, this time to Chios. The island of Chios is off the coast of modern Turkey, in the Gulf of Smyrna. Between 1204 and 1304 it was held by the Italian merchant state of Venice, then Genoa. These merchant states were constantly in threat of attacks from pirates from Italy. One such attack was led by Captain Leone degli Acciaioli, who sacked the island. While Thomas had never visited Italy in his lifetime, he would, or at least his head and some bones, would eventually reach Italy. His bones arrived on September 6, 1258, as part of the booty brought back to Captain Leone's home port of Ortona. This day is celebrated in modern times as well, although it is not as great a celebration as the *Perdona* in May. The most celebrated part of the apostle Thomas was his finger—the finger with which he inspected the wound of Jesus caused by the spear. To Thomas it was the only way his faith might rule over his skepticism.

Jesus allowed him to poke into his wound and then Thomas knew Jesus was crucified. On the Esquiline Hill in Rome is the Church of Santa Croce in Gerusalemme. It holds among other things the largest hunk, a five-foot section of the cross that held the "good thief" and some of the True Cross. It also holds the largest fragment of the inscription that was put on the Cross, two spikes of the Crown of Thorns, a nail, and a part of the Pillar of Scourging. The collection of relics is complete with the finger of St. Thomas, enclosed in a glass reliquary.

James, the Son of Zebedee

The Camino de Santiago, the Way of St. James, was from medieval times one of Europe's greatest pilgrimages. The five-hundred-mile journey started in a Pyrennes border town where Charlemagne would build an abbey. From there the road, as well as the path, works its way over peaks and valleys through northern Spain before reaching its goal, Santiago de Compostela. In medieval times 500,000 pilgrims might make the torturous trip in any given year. In the twentieth century there are still tens of thousands who make the journey every year. While the pilgrimage did much to increase tourism, it was meant to be walked, not driven, and much of the journey from village to village is on footpaths.

To officially make the pilgrimage, one must start at the Augustinian Monastery of Roncevalles, where a passport is issued to those with a letter of introduction. The passport is a requirement for staying at some of the hostels along the way in true pilgrim fashion, although the hostel environment is not every tourist's dream. Then again, following the scallop-marked pathways over mountains can take a bit more than a tourist state of mind. The walk generally takes six weeks.

Just before reaching the final destination, one reaches Galicia, the province of northwestern Spain that ends with the Atlantic coast. There the town of O Cebreiro holds one of those hostels reserved for pilgrims. A silver reliquary holds the sacred blood of Jesus, donated in 1486 by Ferdinand and Isabella. In the early fourteenth century a miracle was said to happen here that is remembered still. A mass was being said by one monk and attended by one Christian, who had braved the weather. During the mass the bread of the host turned into actual flesh and the wine turned into actual blood. It so unnerved the priest that he died of shock. His one parishioner died shortly afterward. Both are buried in the church. The chalice used in the mass is said to be a Galician Holy Grail, the receptacle of the Lord's blood. Two papal bulls declared it authentic.[10]

Other miracles and legends permeate the sacred pilgrimage, but to many, the question remains: how could James have traveled to Spain?

James, the son of Zebedee, if his legends are to be believed, was one of the most remarkable apostles. He was the first of the twelve to be martyred, and his execution took place in A.D. 42. He was beheaded by the order of King Herod Agrippa. What is remarkable is that in the short amount of time between the death of Jesus and the death of James, he was said to have traveled to Spain, where he preached.

James, usually called James the Greater, was the brother of John the Evangelist. He is not to be confused with another James (the son of Alphaeus), who some believe was the brother of Jesus and called James the Lesser. James and John were considered to be the third and fourth apostles. These two seem to have a higher degree of importance than some of the others, as they are witness to some of the major events in the Gospels. James may have come from a wealthier family than the other apostles, and he (and his mother both) asked Jesus to provide a higher place of honor in his future kingdom.

After the Pentecost, James supposedly headed for Spain. Along with a handful of his disciples he was near Saragossa when the Blessed Virgin appeared to him. At this time she was not yet recorded as having died or been Assumed into heaven. A church was built at this site, and the mother of God left a jasper column to commemorate her visit.[11] James then went back to Jerusalem, where he was executed.

After his death his bones were carried back to Spain along a circuitous route that finally ended in Compostela. For a while it was believed that this name was derived from the word for *apostle,* but more likely it was the *campo* (field) of the *stella* (stars).

Despite the great amount of faith it seems is required to accept the St. James-in-Spain story, Compostela became one of Europe's greatest pilgrimage sites.

For the first nearly eight hundred years after his death, his tomb was said to be in Palestine or Marmarica. But from A.D. 830 the story of James having come to rest in Galicia began.[12] The Moors had conquered North Africa and most of the Iberian Peninsula before their invasion was turned around in France. Then began what in Spain is called the *reconquista,* the reconquest of their homeland. The battle cry of the Spaniards was "Santiago de Compostela," *Santiago* meaning "Saint (San) James (Iago)." Just how much of this is myth and how much is reality is impossible to determine.

In the shrine to James at Compostela there is an imposing figure of James seated on a throne. He has a scepter in his hand, and his clothes are made of silver and gold. Scallop shells decorate his cape, and pilgrims can climb behind the altar to kiss the shells. Pilgrims were allowed to bring home, most likely purchase, scallop shells from his tomb as souvenirs of their pilgrimage.

Underneath the statue is a crypt reached by a narrow stairway. The bones of James are in a silver reliquary on a marble altar.[13] They were last examined in 1879.

Not everyone agrees that James's remains are at Compostela. Some believe that he did travel to Spain. Others believe the entire myth was created to rout the Islamic invasion by creating a rallying point. A third explanation is that a Celtic site was assimilated to convert the indigenous population. The church would continually transfer the holy places of the old pagan worship to the new. In many cases the symbols and sometimes even the myths were absorbed.

In the seventh century the church in Spain took over the shrine, which had previously been dedicated to the Brigantine sea goddess, Brigit. This

Celtic goddess was worshipped all throughout the Atlantic Coast, and her symbol was the scallop shell or a cowrie shell, which had a distinct fertility implication. This same goddess symbol was incorporated in Botticelli's *Birth of Venus,* where the goddess emerges floating on a scallop shell.[14] Celtic Brigantia would give way to Christianity, and in Ireland where Brigit was also worshipped, she may have become the basis for St. Brigit. Her feast day, February 1, remained the same, the first day of the pagan spring called Imbolc. It celebrated the lambing of the ewes, a pastoral festival, although Brigit was much more. She was a goddess of healing, poetry, and smith-craft (the art of working with metals). She was also a goddess of war, and her soldiers, called brigantes, later were reduced to the status of outlaws as she became a saint, rather than a most revered goddess. In Italy too Venus was celebrated in early February, although her résumé did not compare to that of the Celtic Brigit. Rome had military heroes and did not need a woman leader.

Christianity reached Spain through Rome. Conversion would take two forms: that of the vengeful St. Martin, who chopped down the trees where pagans worshipped, and the more gracious assimilation of pagan aspects into the faith. In Ireland the Christianized St. Brigit appeared to the army at Leinster in 722, as the Christian cross had appeared to Constantine at the Milvian bridge. The now-Christian soldiers of Leinster routed the pagan forces of Tara. Brigit's sacred flame at Kildare became St. Brigit's. It would burn for eight hundred years after Ireland was converted. The flame would be tended by a college of women, very much as the vestal virgins of Rome had tended their sacred fire.[15] The only difference was that they were now nuns.

Like the Virgin of Guadeloupe, the veracity of the story of James in Spain may be less important than its results. James brought converts to the church in the tens of thousands.

James, the Brother of Jesus

James the Lesser, also known as James the son of Alphaeus, is a theological problem. Because of the problem, there are conflicting stories of both his life and death. He was the brother of Jesus, the cousin of Jesus, or unre-lated. While there is one claim he was hung on the cross, there are many others who say he was thrown from a parapet of the Jerusalem temple and stoned to death.

Recently, a small box was unearthed bearing the inscription "James, son of Joseph, brother of Jesus." The inscription was in the Aramaic language spoke in the first century A.D. The box, measuring ten inches by twenty inches by twelve inches was a bone box, also called an ossuary, may have once held the bones of this important figure, easily recognized by his well-known father and brother, Joseph and Jesus.

In October 2002, at a Washington press conference held by the *Biblical Archeology Review,* Andre Lemaire, described as "one of the world's foremost scholars of ancient scripts," gave his seal of approval. "It seems probable" that the box contained the bones of James. Others were not ready to approve as quickly. To some the problem was the lack of scientific verification. The box was not yet dated, and the inscription had not been proven to be that of a first-century scribe.

The inscription itself created more than one problem. First, the beginning of the inscription has fewer scratches of wear and tear than other areas of the box. Some believe this indicates it was added later. In addition, others claim the second half of the inscription was produced by a hand different from the first half. The Royal Ontario Museum discounted both opinions and points to modern cleaning as the culprit rather than ancient authors.

They believe the box was sanded two thousand years ago and then inscribed and even painted. Experts produced evidence of three concentric circles with six-pointed stars called rosettes to back up the claim that it had been painted.

The other part of the problem is a theological issue. The church believes that Jesus had no brothers.

It is the Gospels of Mark (6:3) and Matthew (13:56) that disagree. Both state that Jesus had four brothers and name them as well. They were Jacob (James), Joseph, Judas (who becomes Jude), and Simon. Official doctrine says James was a brother by a different mother, implying Joseph had children from a previous marriage. Josephus, the Roman first-century chronicler, also mentions Jacob as the brother of Jesus who gets executed by the Sanhedrin. The church later decided that a family, especially one that could claim being heirs to a royal (Davidic) bloodline, would not be accepted by Constantine. They then had to backtrack and eliminate such embarrassing siblings.

The church writer Jacobus de Voragine says James was called the brother of Jesus because he looked like him. His mother was Mary who married Cleophas, whose brother was Joseph. Two brothers then married two women named Mary. He is also called James the Lesser not because he was less worthy or shorter than James the Greater, but because he was the second James to join their small religious community. Hegesippus, however, does not have a problem in saying that James was the brother of Jesus. "From his mother's womb he was holy. He drank no wine or strong drink, never ate meat, no razor ever came near his head, no oil anointed him, he never bathed." Voragine says he was among the first apostles to celebrate the mass after the Last Supper. Other mentions of him are not as charitable, as he was in direct conflict with Peter and Paul over the direction of the new religion. James felt that the message was solely for strict observers among the Jews. Paul felt that the message went to all who would listen, including those who would not accept circumcision as a requirement. He was on shaky ground in Jerusalem, where Jews consider James a very holy man who must be revered. Peter was finally won over to Paul's thinking, and both left Jerusalem to preach to the Gentiles.

For the sake of history, James represents the bridge between first-century Jews and Christians. But he also represents the chasm. Jesus apparently named Peter to be the rock on which the new church was to be built. The apostles may not have been so sure, and Clement of Alexandria (A.D. 150–215) says the apostles elected James to lead. James and Jesus appear to have been at odds. James was for strict adherence to the law, which meant that breaking one law was the same as breaking all the laws. Jesus taught the law was made for man and should accommodate man.

As early as seven years after the Crucifixion, James was forced to deal with another confrontation. He was preaching to his fellow Jews in the temple from a platform when he was thrown off and injured. He survived this violent encounter, but it would not be the last. One apocryphal work says this attack before A.D. 50 was the work of Paul. While this is doubtful, it does reflect the early hostility among some of the followers of Jesus.[16]

While Pauline Christianity and rabbinical Judaism sought to find accommodation with Rome, zealous strict observers like James sought no such compromise. James too then was a danger to the peace. He was at odds with the Pharisees and the Sadducees. A second attack had James thrown off a pinnacle of the roof of the temple while preaching. This second attack would turn fatal, as the crowd then stoned him for preaching about Jesus. The death blow came from a fuller who struck him with a crowbar. This was in A.D. 62.

The owner of the box says he bought the box in the 1970s for a few hundred dollars. It had been in the town of Silwan where Arabs live in a densely populated, poor Jerusalem suburb. Underneath the cinder block houses is a virtual graveyard of ancient interments. Residents can strike gold or at least make a profit by excavating their own basement. The area has yielded literally thousands of these burial boxes. Some are ornate, others carry no decoration or inscription. The James box is simple, deceptively so in light of the inscription.

The forty-five-pound box has so far been tested for chemical traces, which, if present, would date it differently, and for tool marks that could imply it was carved later. The Israeli Government Geological Survey had two scientists conduct a detailed microscopic examination of both the surface patina and the inscription. Both agree there is nothing scientific that would disprove Lemaire's conclusion. Lemaire's work in reviewing the inscription centered around three characters written in cursive. They were written in a style that developed around A.D. 25. The burial box–style ossuaries mostly date until A.D. 70 when Rome unleashed a reign of terror against a Jewish revolt, and much of the population left the Jerusalem area. So the "window" of A.D. 25–70 narrows the date and epigraphic style. Because there are no organic remains attached to the inscription, carbon dating cannot be used to estimate its date.

Lemaire also believes, after a study of the incidence of names, that the James son-of-Joseph, brother-of-Jesus combination would allow for possibly twenty individuals who could meet that description. Since the Pharisees, not the Sadducees and others, were the Jewish sect that employed such ossuaries, that number could be reduced further. Naming the father is a typical inscription, but naming the brother as well is very unusual. A likely conclusion is that the brother was someone important. This reduces the number much further.

Reverend Joseph Fitzmyer, a professor emeritus of New Testament studies at Catholic University in Washington, agrees that both the style and the mention of Jesus are very important, but he stops short of saying that nobody can prove the Jesus is the Jesus of Nazareth.

If it is the same Jesus, then it is one of the first inscriptions using his name. There is unfortunately a wealth of such ossuaries, and one has to wonder about authenticity. In 1980 in the East Talpiot section of Jerusalem, excavations unearthed what appeared to be a family tomb. Individually inscribed was a box for a certain "Jude" (the name of a brother of Jesus), a Mary (possibly a sister of Jesus), Joseph (as in his earthly father), Mary (as in his mother, the Blessed Virgin), and even a "Jesus, son of Joseph." No bones were found in any of the boxes, and the find, possibly considered dubious, received little attention. In 1996, sixteen years later, a British team with a documentary in mind came to Jerusalem to investigate.

The James ossuary box, however, received a great deal of attention. It went on to be displayed in the Royal Ontario Museum in Toronto. It fared poorly during the voyage and developed several cracks that had to be mended. At the same time cracks developed in the scientific community. Not only is determining authenticity a problem, but also, as always, an undetermined provenance also invites doubt. The old saw of the research community is that whenever something is unscientifically unearthed it is suspect. While to an outsider this concept is ridiculous, to an archaeologist it is job security. Provenance often aids the determination of authenticity, but the many new discoveries of ossuaries that have been buried for two thousand years would have no such authority. In 1873 a wealth of ossuary boxes was uncovered. Effendi Abu Saud was constructing his house near the road to Bethany. He found over thirty burial boxes, including three with very familiar names—Lazarus, Martha, and Mary. Others had the name Jesus or a cross inscribed on them, which would serve as evidence that they were Jewish-Christians. Jews during that period often buried their dead in caves and tombs only to later remove the decomposed body and place the cleaned bones in an ossuary box.

An 1874 paper by the French archaeologist Charles Claremont-Gannueau listed numerous names recognized from the Bible. His body of research was complemented by the Italian scholar P. Bagatti, who discovered in a catacomb near the Catholic Chapel of Dominus Flevit over one hundred boxes with another host of New Testament names, including Shappira, who is found only in Acts 5:1.

In 1953 an ossuary box was found inscribed in Aramaic with the name Simon bar Jona, the original name of St. Peter. Some believe this casts doubt on the bones of St. Peter in Rome, although others believe because Simon was a very common name it may have been given to another son of a different Jona.

Worse than a lack of provenance for authenticating the James box was the fact that it was looted and came to the public attention through the antiquities market. To inhibit such markets, which are mostly illegal, the scientific press and associations generally ignore artifacts such as the James box.

Bones found in ossuary boxes are generally femurs, and some may include very small fragments of other bones. The femur itself is considered to be very important. The "James box" did not contain any bones, and only through use of a scanning electron microscope could analysis of interior deposits be investigated. The finding of a chemical encrustation rich in phosphate tells scientists that the box indeed once held bones, as bones can leach phosphate. Its usefulness stops at that point, however, as just whose bones they were cannot be determined. Even if bones had been included in the discovery, DNA testing would be unlikely to provide new evidence. DNA must be compared to some other DNA to have meaning. Since there is no known deposit of DNA to be used in comparison, the bones would have to wait for a further discovery.

By April 2003 the debate over the James ossuary box had both proponents of authenticity and critics lining up against one another. Ben Witherington, a professor of New Testament studies and the author of *The Brother of Jesus* declared that "the artifact had passed all tests with flying colors"[17] for a *National Geographic* news article. At the same time Joe Nickell of the Committee for Scientific Investigation of Claims of the Paranormal was first to argue in the March/April edition of *Skeptical Inquirer*[18] that the inscription was a forgery. By late summer it emerged that while the proverbial jury was still out, a real jury might soon be called.

Israeli police raided the home of the owner, Oded Golan, and arrested him on suspicion of possessing ancient artifacts. He was released four days later and no charges were immediately filed. The Israeli Antiquities Authority then published a report that declared the box real but the patina a forgery.

St. Jude Thaddeus

Vincenzo Pullara was a man who needed a saint's intercession as much as anyone could. Alleged to be a Gambino family crime boss by the FBI, he had Louis Freeh (soon to be the director of the FBI) and Rudy Giuliani (a Justice Department prosecutor at the time) on his case. It was during the now-famous Pizza Connection prosecutions, and Mr. Pullara was accused of being a murderer for hire and killing a witness. He needed a miracle, and as a fugitive from justice, he needed it fast. Along with forty of his closest friends and family, he made a pilgrimage by bus to the shrine of St. Jude in Baltimore.

St. Jude, in Justice Department terminology, "allegedly" interceded on Mr. Pullara's behalf. Charges were dropped.

Modern miracles still happen within the church, although they are often limited to either the Blessed Virgin or more modern saints. The one exception is the saint that has become known as the patron saint for lost causes. St. Jude is regarded as the saint for the otherwise hopeless, the last resort for those whose prayers remain unanswered. From St. Jude's Children's Hospitals to the shrine of St. Jude in cities like Baltimore and New Orleans, miracles are a regular occurrence. As a result St. Jude is the subject of more than one modern investigation.

Believed to be the brother of St. James the Lesser, St. Jude is one of the minor apostles whose role in the Gospels is very small. Depending on the interpretation, his relationship to James makes him either a cousin or a brother of Jesus, but the Gospels do not elaborate. The Last Supper is actually the first time he is mentioned. His true name was Judas, but that name fell out of favor as quickly as Adolf did in the twentieth century, so he is always referred to as Jude.

The church has done everything to make the faithful believe Jesus was an only child, even disputing two of the accepted Gospels. One of the earliest church writers, Eusebius, wrote well before the Gospels were then edited to play down or eliminate Jesus' family. Eusebius was born in 260 in Caesaria on the Palestinian coast. It was a pagan city with a large Jewish and Samaritan population. He went to an academy that had attracted Christian pupils by having the most extensive writings in its library. Unfortunately most of the library did not survive. But Eusebius did get to write a history of the church on the research he garnered from texts that now no longer exist. One such early Christian text was written by Hegesippus. It was Hegesippus who wrote that Jesus did indeed have a family and mentioned Jude as the brother of Jesus. As mentioned earlier, the grandsons of Jude survived into the time of Domitian. They in fact met with Domitian and were asked if they were in the direct line of David. They admitted that they were. He also asked them what assets they held, and they described a large tract of farmland that provided them with enough to pay their taxes. The emperor is described as looking at their hands. When he found them hard from manual labor, he decided they were not a threat to the Roman Empire and let them go.[19]

What matters most is not the details themselves but the amount of detail, which would indicate that the story was not made up. It certainly is not the result of any embellished storytelling by Hegesippus or at all politically motivated by Eusebius. Simply stated, it rings true. And if Jude was the brother of Jesus, there is no longer a reason to say James was not.

There is also evidence that leaders of the early church prohibited neither marriage nor children. Jude's grandsons as real people also indicate that yet another apostle was married, although only the wife of one, Peter's wife, is mentioned by name.

At the Last Supper, Jude asks Jesus why he will not reveal himself to the world. It is again very telling in that the brother of Jesus believed, at least by that time, that Jesus was the Son of God.

Tradition has Jude and Simon preaching together after the Crucifixion and both being executed, possibly in Odessa, or Arata in Armenia. St. Jude was also reported to have died either a natural death in Boeotia in central Greece or was hung from an olive tree in that country. Jude's remains are alternately described as being located in Edessa, Reims, and Toulouse, and small fragments of St. Jude's bones were distributed to numerous churches. Jude is one of those saints whom Armenians hold in the highest regard. The greatest American church to St. Jude may be his shrine on South Ashland Avenue in Chicago.

The Baltimore shrine, on Paca Street in that city, is the subject of a book by the *Washington Times* reporter Liz Trotta. An award-winning journalist whose experience ranges from her days in Vietnam to modern political jungles, Trotta describes herself as a lapsed Catholic. In that sense she starts with a degree of skepticism as well as an eye for the improbable. Her treatise, *Jude: A Pilgrimage to the Saint of Last Resort*, has both sentimental stories and often funny anecdotes, including the pilgrimage of Vincenzo Pullara. Another story is about a woman who travels by ambulance from New York City to Baltimore to receive a blessing from a priest at St. Jude's. Within a year she is cured of the debilitating effects of a stroke and blessed by the return of a long-lost daughter.

The New Orleans shrine too has been the epicenter of numerous miracles since a relic bone of St. Jude was brought to that city in 1935. A Web site (saintjudeshrine.com) displays a multitude of letters of thanks. The favors include help in overcoming infertility, procuring jobs, obtaining promotions, getting negative test results, overcoming chemical dependency, and again, dropping of felony charges.

Simon the Zealot

Little is known of Simon the Zealot, who was from Cana in Galilee. Dubbed the zealot, he may have been in a militant ultrapatriotic group that wished to return to strict religious rule in his homeland. The Zealots had a fanatical emphasis on purity and were connected to the Baptist movement. Tradition has Simon preaching in Africa, in Persia, and even

Brittania. Some believe he joined St. Jude in Mesopotamia, and they were both executed together. It is said that his bones, along with those of St. Jude, were brought back together and interred in an altar in St. Peter's.

The idea that he might have made it to Britain is not so far-fetched. A book entitled *Synopsis de Apostol* written in A.D. 303 by the bishop of Tyre has Simon reaching England. He would be that country's second martyr.

Another text, the twenty-ninth chapter of the Acts of the Apostles, makes the claim that Paul too reached England. Paul was not an apostle and in fact was one of the Greco-Roman persecutors of very early Christianity. After participating in or possibly instigating the stoning death of Christianity's first martyr, Stephen, Paul, then called Saul, was blinded by God. He had a vision and saw God asking him why does he persecute the Christians. Saul, cured of his temporary blindness, converted and became the most evangelical of all the apostles. He was the first to bridge the gap between the Gentiles and the Jewish-Christians. He soon had a falling-out with James, the brother of Jesus. Paul took his message through Asia Minor and to Rome, and possibly much farther afield.

The Acts of the Apostles was possibly the first text written about the church, as early as A.D. 40. It describes in realistic detail the problems of the early church. Its chapters were compiled, like many of the Bible texts, as being old and new. Various versions were found and edited before becoming the canonical, or approved, texts. The twenty-ninth chapter of Acts would turn up in the archives of the Greek Orthodox Church in former Constantinople, now Istanbul. A Frenchman, C. S. Sonnini, was traveling through Greece and Turkey in the late 1700s when he found it. It describes Paul landing in Raphinus, the Roman name for Sandwich in Kent. It also has him arriving in Roman Londinium and standing on Ludgate Hill, where St. Paul's Cathedral now lies.

Philip

The third apostle to come from Bethsaida, the town of Peter and Andrew, Philip too is only briefly mentioned in the Gospels. The first time is when he is called to join the small group of apostles. He then recruits Nathaniel. The second mention is when he asks just how they are to feed the multitudes with very little food or money. At the Last Supper he was apparently unsure of what was about to take place. He asked Jesus to show him the father. He was mildly rebuked for his lack of faith.

After the death of Jesus he preached the word of the new covenant for twenty years in Phrygia. Then the pagans took hold of him in an attempt to force him to pay reverence to a statue of Mars. A dragon then appeared out from the base of the statue and killed the son of the pagan priest. Philip rode away to safety.[20] He later turns up in Hierapolis. Polycrates, the bishop of Ephesus, wrote of Philip's death in that city along with two of his daughters, who had remained virgins. A separate legend says he was crucified upside down during the reign of Domitian and buried there. His remains were taken from Hierapolis to Constantinople and in 561 to Rome. It was Pope Pelagius who built a church dedicated to Philip and James the Lesser[21] and there entombed his bones. Within the church the actual location of the bones is uncertain. In 1869 renovations to the church started, and four years later the bones of two adult males were interred. They were declared to be those of Saints Philip and James. The Basilica of the Holy Apostles in Rome now preserves what is said to be the remains of St. Philip in a translucent marble sarcophagus in the crypt beneath the high altar (with James).

Nathaniel Bartholomew

Recruited by Philip, Nathaniel Bartholomew became one of the apostles. His surname, Bartholomew, means "son of Tholmai" (which can also be interpreted as "son of Ptolemy"), and he is often called by this name. Some believe this implies that Nathaniel had a Greek-Egyptian heritage, for as Ptolemy was the name of the dynasty Alexander the Greek conqueror left behind to govern Asia and Egypt.

He is mentioned as sitting under a fig tree reading Scripture. The Scriptures did not mention that Christ would come out of Nazareth, and when he heard of Jesus his comment was "Can any good thing come out of Nazareth?" He too was from Cana, in Galilee, which was a hotbed of anti-establishment feeling in the first century, directed against both Rome and Jerusalem. There is a curious dialogue with Jesus recorded in the Gospel of John (1:47–50) where Nathaniel may have had his doubts. Jesus said he had seen him before they first met, the recruit having been under a fig tree. It apparently rang true to Nathaniel, who then said he believed Jesus had to be the Son of God. Jesus promised much greater things to come.

After the death of Jesus, Nathaniel went to Hierapolis. He and Philip were to be executed together, according to tradition, but Philip prayed that his fellow apostle be released, and he was. Nathaniel then traveled into Lycaonia and finally to India. India at the time was a catchall place-name that could include anywhere from northern Africa to Persia to the subcontinent. From wherever in India he then headed north to greater Armenia, where he was either beheaded, clubbed to death, killed with a sword, put in a bag and thrown into the sea, or crucified upside down in Albanopolis. The city of Albanopolis is now Baku and once claimed possession of his bones. But since there is little agreement regarding a final place of death, it makes authenticating his bones difficult.

One tradition claims that the Eastern Roman emperor Anastasios (491–519) brought the relics to a city named in his honor. This city was then taken by the same Persian emperor who once held the Spear of Destiny. The relics escaped being destroyed, only to be thrown in the Black Sea. This might account for that tale of the saint's demise. Through miraculous intervention, the chest washed up on the island of Lipari. When the chest was opened, myrrh flowed from them and was used in healing.

In 809, when the Lombards ruled in southern Italy, Nathaniel's bones were reputedly brought to the mainland of Italy. Part of them went to Benevento near Naples, where a very small church to the apostle is shadowed by much larger churches and even a temple to Isis. Once known as Maleventum, meaning "the ill winds," the name was changed to Beneventum, "good wind," before the Lombards reached the south of Italy. The area is known to cling to ancient beliefs, and for centuries it was the Egyptian deities who were honored in this small region. No greater quantity of Egyptian-style statuary is found anywhere else in Italy. When Christianity penetrated the south during the reign of the Lombards, pagan belief and witchcraft were commonplace and somehow accepted. The Italian liquor *strega* is named for the word *witch* in Italian. The liquor, which can be found almost anywhere in the country, is manufactured here.

From there the rest of the apostle's bones were brought to Rome years later and housed in the Church of San Bartolomeo. Canterbury Cathedral claims to have an arm, and his skull is said to be in Greece.

Judas Iscariot

There is one apostle, of course, who did not go on to becoming a saint. That is Judas Iscariot. Some scholars believe his name means he is Judas of Kerioth, although others believe his name has a more sinister meaning: Judas Sicarii. The Sicarii, like the Zealots and other radical groups, were named after the curved knives they used to assassinate their enemies.

Judas played a very important role in the Crucifixion. The prophecy of the execution of the Son of God could only be fulfilled through the betrayal of Judas. At the Last Supper, Jesus let it be known that he knew his betrayer sat with the others. After Judas left, the apostles and Jesus gathered in the Garden of Gethsemane and waited for the arrest.

Judas betrayed Jesus with a kiss, identifying him to those who came to arrest him. His fate after the infamous betrayal is uncertain. In Matthew the Gospel author says Judas hung himself. In Acts he died after a serious fall that caused his body to burst. A medieval account even had him living forever, cursed by his deed. In any case the message is that because of his guilt he suffered enormously.

He flung the pieces of silver earned by his betrayal of Jesus into the Aceldama, the Field of Blood, where legend says they were recovered and used to create a "potter's field," a cemetery for those who could not afford a burial plot.[22]

It would not be surprising if relics from the traitor were not collected, but they were. Rome claims to have several of the thirty pieces of silver Judas earned for his betrayal. A church at Aix (Aachen) claims a footprint of Judas, as does the church of St. Corneille of Compiegne.

At the Last Supper, Jesus began by washing the feet of the apostles. Judas was the first and presented no objection, although Peter who was second objected strenuously. After completing his task Jesus remarked that despite washing everyone, they were not all clean. The implication being that one would betray him. It was Judas, and because he was not clean his foot stained the towel that Jesus used. Calvin's *Treatise on Relics* used the example of there being more than one such towel, which proved that at least one church was guilty of fakery.

9

THE GOSPEL WRITERS
(MARK, MATTHEW, LUKE, AND JOHN)

The Bones of St. Luke

After resting in peace for centuries in a powerfully built coffin, St. Luke has become a source of controversy. In October 2001, near the feast of the saint and Gospel writer, it was announced by Professor Guido Barbujani, a population geneticist, that he had confirmed the authenticity of the bones of St. Luke. The bones had actually been identified two years before and the work of Professor Barbujani was actually further confirmation. This University of Ferrara scientist was not seeking headlines, although his news made headlines around the world. And he cannot be accused of being biased; as he himself points out, he is an atheist.[1]

As a scientist he declared there is no way to say for certain that the man is St. Luke. Historical research provides the basis for the background of St. Luke. Genetic science can confirm that the Gospel writer Luke was of Syrian origin, and his DNA matched most closely that of modern residents of ancient Aleppo. To come to that conclusion he analyzed DNA taken from the teeth and compared it with that of living descendants of residents of ancient Antioch. The data convinced him that the bones he examined confirmed a case already established. Is the man then St. Luke? Professor Barbujani is 99.9 percent convinced.

Luke was a companion of Paul who made one of the most lasting effects on Christianity by promoting his newfound religion to the Gentile world. Extending Christianity to the Gentiles was a source of contention for several in Jerusalem, and early factions were created because of issues such as circumcision.

Luke was Greek and most likely born in the city of Antioch in Syria. His writing gives evidence that he is very familiar with that city. Besides speaking Greek, his first language, he studied as both a physician and as a religious man, through which he learned Aramaic, a language much more widespread during the first century. The Gospel of Luke and the Acts of the Apostles are credited to him.

Luke preached throughout modern Turkey, and when Paul headed to Rome, Luke went with him. They were shipwrecked off the island of Malta, where it is believed Luke remained. Later he went to the Greek mainland, where he lived out his last years. Two hundred years after his death, his body was sent to Constantinople. Emperor Constantius was interested in collecting the bodies of saints. His successor, Julius II, had other ideas and wanted to wipe out Christianity and rid his kingdom of churches and shrines.

Well before the Crusades, when relic-hungry Europeans were carrying back saints by the boatload, Luke was rescued by being brought to Padua. Four hundred and thirty-six years after St. Luke's bones were brought to the Basilica of St. Justina in Padua, forensic science made the first confirmation of what the faithful already knew: St. Luke's bones were St. Luke's bones. They were not actually in a sarcophagus in the basilica but in a lead casket in a storeroom. The lid of the casket was inscribed "S. L. Evang." It did contain the saint's bones, although not the skull. This acknowledgment was made through the research of Vito Terribile Wiel Martin, a forensic pathologist.

It was believed that St. Luke lived a much longer life than the average man of his times, especially one preaching a religion that was persecuted. Legend has it that he was eighty-four when he died and that he had suffered greatly in his old age. Forensic evidence confirmed that the bones of the man in the elaborate sarcophagus were of a man who was over the age of seventy and under the age of eighty-five when he died. The evidence also confirmed the tradition that St. Luke suffered greatly in his old age. He suffered from acute osteoporosis as well as arthritis of the spinal cord. He also had pulmonary emphysema, a condition evidenced in the curvature of the ribs.

While the sarcophagus itself was protected under a huge marble slab, possibly because of rampant relic theft, the saint's remains were housed in a solid lead box. Wax seals, several coins, and parchments all add evidence to the authenticity of St. Luke's bones. The coins date to A.D. 229 and provide further evidence that as far back as the third century the bones were venerated as a relic. As such, the bones of a saint were on occasion gifted to other churches and cathedrals. The skull of St. Luke had been missing part of the cranium, which corroborated historical evidence that part of Luke's skull had been gifted to the Cathedral of St. Vitus in the city of Prague. Placed together, the skull fragment from Prague matched what was missing from the cranium.

The preservation of the teeth of the saint allowed further testing, and the carbon dating was borderline. Radiocarbon dating, which can often be thrown off by quirks of nature, indicated the teeth were from someone who died between 416 B.C. and A.D. 72, a few years short of the reputed death of Luke in A.D. 84.

The scientists involved believe the evidence is strong enough to make the case. So does the Greek Orthodox Church. They want him back.

St. Mark's Body

During his life, St. Mark went to Rome but most likely never Venice, a fact that didn't stop Venice from claiming him. In 827 St. Mark's body was in Alexandria. It was a time when the Muslims were in an expansionist mode, and relations with Christianity were not always friendly. In general, Muslims respected Christian sites and saints, but Venice, claiming to be acting in Mark's best interests, would steal his body. To ensure that a check of their cargo wouldn't reveal any kidnapped saints, they packed his body in a cargo of pork. After a rough sea voyage, his body arrived in Venice. The Christian Coptic Church would survive Islam and instead contend with Rome itself for eleven hundred years to get their most holy saint back.

There is much more to the story than saving the saint from Islam. Venice, as a city state, was limited in military power as well as in population. The Carolingian empire was expanding throughout Europe in every direction. Venice wished to remain independent of the growing empire. Venice was fully capable of maintaining a balance with the Byzantine empire in the East, but the Franks in the West were a threat. When the threat came, it was in a diplomatic action rather than a military maneuver. A court in Mantua decided that the area bordering Venice, Istria, was in danger of being absorbed by the Greeks. The Carolingian answer was that it should take it over, which was a direct threat to Venice. Venice needed a way to raise her own importance.

In France and Italy those churches that held the relics of the apostles exerted a superiority over those that didn't. Venice needed to claim her own apostle as a means of raising her status and importance. What better saint than Mark? Mark was almost an Italian apostle, even having written his

Gospel in Rome. Two Venetian merchants, Bonus and Rusticus, set out on a mission to Alexandria. They arrived at the time when Saracens were taking the statuary from Christian churches and preparing to build a mosque. They first approached the Greek custodians diplomatically, but the Greeks were dismayed. Mark was the first apostle to Alexandria, and they had no intention of giving him up.[2]

The Venetians decided they would have to take decisive action. In the middle of the night two Greeks and the two merchants stole Mark's body and switched the remains of a minor saint into his tomb. Mark's body reputedly gave off a fragrant odor that could be smelled all over the city. Other clerics checked his tomb and found remains that were assumed to be Mark's.

The body was packed in pork and loaded aboard the merchants' ship. When the Saracens came to inspect the ship, they reeled in disgust at the pork and did not search further.

The church writer Jacobus de Voragine records the voyage in great detail. The ship had pulled alongside another ship, and the sailors, so happy that they had the saint aboard, told the sailors of this other ship. Instead of awe they were greeted with doubt. "Maybe they gave you the corpse of some Egyptian," said one of the other crew members, laughing. The ship bearing Mark then rammed the other ship of doubters and could not be pulled loose until all aboard swore they had the real saint. If that was not enough, a storm threatened the ship so badly they were in fear of sinking. In the middle of the night Mark appeared to the monk guarding his body and instructed him to lower the sails quickly, as they were close to land. While none could see land, as soon as they did as they were instructed, an island appeared.[3]

After an adventurous voyage the merchants brought Mark to Venice and were welcomed by the doge as sons. Venice accomplished what she had planned. Her superiority over her neighboring cities was established. She kept her independence. The doge was so elated over having Mark's body that it was housed in the Ducal Palace rather than in a church. It was only after the independence issue was put to rest that a succeeding doge built the Basilica of St. Mark. Today the Piazza San Marco is the heart of the city.[4]

Numerous miracles attributed to Mark began to occur. A knight who was wounded so badly his hand needed to be amputated came to St. Mark's. His hand immediately reattached itself, leaving only a scar as evidence of his wound. In nearby Apulia a drought ravaged the land. Nothing could bring rain until it was told that they had neglected to observe Mark's feast day. The people prayed and promised an annual observance, and the rains came.

Mark had been a part of the early Christian community, and his mother's house served as a meeting place, most likely in secret. It was Paul who baptized him and from then on referred to him as his son. In A.D. 44 Paul and Mark's cousin Barnabas left for Antioch, and Mark joined them. He would eventually wind up in Rome and stay with Peter, who imparted to him the stories of Jesus that Mark recorded as one of the four accepted Gospels.

He is also said to have written a secret Gospel. According to Morton Smith, it was discovered in a letter from Clement, the early church writer and bishop. It was said to be directed only to those followers who were "perfected" or initiated into the mysteries. This led Smith to write that the story of Lazarus rising from the dead was actually a death-rebirth initiation rite that was required for someone to be among the "perfected."

From Rome, Mark went to Alexandria, where he became bishop of that city. He was arrested, tortured, and after an apparition of Jesus visited him in his cell, his body expired, and Mark went on to heaven. When his body was brought to Venice, the invented biography of Mark began to include his ministry to Venice. His body was kept in a mausoleum under the altar until 1808 when he was moved into the high altar.

In 1968 the Coptic Church struck back. Mark had been the first patriarch of Alexandria, and an entirely separate Christian Coptic Church begins its line of patriarchs, also known as popes, from Mark. The pope of Alexandria, Kyrillos VI, is the 116th in line from Mark. The Coptic Church had been negotiating for years, and finally the Roman Catholic Pope Paul VI agreed that some of Mark's relics be returned. June 22 of that year was marked with an unusual reception and solemn gathering where high-ranking dignitaries of both branches of Christianity met in Rome. Then on June 24, a special plane from Cairo picked up the Coptic delegation with their sacred cargo and headed home. Greater celebrations awaited as thousands turned out to greet the plane, Christians and Muslims alike.

As the relics of Mark were handed to the Coptic pope, it is said that three doves flew overhead.

St. Matthew

The breakup of the former Soviet Union has allowed the eastern churches to again openly exhibit their faith. It is only natural that they too would now require relics and pilgrimage sites to help appease the faithful and focus devotion. So recently the tomb of the Gospel writer Matthew has emerged from obscurity. The problem is that it is submerged.

Sergey Melnikoff claims that he has found the area where the saint's tomb lies but that it is underwater. Legends that Matthew, like others of Christ's inner circle, left and headed for India have Matthew founding churches along the way. One such community founded by Matthew was in what is now the territory of Kyrgyzstan. The journey was arduous, and by this time Matthew was much older. He fell ill and died and was interred on the shore of Issyk-Kul Lake. A monastery was built to mark the spot. Unfortunately, the Issyk-Kul Basin soon flooded, possibly the result of an earthquake, and Matthews's burial site is now underwater. The archbishop of Bishkek and Central Asia, Vladimir, supports the research, while both Russian and American teams dispute Melnikoff's claims. Others from the Kyrgyz Academy of Sciences have their doubts. To date, no excavation has begun.[5] While the debate continues, several other locations claim the saint.

Matthew, as may have been customary, had two names; his other was Levi. He was a "publican" or a tax collector in the town of Capharnaum, and the Pharisees regarded this occupation as very close to being a thief. When Matthew was called to be an apostle, he shared a meal in public with Jesus, which earned the criticism of the Pharisees. He wrote in Aramaic and began recording the words of Jesus twenty years after his death.

While tradition has Matthew writing in Aramaic, the early Christian writer Papias, whose works barely survives in fragments, says Matthew wrote in Hebrew. The language of Judea, however, was Aramaic at this time. There are some who put forth the idea that all of the Gospels were composite, and they point out that Hebrew texts rarely included an author's name.

Matthew established the genealogy of Jesus and described his family, including brothers and sisters of Jesus (13:55). He was nationalistic and possibly would not agree with Mark's pro-Gentile attitude. The non-Christian Jews were hostile to the Christian Jews, as they did not participate in the anti-Roman rebellion. The Romans, of course, were hostile to both. Authorship then was not without risk.

Matthew, like John, would not refer to himself directly, but in his fifth chapter on loving ones enemies, he includes "even the publican," the tax collectors like himself so often hated by the common man.

It is said that after the Resurrection, Matthew headed to Ethiopia. This could refer to anywhere in Africa. He wrote his Gospel in Aramaic, and it was translated into Greek. In Ethiopia a prince had him tortured and put in a leaden casket and buried at sea. It is also said he was killed with a sword in Hierapolis and buried in that city. It is also said that he traveled north of the Alps, the only apostle to reach that far north, and was buried in what is now Germany.

His grave was forgotten until the city of Trier in 1127 decided to rebuild a church to St. Eucharius. During the construction an ancient crypt was discovered to be holding the apostle and evangelist. The crypt is preserved and is open to the public, although Matthew's remains merited a cathedral. Trier is one of Germany's oldest towns and was the residence of Constantine for six years. Charlemagne made it an archbishopric. Among its many churches, the Church of St. Matthew is now an important pilgrimage site in that country.

John, the Evangelist

A native of Galilee and the brother of James the Greater, John like several other apostles, had been a follower of John the Baptist. He composed his own Gospel and, notably, the book of Revelations. He was the youngest of the apostles and referred to himself in his Gospel not by name but as the "apostle that Jesus loved." He was present at the Last Supper, where he has been depicted as leaning his head against Jesus. He was in the Garden at Gethsemane, where Jesus was arrested. Just before his death Jesus had asked John to take care of Mary, his mother. John and James seem to have had a more aggressive style than the other apostles, and among John's exploits was one where he told an exorcist to stop casting out devils. When Jesus heard this he told John, "The man who is not against you is on your side." In Samaria, where doors were shut to Jesus, John suggested calling upon heaven to destroy the Samaritans.

It may have taken experiencing the Pentecost to gain enlightenment. From that moment the apostles went forth to preach the new covenant. John was close to Peter and was thrown into prison with him for praying in the temple. He then went to Asia, where he founded many churches. The Emperor Domitian summoned him to Rome. In an attempt to kill John the emperor ordered him thrown into a vat of boiling oil. The attempt was miraculously unsuccessful, as John emerged uncorrupted. He was then banished to the island of Patmos, where he wrote the Apocalypse, or Revelations. Patmos is a tiny island, thirteen square miles, that remembers John until this day. A fortified monastery on a rocky hill that dominates the town still bears his name. Another monastery, the Monastery of the Apocalypse, is a theological college. It is built over the cave in which John spent his exile.

The exile was not to be for long. The same year he arrived, Domitian himself was murdered, and so John's exile ended. He then went back to Ephesus in Asia Minor. On the day of his arrival he resurrected a faithful Christian woman from the dead. It was not the last such resurrection he performed or miracle. Reminiscent of his desire to call the fire of heaven down on Samaria, in Ephesus he finally had his day.

Pagan Ephesians had dragged John to the Temple of Artemis. They wished to force him to pray to Artemis, but instead, John called down heaven on her temple. It collapsed through John's command, and her statue turned to dust.

He lived out the rest of his years as the protector of Mary, the mother of Jesus.

Ephesus was one of the great cities of the classical world, and only Alexandria was larger. When the Ionians colonized it in the eleventh century B.C., they replaced the worship of the goddess Cybele with their own goddess Artemis. The Temple to Artemis was one of the Seven Wonders of the World. Both St. Paul and St. John preached there during its golden age as part of the Roman Empire. At the time, it served as the capital of Roman Asia.

The youngest apostle when he joined Jesus, John lived out his life in Ephesus to a possible age of one hundred years. He had fulfilled his promise to protect the mother of Jesus. The house where the Virgin lived is called the Meryemana and was rediscovered in 1891. Clergymen searching for the house were guided by a German woman whose directions were the product of her visions. On the first-century foundations of the house a chapel was built, and Ephesus is now the center of an annual August 15 (Assumption) celebration. Two popes, Paul VI and John Paul II, have said mass at the sacred site.

St. John's Basilica was built in the sixth century by the Emperor Justinian over the tomb where the saint was buried. Being the burial place of an apostle elevates a site to be considered most sacred, although today the church is in ruins. It may also be one of the few burial places that is not in dispute. The government has begun a campaign to restore some of the country's most remarkable archaeological wonders.

10

THE MIRACLES AND
THE RELICS OF THE SAINTS

Occasionally the body of a deceased holy man or woman will exhibit miraculous phenomena that in itself can be a reason for considering that person
to be a saint. A high rank in the church, death by martyrdom, or just a particularly religious life is a start on the road to sainthood. In death, however,
there are other pieces of evidence that can become cause of canonization:
bodies, or body parts, of the saints are found that seem to never decom-
pose; blood that can liquefy or solidify seemingly on cue; bones that produce powder or oil that is called manna. Such a postmortem display is
regarded as a sign and is never ignored, and only in the last century have
these signs ever been challenged by science.

The manna of the saints is a broad name given generally to oil that has
flowed or still flows from the bones of certain saints. Oil exuded from relic
bones has been used by believers to cure both physical and spiritual ills.
The church cautions that it is through the intercession of the saint, not
the substance itself. One of the most famous oil-producing saints is St.
Walburga in Bavaria, who is recorded exuding the sacred manna from as
early as the ninth century. The manna was tested and basically is made up
of water. It constantly flows from the saint onto her slab and into a silver
cup. Other saints inexplicably produce a powdery substance. The church
recognizes over a score of manna-producing saints.[1]

Another phenomenon is incorrupt bodies. To the church this state
of remaining incorrupt defies nature and is therefore a sign of holiness.[2] On occasion, saints' bodies have remained incorrupt for centuries, only to begin decomposing much later than natural bodies.
St. Bernadette, one of the three children to whom the Blessed Virgin

appeared at Lourdes, died in 1879. One hundred and twenty years later her incorrupt body lies in St. Gildard Convent in Nevers, France. St. John Vianney, who died in 1859, similarly lies incorrupt over 140 years later, encased in glass on a marble altar in Ars, also in France. St. Francis Xavier, who died in 1552, was a colonial Jesuit apostle to Asia. His body remains incorrupt after hundreds of years. Parts of his body have been taken as gift relics to other churches, but most of his body remains in a silver casket. Occasionally only the skeleton remains intact. St. Clare of Assisi died in the mid-thirteenth century. Her clothes and flesh turned to dust.

St. Catherine of Bologna, who died in 1463, appeared to a sister nun sixty years later. She requested that her body be exhumed and left in a sitting position in the cell that she lived in before her death. Her face and hands today are darkened, but it is said that this has been caused by the burning of candles. In some cases there is reason to believe that such an incorrupt state has been assisted. St. Bernadette was injected with formaldehyde. Some saints had wax coverings placed over the face. Others had been buried in lime, which actually has a preservative effect on a corpse.

Finally there is what has been referred to as the Odor of Sanctity. This phenomenon can be exhibited by corpses that have been dead for hundreds of years as well as by living humans. Hundreds of saints have demonstrated the effect. St. Teresa of Avila, Christianity's most mystical woman saint, is said to have exuded a pleasant fragrance throughout the hallways and rooms of her convent. St. Catherine dei Ricci, who died in the sixteenth century, exuded a fragrance described as more pleasant than any perfume. St. Gerard Majella, who died in the eighteenth century, also gave off a very sweet smell, even when he was near death. Padre Pio, whose life was equally simple outside of his miraculous demonstration of stigmata, often gave off a pleasing fragrance when his stigmata wounds were open. His own doctor, Giorgio Festa, who had no sense of smell, brought a cloth dipped in Pio's blood to Rome. Despite the cloth being in a box, others could smell the perfumelike odor and commented on it, to the doctor's surprise. For a long time afterward he kept the cloth in a cabinet, and his patients often commented on the source of the fragrant odor.

Many such remarkable powers are explained away as the power of suggestion, others as pious hoaxes. But there are some that science has had a tougher time explaining.

St. Gennaro

Southern Italians have an unusually deep superstitious side. Naples, it seems, is as full of superstitions as any third world nation. Belief in the power of saints is an integral part of the Christian religion. Here amulets, charms, and Madonnas decorate cars and houses. In such a place only a true miracle could make anyone sit up and take note. In Naples such miracles take place three times a year. These regular miracles occur like clockwork on the first Saturday in May, on the nineteenth of September, and on the sixteenth of December.

On those dates the blood of the city's patron saint, San Gennaro, also known as St. Januarius, is brought out in public for all to see. The blood is in a solid state, but it almost never disappoints the thousands from all over the world who come to view the miracle. The blood liquefies. Every year since 1389, the blood of the city's patron saint has liquefied, with a few remarkable exceptions.

In Italy alone there are two hundred blood relics, and they are mostly in the southern part of the country. A small number of these blood samples can seemingly liquefy from their normal clotted state. Science has attempted to explain the phenomena by proposing that thixotropy may explain the seemingly miraculous change in the blood matter. Thixotropy is the opposite of isotropy, and both scientific terms have an easy explanation.[3]

Isotropy is the property by which a liquid becomes solid by being agitated. Thixotropy, the opposite, allows a solid to become liquid by the same means. Striking a bottle of ketchup to get the seemingly solid mass to pour out of the bottle is an example of thixotropy.

Three times each year there is a celebration or feast for St. Gennaro. During the feast the ritual liquefaction would hopefully take place. While the church does not take a stance on authenticity, and no one has ever been allowed to perform physical tests on the blood, it does liquefy in front of numerous witnesses. The ritual starts with the cardinal bringing out the two vials from a safe behind the altar. The substance in the vials is dark and solid. The cardinal will raise the vials in the air repeatedly until they turn liquid and red. Not everyone has always been convinced that the liquefaction is real. Mark Twain denounced it as "one of the wretchedest of all religious impostures."[4]

Thixotropy as an explanation would be a kinder answer. A reaction occurs when blood drawn from a living body is poured into a container. The soluble serum protein fibrinogen is turned into insoluble fibrin, or simply put, the blood clots. The clot can be broken down, that is, reliquefied. However, once this happens it is unusual for it ever to clot again.

The act of vigorously shaking the blood of the saint can explain a one-time liquefaction, but it cannot, in general, explain how the transformation occurs three times a year.

The story of St. Gennaro starts in A.D. 305 when Genarro, then the bishop of Benevento, was comforting Christian prisoners arrested by the Romans. He too was arrested and was sentenced to death in the amphitheater of nearby Pozzuoli. With six companions, he was sentenced to be beheaded, but first a finger was cut off. His followers filled two vials with his blood. Later, in the time of Constantine, Bishop Severus brought the saint's body to Naples, where it too is preserved in a cathedral.

Mount Vesuvius, the nearby active volcano, would occasionally threaten to erupt, and San Gennaro would be called upon to intercede. The amalgamation of people that make up southern Italy were the result of the Italian boot being a trading center for the world. A decidedly ancient attitude took hold, and during an eruption the saint's statue was placed in the path of the lava flow. The implication was: save us or die with us. After St. Gennaro performed the miracle of saving Naples in 685, it was decided that every year an annual feast to the patron saint would be held.

Today the blood of the saint and a gold reliquary bust containing his skull are protected in the Cappella del Tesoro in a cathedral called the Duomo. Built between 1294 and 1323, the exterior of the cathedral has a nineteenth-century facade. Inside, however, the nave is lined with ancient columns and monuments to past rulers. The Cappella Carafa, which is also in the Duomo, is an ornate structure built around 1500 containing the tomb of the saint. Connected to the church is a fourth-century basilica built over a temple to Apollo.

While Mark Twain would consider it typical of religious hucksterism in Italy, others would be convinced it was truly miraculous. In 1902 light was shined through the liquid, and it gave off the same spectrum as blood. Later, a Jesuit debunker of false miracles declared it to be the real thing. To paraphrase Galileo: nevertheless, it does liquefy!

And woe to Naples when it doesn't. It is said that it failed to liquefy once during the French occupation under Napoleon, nearly causing a revolt. Then the French commander threatened to shoot the bishop if the miracle did not occur. On cue it did, and the bishop was spared.

In 1944 the miracle failed to happen. This was an evil omen for Naples, and the ever-threatening volcano Vesuvius erupted. Lava was spewed two thousand feet from the central crater into the sky, and a column of ash rose nearly a mile into the atmosphere. Lava flowed into two towns, Sebastiano and Massa, and destroyed them.

In 1980 the liquefaction failed again, and an earthquake hit the area. In Naples the ground shook and buildings collapsed. The city proper was spared the worst, but a string of bad news followed. Nearby Irpinia was almost completely destroyed, as it had been the epicenter of the quake. Three thousand lives were lost. Billions of dollars sent to rebuild the many destroyed buildings and homes in Naples were put in the hands of corrupt politicians who seemingly just split it with the Camorra. This Calabrian version of the Mafia controlled the construction business that reputedly stole the relief funds. Years later many of the projects contracted for were still not completed. A reporter for a Naples daily was gunned down while investigating the corruption. And the number of new homeless added to an already impoverished city.

Napolitanos, however, accept their patron saint even with his imperfections. Even the soccer fans scream for their saint to protect them.

As if performing one such regular miracle was not enough, St. Gennaro performs two miracles at the same time. Nine miles away, housed in a church at Pozzuoli, is the stone column on which the saint was allegedly beheaded. When the saint's blood is performing its thrice-annual miracle in Naples, a depression in the stone reddens. It is said the cause of this is his blood. One time in 1860 it actually exuded blood, if the locals can be believed, when a church dedicated to the saint caught fire. Another time, in 1894, cotton was used to take a sample of the blood. The blood was revealed actually to be blood, although the test was not done until years later. The column itself was monitored and turned different shades of red, even though there were no changes in humidity.[5]

Adequate testing on the column and the blood itself has never been done in a manner that would satisfy skeptics. Until recently the explanation of the changing of the blood from solid to liquid was said to be caused by the heat and humidity. The effect took place, however, in both May and December. It was in 1994 that the more logical explanation of the thixotropy effect was proposed. The faithful simply ignored the scientific explanation. The explanation itself, if true, would then make it harder to explain the miracles of numerous other saints. Southern Italy has no fewer than twenty saints who perform blood miracles, and their blood does not require being shaken.

St. Lawrence (San Lorenzo)

One hour south of Rome lies the town of Amaseno, where the blood of St. Lawrence is stored. Martyred on August 10, 258, under the Roman emperor Valerian, St. Lawrence died in a particularly gruesome fashion. He was charred on a grill. It was punishment for his tricking the prefect of Rome. Tradition has St. Peter bringing the chalice that would be called the Holy Grail to Rome when he became the first bishop of that city. It survived in Rome through numerous persecutions that kept the life spans of the popes very short. There had been twenty popes that served as bishop of Rome in two hundred years. They all guarded the chalice of the Last Supper. Pope Sixtus II was the last.

The Roman emperor Valerian was particularly cruel. He was also in need of funds, and as other kings would do later in history, he targeted a convenient scapegoat. In this case the Christian church. Sixtus II was called to appear before the emperor. Anticipating his execution, he gave the chalice to St. Lawrence and asked him to protect it.

For Lawrence it was a death sentence, but he too acted to protect the chalice. He gave it and other important relics to a Spaniard to protect from the avaricious Romans. Next it was St. Lawrence's turn to appear before Valerian, who had demanded the treasures of the church. Lawrence, as the holder of the church's valuables, asked for time to gather them together. Granted the time, he sold everything that was left and gave the proceeds to the poor. When he returned, the magistrate asked where the treasures of the church were. Lawrence pointed to the beggars. And earned his punishing death.

Even during his execution, St. Ambrose records Lawrence kept his sense of humor. He was subject to the horrible torture of being roasted on a grill. He apparently felt no pain, and he is said to have instructed his executioners to turn him over, as he was well done on one side. Despite the cruel execution, his bones and blood were preserved, and during the Middle Ages he became a very popular saint.

He would serve as patron to students, brewers, cooks, cutlers, glaziers, and launderers.

On his feast day his blood, normally housed in a locked silver tabernacle in the right wing of the Church of St. Maria, is brought out and inspected. Then it is placed in a glass cabinet near the altar of the church. Any transformation of the condition of the blood that takes place is visible to the worshippers who crowd the church. The miraculous conversion takes place without it being shaken, or stirred, and therefore thixotropy does not explain the phenomenon.[6]

Unlike their more superstitious neighbors in the south, the people of Amaseno actually allowed testing to take place on their patron saint. Father Italo Pisterzi of the Church of St. Maria presented the sacred relic to Dr. Luigi Garlaschelli of the University of Pacia to conduct testing. The condition was that the testing be done where everyone can see it. The solution? The event would take place on national television. On August 10, 1996, the feast day of the saint, the Italian state television, RAI 2, presented this most remarkable event.

Dr. Garlaschelli brought a camera, a caliper, an electronic balance, a test tube whirler, and various clamps, stands, beakers, and measuring devices. He was given a bottle in the shape of an inverted cone closed with a cork, secured with red wax seals, red string, and a bishop's label. He whirled the mass in a test tube mixer, heated it, cooled it in an ice water bath, and reheated it again. The transformation of the blood took place as the faithful believed; however, Dr. Garlaschelli had an explanation that wasn't welcomed by all.

The liquid contained in the vial was reacting to a change in temperature. Furthermore, he expressed his opinion that the blood was not blood at all but a mixture of waxes, fat, and an oil-soluble red dye. In his report, which followed, he believed that in the seventeenth century, which was when the "blood" was first exhibited, some kind of substitution had taken place. The relic had originally contained a scroll dating from the twelfth century describing the contents as *de pinguedine* of the saint, which is the fat of the saint. Such a relic may not have been as welcome in more modern times, so the relic was doctored.

If the results of the testing were disappointing to St. Lawrence's faithful, his "incorrupted" head is on display every August 10 at the Vatican. The body of the Roman martyr was discovered to be in this incorrupted state in A.D. 460 when the bones of another martyr, St. Stephanus, were brought to Rome to be buried alongside Lawrence. On opening his tomb the body looked "as if it had come to life again." During a thirteenth-century renovation his tomb was opened again. At this time his head was removed from the rest of the corpse and brought to the Pontifical Palace. So far no explanation, scientific or otherwise, has been given for its condition.

St. Anthony of Padua

Every June pilgrims from all over the world come to honor the saint at the Basilica di Sant Antonio in Padua. The chapel inside contains the revered saint's tomb. It also contains his tongue, jaw, and vocal cords. They were preserved separate from the rest of the saint because he was one of Christianity's best speakers. St. Anthony was well-known for his speaking ability and was renowned as a gifted preacher. Years after his death in 1231, his relics were transferred to a new resting place. When the vault that held his body was opened, the flesh was found reduced to dust, but the tongue was as fresh, undamaged, and red as a living person's. St. Bonaventure witnessed the wonder and declared it to be a miracle.

His skeleton too is exhibited in the church, although it is missing a left forearm and some other minor bones, which were given out as relics to other churches.[7]

St. Anthony of Padua started life as Fernando de Bulhoes in Lisbon, Portugal, in 1195. He took the name Anthony when he became a Franciscan monk in Coimbra. He had a captivating voice and charisma to match, and his teaching attracted much attention. He felt that people may have paid him attention only because he was from a wellborn family. He traveled to Toulouse and Paris, where he continued his education. Then, in imitation of St. Francis of Assisi, he traveled to Africa to convert the Moors. Leaving Morocco, he was shipwrecked in Sicily. And most likely, as one believes everything happens for a reason, he finally met St. Francis. His preaching earned him the title Hammer of the Heretics.

He also took up social causes and pushed the city of Padua into enacting a rule, in the year of St. Anthony's death, that a person could no longer be deprived of their liberty because of a debt. It would be centuries before such rules were passed elsewhere.

Back home he is still remembered as Lisbon's favorite saint, even though St. Vincent is the city's patron saint. On the eve of St. Anthony's feast is a celebration of eating, drinking, and folk dancing, and neighborhood feasts continue late into the night. No doubt the feasts incorporate some vestiges of an older pagan custom. Women carry around small earthenware pots with fresh basil and a love poem. The custom is that as the basil grows, so will the buyer's love. The next day starts off more quietly, as the statue of St. Anthony is carried throughout the city as part of a procession that all parishes participate in. The celebrants kneel in prayer or throw coins and flowers in advance of the saint.

What some may regard as an inappropriate way of showing reverence has allowed science to help in seeing the real St. Anthony. Anthropometric information suggests that St. Anthony was five foot six inches with a long face and deep-set eyes. He had well-developed legs, most likely from a great deal of traveling on foot, and enlarged knees.

St. Nicholas

St. Nicholas has been giving the faithful a very unusual gift for sixteen hundred years. Not from a sack but from his bones. They constantly produce a liquid substance referred to as manna. They started to do this soon after his burial in Myra, Turkey, and continue to do it today, in his new resting place in Bari, Italy. The "manna," a combination of hydrogen and oxygen, is biologically pure and not the result of seepage, rain, seawater, or any known agent. The substance is found only on his bones, not on the walls of his tomb, which would indicate a more natural cause. His tomb, partially marble, is said to be unaffected by the outside atmosphere and shows no signs of humidity. The liquid oozes out of the pores in his bones and is regularly collected. Supposedly a knight took a tooth from the saint's body that also oozed manna when placed in a golden case. Because this paranormal phenomenon has occurred in two separate places, local climate as well as the conditions within the tomb are eliminated as possible causes. Similarly, bones taken from the tomb in a sack soon left the sack wet with manna.

To the believers, what is called manna is often a sacred liquid, at times oily, with thaumaturgic powers.[8] In plain English the clear liquid produced by the bones of the saint can ward off danger and cure sickness. The sacred liquid produced by St. Nicholas is sold in bright hand-painted bottles produced in Bari (and has been diluted with water). Anyone with three dollars can buy a gift of St. Nicholas to bring home. The sacred oil is also used in annual blessings of the waters, in Bari and even in Lake Michigan, where a ceremony precedes pouring some of the saint's oil in the water to protect sailors and provide fishermen with a plentiful bounty. The ceremony has taken place in Italy for centuries and has just started in Chicago in June 2000.

The church plays a prominent role in the ceremonies but cautions the faithful that the oily water has no power of its own but just acts to help the intercession of the saints. An odd gift indeed from the saint who had much to do with the modern Christmas celebration.

The real St. Nick did not wear red or fur, drive a sleigh, or live or even travel anywhere near the North Pole. He was a fourth-century bishop in a southwestern Turkish coastal town. He is, however, remembered and revered by Christians and Muslims alike for his generosity. Today this town is in the middle of raising funds and fighting bureaucracy to rebuild St. Nick's home church.

It will have everything a fitting shrine should have, except for the bones of the revered holy man. They were stolen by Italian tomb raiders one thousand years before. The year was 1071 and the Normans, a collection of adventurers, mercenaries, and pirates from France, had just reached the city of Bari on the Apulian coast of southern Italy. Italy's south was divided between pro-Normans and pro-Byzantine factions. Both Norman and Byzantine invaders had settled here. To unify the city and to raise its status as well, it was decided that Bari needed a patron saint to bring peace and prosperity. Merchants and a crew of forty-seven sailors headed to the Byzantine coast of Asia Minor. It was at a time when the Turks were invading the coast and threatening Christian sites. The Barese sailors went to the church of St. Nicholas and requested the monks show them his tomb. The monks, acting as curators, were suspicious. The theft of relics was at its height throughout Europe, and no doubt churches and monasteries everywhere were on their guard. Myra was isolated, however, and after threats of violence, one monk led them to his tomb. A sacred oil is said to have flowed over the tomb, and when the Italians opened the tomb, the fragrance spread throughout the town. The merchants from Bari were soon confronted by the townspeople who smelled the fragrance and became curious.

The crowd was pacified, however, after being told by the merchants that they had been guided by a revelation that brought them to Myra to save Nicholas. One monk even claimed Nicholas appeared to him and told the monk he wanted to leave. The townspeople gave their consent, and the sailors departed before they changed their minds.

St. Nicholas was then brought to Italy.[9]

Nicholas was born in the small town of Patara in what was then Asia Minor sometime before the year A.D. 300. It was a Lycian (Greek) port city that today is still covered with Roman ruins along a beautiful sandy beach. Nicholas was said to have started praying immediately after he was born. Even as an infant he was so pious he fasted. His childhood served as an example of piety to other children. His parents died while he was still a young man, and despite a large inheritance, he joined the church and moved to Myra, also on the coast. In Myra he was appointed bishop and stood guard against paganism, even to the point of destroying a temple to Artemis. During the Roman persecution by Diocletian he was tortured, chained, and thrown into prison for his efforts. The Roman Grinch who had the future Santa thrown into prison was soon replaced. When Constantine took over in Rome, he had Nicholas freed. Nicholas returned to Myra to finish out his life as bishop. His legend grew far and wide during his life and after his death. The small town of Myra, as remote as it is, still exists today as Demre. It is reached by road from Antalya, the nearest place with an airport. The coastal drive has been described as the California Big Sur, although this stretch of the Turkish coast shares little else with the California coast. Ninety-eight percent of the population is Muslim today, and the area is an archaeological paradise.

Bishop Nicholas would become the source of the modern Santa. The people of fourth-century coastal Turkey had seen better days, and one man was so poor he had no money to provide dowries for his three daughters. Instead the daughters were ready to be sold into slavery. Nicholas threw gold coins into their chimney, at least one coin landing in their stockings. The women then had enough for their respective dowries and were able to marry.

It wasn't his only good deed. He is said to have traveled around, putting gifts in houses through open windows, saving ships in distress, saving towns from famine, and saving unjustly condemned men from their fate. His most miraculous undertaking was accomplished on the way to the Council of Nicaea. He stopped at an inn where the evil innkeeper had murdered two boys, which he was then going to serve up as food. Nicholas became aware of what had happened. The bishop restored the boys to life and converted the murderous innkeeper.[10]

After his death he became the patron saint of children, merchants, bakers, mariners, and pirates. A sailor's wish on departure was "may St. Nicholas hold the tiller." Prisoners and captives invoked the intercession of Nicholas for their freedom. He is even said to protect city dwellers from being mugged, no small feat in the winding narrow alleyways of the old city in Bari. He also became the patron saint of many nations, including

Greece, Italy, Russia, and Holland. By the Middle Ages there were already four hundred churches in England dedicated to St. Nicholas.

Other priests and bishops all through Europe preached about the generosity of Nicholas without realizing the persona they would ultimately create. St. Nicholas's example was a motivation for everyone, but he also had a special focus on children. His feast on December 6 was soon celebrated in northern Europe with gingerbread, multishaped biscuits, and other confectionery items. A man in each village dressed up like a bishop and would inquire if local children had been bad or good. The good, especially those who had learned their catechism, might be rewarded with gifts.

Just in case the children didn't know where they stood, they left out a gift for St. Nicholas, as well as hay for his horse and a glass of schnapps for his servant. In some towns the tradition had an ogre accompany St. Nicholas carrying a rod to punish the bad children. The Dutch name for St. Nicholas was pronounced Sinter Klaas when they brought his legend to seventeenth-century colonial New Amsterdam. In the early 1600s the Dutch had landed in the New World and colonized most of the area along the Hudson River, from modern New York City to the state capital in Albany. They planted farms throughout the Hudson Valley and into what is now New Jersey. Only a half century later the English took over and renamed the small city of New Amsterdam as New York. But the Dutch influence would remain. When the English began their own efforts to colonize New York, they brought their own brand of the Protestant religion, which was a bit more strict than the Dutch, although not as severe as that of the Massachusetts Pilgrims. They did not encourage the practice of gift giving on the eve of St. Nicholas's feast day.

The Dutch combination of St. Nicholas and Christmas was established in America as the practice of giving gifts was moved up to Christmas. Washington Irving, who is more famous for Rip Van Winkle, preserved the early New York legend of St. Nicholas as an old man riding a flying horse to bring gifts to children.

As the legend grew, his horse had become reindeer, his servant became an elf, and happily for many of us the ogre with the rod was left behind in Europe.

There are many pagan influences in the modern Christmas celebration. The pagan Sol Invictus of Constantine was left behind, but like other ancient practices it placed importance on the shortest day of the year, December 21, as a solar celebration. Another Roman feast called Mothers Night had been celebrated between December 25 and January 1. The pagan

name for that old month was *giuli,* which became *yule* in England. The custom of carrying in evergreens and the burning of a yule log were pre-
Christian. Attempts to trace the tree origin include a decidedly barbaric
Celtic custom of decorating a particular tree with the skulls of sacrificed
animals, and Martin Luther's own invention of putting lighted candles on
a fir tree. The first seems most un-Christmas-like, the second a recipe for
disaster. Holly and mistletoe too have their roots in pagan worship, as both
were revered by the Druids as preserving the spirit of the tree. Mistletoe
could be a poison as well as a healing agent, and the benefit of kissing
under the decoration is unknown. The custom started in England.

While some claim a Norse infusion of flying gods as the source of modern
Christmas, the final step to the modern version was a Dr. Clement Moore,
who wrote " 'Twas the Night Before Christmas" while on his way to Green-
wich Village in a carriage back in 1822. The saint in Dr. Moore's poem had
become a tiny elf with a miniature sleigh driven by eight tiny reindeer. Most
likely it was the only way to fit him in a chimney. The illustrator Thomas
Nast may have had Dr. Moore's poem in mind when he included several
styles of Santa in *New Yorker* magazine, where he created cartoons for over
twenty years. One hundred years after " 'Twas the Night Before Christmas," Coca-Cola advertisements restored Santa to the full-size, red-faced,
and bearded image we have today.

Along the sunny blue waters of coastal Turkey there is not much evidence of red fur or reindeer. But there is a great deal of generosity, thanks
to the universal love of St. Nicholas, who is Father Christmas to the Western religions and Noel Baba to the Muslim Turks. The Father Christmas
Foundation along with the Foundation for the Preservation of Turkish
Monuments is raising the millions it will take to restore the ancient
church. The church now lies behind a grove of trees in a ditchlike area. It
has been destroyed by earthquakes, battered by floods, sacked by Arabs,
and rebuilt in a conglomerate style. The silting of the harbor has caused
the land the church was built on to sink seventeen feet below sea level. After
a strong rain eight pumps are required to pump out as much as two feet of
seawater.

While the funds for restoration have been forthcoming, the various
plans for the actual work of restoration are the source of conflict. So far,
well-meaning architects and engineers have done little more than debate
just how the church can be saved. One archaeologist is holding up the

plans from becoming reality. The government, unable to fix the impasse, has big hopes for the church once it is finally restored. The Turkish Culture Ministry, which technically owns the site, wishes nothing more than getting any form of restoration started. Last year several thousand Turkish children visited the site at Christmas. Tourism, however, brings more dollars, and it is hoped that an attractively restored site will add Myra to the must-see destinations along Turkey's sunny coast. The small town has also petitioned Bari for the return of their patron's bones.

Meanwhile the sister-city of Myra in Bari, Italy, has fared better. It is still a commercial port, with ferries calling on Greece, Albania, Croatia, and Turkey. It is one of the most important commercial centers of the south, with regular trade fairs that fill the hotels as full as the annual St. Nicholas festival days.

When Nicholas arrived, he was placed in a church dedicated to St. John the Baptist. Immediately plans were made for the saint to have his own basilica, which was started within two years and is now the center of the Old City. Despite Bari being a crossroads between the Norman invasion and Byzantine interests, it was a wealthy seaport. Unlike Genoa and Venice, which were closed from the interior by high mountains, the merchants of Bari had direct access to the farmlands of the countryside. Nobles, often from families with large landholdings, and merchants enjoyed a cooperative relationship. St. Nicholas may have helped cement the relationship between the nobles and the merchants, which might have been hurt by the influx of any newcomers. In 1105 the Society of St. Nicholas was formed, and those who played a role in the theft of the saint were honored. This group—including merchants, nobles, and common sailors—altogether added up to sixty-two individuals, although not all were present on the voyage. Members are still honored figures at the modern celebrations and display oversize St. Nicholas medallions hanging from a bright yellow collar.

The basilica, which is entered through a finely carved door, includes a large crypt and stairways that lead to the crypt from the aisles of the church. Bari now had a patron saint and became a magnet for pilgrims from all over. One of the greatest sculptures from medieval times is an eleventh-century throne that is off at the side of the altar. In 1319 the king of Serbia presented the basilica with a Byzantine icon of Nicholas, which is still displayed in the central apse of the crypt. In the early 1400s three great transept arches were added. In the sixteenth century the duchess of Bari, who was also the queen of Poland, was interred in the basilica. An orthodox chapel was added to accommodate pilgrims from Russia and Greece.

At the same time reinforced concrete and steel grilles (and a pair of angels) were added to protect Nicholas from unwanted intruders and potential modern-day tomb robbers. For their part Bari will not entertain the return of their saint. Dominican Father Matera pointed out that Turkey, after all, is predominantly Islamic, and his reply—"They won't get him back, ever"—allows for no compromise.[11] The tomb of St. Nicholas attracts visitors from all over the world, as many as 100,000 each year. Their ranks have even included Princess Diana and Prince Charles.

Today Bari still celebrates both the feast of St. Nicholas and another holiday, the day he arrived. That celebration starts on May 7 with a procession in traditional garb through the streets of the Old City. At the first mass the next morning the name of which boat gets to carry the saint's effigy, ahead of the other boats, is announced. A procession of boats to the harbor takes place, and by nightfall the celebration is at its height when an icon is displayed from the lead boat to the celebrants onshore.

Remarkably, after one thousand years St. Nicholas's bones still exude gallons of the liquid called manna. Miracles have been attributed to this strange substance, and many locals keep a vial of it for luck. Visitors bring some home. And science until recently did not have a chance to test the manna. Between 1954 and 1957 there was an effort to provide an explanation. During a renovation the bones were taken out of the tomb and placed in the Hall of the Treasures. They visibly "perspired" in front of the faithful. When placed on linen, they could soak the cloth in a short time.

Because the manna is actually a hydrogen-oxygen combination, it is safe to call the gift of St. Nicholas water, although a better description is pure water. Just how the bones produce such a liquid over a thousand years after the death of the saint, and in almost any atmosphere, has not been answered by science.

11

NOAH'S ARK

The search for the biblical Noah's Ark has been going on for centuries, and technology may finally serve to locate the legendary ship. A series of American spy satellite photographs that range from 1949 to the present are being declassified and for the first time made available for nonmilitary review. In November 2002 documents released by the CIA reported that an unidentified shape had perked up interest not only at the agency but also all the way up to the White House when George H. W. Bush was president. The image showing the Mount Ararat area reveals something sticking out of the ice and snow, but it could be anything. The CIA director James Woolsey asked what an exhaustive review would cost and just how long it would take. The project never got off the ground.

Today the investigation and search for the Ark of Noah remains in private hands. One group, working under the corporate name of ArkImaging, is studying the satellite photographs. According to Porcher Taylor, a senior associate of the Center for Strategic and International Studies in Washington, who pushed the CIA for years to declassify the images, there is a six-hundred-foot-long boat that has been depicted since 1949. Taylor, who is now a university professor in Virginia, had first heard about the spy pictures as a cadet at West Point. With help from the Freedom of Information Act, Taylor's persistence finally bore fruit, and the first photos were released. There are others that may not be released anytime soon, as they are from the most sophisticated satellites.[1]

Remote Ararat

The Bible states that Noah's ship, with dimensions almost as large as a modern cruise ship, came to rest in the mountains of Ararat. The size of the ship, as determined by the Old Testament, is 450 feet long, a size unrivaled by any other ship on earth until 1884 when the Cunard line's *Eturia* was built. The place where it landed, Ararat, is a derivative of an ancient Assyrian word *Urartu*. As an individual mountain, Ararat is the location given. As an area, Urartu designates a large landmass that would later be called Armenia. Other references from as early as the third century B.C. suggest that at least at that time the Ark could still be sighted. In fact, the Ararat region has been known to be the final resting place for the Ark for literally thousands of years.

Mount Ararat is in the extreme eastern end of modern Turkey. This country covers a vast area stretching nearly one thousand miles from modern Istanbul in the west to the mountainous border country in the east. While the cosmopolitan aspects of Turkey's key city and the attractive seaside resorts in the south may be accommodating to travelers, the east is anything but accommodating. Ararat, known in country as Agri Dagi, is part of a mountainous region of Karasu-Aras (a.k.a. Zagros). Ararat is Turkey's highest mountain, at 16,950 feet.

Reaching Ararat can be done by taking a plane from Ankara to an ancient town called Erzurum. This ancient town kept its name, meaning "Land of the Roman," from one of the many times it was conquered. Conquest is the price of being a crossroads town, and Romans, Arabs, Seljuk Turks, and Byzantine emperors have all ruled this mountainous town. From there a bus ride of nearly 150 miles into the mountains brings the visitor to Dogubayazit, a dingy town with a wealth of history. Nearby mosques date from the thirteenth century, and fortresses date from thousands of years earlier.

Before braving snowstorms, bears, and packs of wild dogs, the visitor who wishes to climb Ararat must first seek the permission of bureaucrats back in Ankara. Taking a lesson perhaps from Everest, visitors are allowed only when accompanied by local guides. But though Ararat's location is remote, it is the area's geopolitical concerns that are now stopping all visits.

The reason: it lies near the border of the former Soviet Union republics of Georgia and Armenia and the country of Iran. A little over one hundred miles farther south is Iraq. In June 2001 the Turkish government notified searchers that permission for expeditions planned in 2002 was canceled because of the threat of war in Central Asia. Permission for foreigners to enter the Ararat region of eastern Turkey is now not to be granted until, presumably, conflicts in the area are settled.

Witnesses to the Ark

While a group of explorers known as Ark-eologists wait for peace, they are not sitting idle. Modern technology has served both to help and in some cases hinder, as aerial photographs have produced several "boat-shaped" objects.

To date, no one has conclusively located the vessel. The Chaldean historian Berosus described the Ark as still being visible in his time, which was 257 B.C. In the first century B.C. other Armenians recorded that it could still be seen. The Jewish historian Flavius Josephus mentioned the Ark three times, although he was not helpful in pinpointing its location. In A.D. 180 Theophilus of Antioch testified to the remains still being visible. Later, early Christians built the Monastery of the Ark in nearby Phrygia and celebrated an annual feast to commemorate Noah's landing. Fourth-century Bishop Epiphanius of Salamis described it as being in the country of the Kurds.

The Ark was mentioned by Isidore of Seville in the seventh century and by a monk, Johan Haithon, in the thirteenth century as being visible on Ararat.

The location of the Ark was even reported by the Italian traveler Marco Polo, who mentioned it in his thirteenth-century travelogue. Born in 1254 to a merchant family, the adventurer left for a decades-long trip to China in 1271. When he returned, he was briefly a prisoner of war in an Italian states conflict with Genoa. With little else to do, he dictated the story of his visit to China to Rustichello of Pisa. He declared the Ark to be in the heart of Greater Armenia, on a mountain so large that it takes two days to go around it. He also recorded that the snow on the mountain is so deep it never melts, which prevents anyone from reaching it.[2]

In the seventeenth century it was described by Adam Olearius, a seventeenth-century traveler and writer, as having taken on a petrified form. Olearius was shown a piece that had been retrieved from the Ark while in Persia. In the nineteenth century Haji Yearam, an Armenian guide, described in length a visit to the Ark. Soon after, a British diplomat, Captain Gascoyne, visited with a group of soldiers after an earthquake. Sir James Bryce, a British statesman, visited the site on his own and returned with a five-foot length of partially petrified wood. In 1887 Prince Nouri, an archbishop of Babylon, claimed to have found the Ark on Ararat. He visited the Chicago World's Fair in 1893 to enlist financial support but passed away shortly afterward.

In the early twentieth century George Hagopian, an adventurer, visited the site. He was only eight years old when his uncle brought him on an expedition up Mount Ararat. His first thought was that he was viewing a house made of stone. His uncle showed him the beams and told him they were petrified. Even using a knife failed to cut off a souvenir. He died in 1972. Since he could not read a map, he was unable to show exactly where he had been.

In 1955 the French engineer Fernand Navarra climbed Ararat with his twelve-year-old son. He took photos and brought home a beam that was carbon dated, but the results did not place it near the time the Ark was said to have landed.

The Turkish Air Force conducted a survey of the area, and photos taken miles south of Ararat's peak reveal the outline of a ship at 6,300 feet. In 1960 the Turkish Army explored the area, and dynamite was placed on what was thought to be the wall of the mostly buried Ark. Decayed wood was the only reward for their efforts, and no inner chambers or even wooden beams were uncovered.

Prior to the twentieth century the inhospitable terrain denied access to most Ark hunters, but with the dawn of aviation, the search was on again. A Russian aviator, Lieutenant Vladimir Roskovitsky, reporting on Turkish troop movements, claimed having seen the Ark in 1916 and sent reports back to the czar, who was on the brink of being overthrown. A unit of over one hundred Russian and Turkish soldiers visited the Ark. They are reported as having taken measurements and photographs and sent their results to the czar. All reports of the expedition were lost when the czar was toppled in the Russian Revolution, which began that same year.

American Secret Intelligence

American fliers may have first photographed the Ark in 1943. There are few records and very little that has been revealed to the public. American military were stationed in Turkey at the Adana Air Base as part of a NATO operation in 1960. There are records that fliers claimed to have viewed the Ark, although they did not take any photographs. Possibly the best photos may have been taken in secret. Before the NATO operation American cold war spy planes such as the U-2 started flying over the area. These spy flights started in 1949. By the mid-1950s Lockheed had developed a plane that could fly at 55,000 feet and photograph the earth. It was not revealed at the time, but the degree of detail American technology could capture was astounding. It also helped that at that height the fifty-foot plane, with an eighty-foot wingspan, was almost invisible. The flights, however, were not completely invisible and would come to a premature end. The U-2 flights would cause a great deal of embarrassment after a surface-to-air missile was responsible for downing the American pilot Gary Power's spy plane in 1960. It was at the height of the American-Russian peace talks, and the revelation of American spying would lead to a chillier relation between the Soviet Union and the United States.

The flights would at least officially end but most likely not for long. Spy plane photos of Ararat would attract a great deal of attention, although they were kept secret. American intelligence calls the boat-shaped object the Ararat Anomaly.[3] While the government did not want to reveal its high-flying photographic capability early on, the more images of the anomaly, the more interested the CIA became. Dino Brugioni, a retired CIA photographic specialist who was one of the experts directed to study the evidence, claimed that they had very high visibility and it allowed them to measure what they believed could be the Ark. The problem was it did not live up to the biblical dimensions. The CIA's National Photographic Interpretation Center was not the only agency to work on viewing the Ark Anomaly. The DIA, Defense Intelligence Agency, conducted a separate study. In a recent article in the *Washington Times,* Bill Gertz reported that the CIA spokesman Tom Crispell said the agency would begin declassifying its collection of satellite photographs.[4]

From the earliest aerial photographs to SR-71 to the U-2 photographs, they would be available to the public. Now military intelligence is using even greater technology in spying on earth from space. Today spy satellites use high-resolution optical imaging in what is now called the "Keyhole" project. Images are processed on board and downloaded to ground stations when they pass over Greenland or a Pacific Island base. In 1980 they had improved ground resolution to twenty feet, using the KH-9 satellites. Just how much detail was captured from KH-11 satellites remains classified.

If it is any hint, in January 2003 it was reported that Florida's Department of Citrus was requesting that satellite technology be used to view Brazil's orange crop. Brazil dominates the world market, and the forecasts offered by that country are reported to be poor indications of the real size of the crop. Eliminating the tariffs on imports would hurt Florida even more, so they wanted a level playing field.

Using photographs from an altitude of 250 miles, Florida's citrus researchers can accurately see the tops of the orange trees and make their own forecasts. That technology is actually considered to be behind the image resolution available to the military.[5] Any advances that take place in the near future may considerably help survey the mountains of Ararat.

Finding the Ark remains an unresolved challenge. In the late 1970s the location of the Ark and Ararat became an even less hospitable place to search, as geopolitical events prevented organizations from getting the required government clearances. But this did not stop adventurers from the quest.

While modern-day adventurers set out to tackle the mountains of eastern Turkey, historians and scientists probed further into the most important question: is the story true?

There are actually two parts to that question. The first one is: did such a flood ever take place?

The Stories of the Flood

The wealth of worldwide flood stories can cast doubt on the uniqueness of the Old Testament Noah, although not on a dramatic rise in the waters of the ocean. The existence of one great flood that inundated the planet is not agreed upon by scientists. It is historically accurate that a number of very dramatic floods have occurred around the world. Traditions from Southeast Asia, China, American Indian tribes, Australia, and Central America all describe great floods.

The last glacial period lasted from 26,000 to 8,000 B.C., and this ice age may have actually peaked in 14,000–12,000 B.C. Millions of cubic miles of ocean were stored in ice. The sea level was 350 to 450 feet lower than it is today. When the earth began to warm and the ice began to melt, it did not happen in one day. In fact, the breakup of ice led to the steady submergence of land in various areas over the next seven thousand years. The water levels of the ocean at that time rose by 400 feet. What this means is that, at one time, New York City and the beaches of Long Island were one hundred miles inland. On the other side of a widening ocean, the area that would later become the British Isles suddenly became islands. Britain and Ireland were no longer part of the European landmass. They had once been connected to the mainland of continental Europe; after the waters rose, they were separated.

The coast of France, which obviously had extended much farther into the Atlantic, sunk. Once, a traveler could walk from the western tip of Brittany to what is now the southwestern tip of England—a journey of one hundred miles. The same traveler could walk one hundred miles west into what is now the ocean. Or one hundred miles south, into what is now the Bay of Biscay. Then it was a vast plain stretching down to the sea. Now it is a continental shelf, under hundreds of feet of water.

Rows of standing stones, once testament to a vast megalithic building complex, were soon underwater. The North Sea, which had not been a sea, became flooded, very likely as a breakthrough of water flooded a plain the size of the American plains.

Just how fast such a dramatic sinking took place is left for geologists to reconstruct, but the legend of various peoples, as inexact as they are, become a testament to the calamity. Five hundred thousand square miles of land, in Europe alone, were lost to the sea.

It is no surprise that the areas bordering the sunken lands have the most legends. They are often vastly different from the Noah story, yet a moral theme runs throughout—God, gods, or goddesses are punishing the wicked.

In the Cornish legend of the Y's a king named Gradlon returns from war, bringing home his new daughter. His daughter was born of the sea and a Nordic fairy who did not survive the voyage. The king builds a city for his daughter called Caer Y's or Keris. She had rejected Christianity, although her stepfather, the king, was an ardent Christian. Her town too had been taken in the pursuit of pleasure and debauchery to the point where St. Gwennole came to warn the king that the town would be punished. The king left the town, and a storm was unleashed that broke the walls of the city. Soon the City of the Y's was under water and thousands were killed.

The floods that plagued Europe from west to east most likely had stopped before 1200 B.C., but the story itself was updated to what was then modern times and was used to convey a moral lesson.

The Welsh have a very similar tale of Gwyddno Garanhir. Sixteen important families lived along the coast. There, King Seithenhin, in a state of drunkenness, has his way with the goddess of the spring. This caused the spring to overflow and that caused a flood to be unleashed. The survivors, a handful, escaped and settled in Ardudwy and the mountains of Eryri.[6]

The Welsh also have tales of Sarns, or roads, that stretched far out into the sea. Many of these stories date from the first millennium A.D. when the floods should have already taken there fullest effect. One Welsh tradition speaks of a causeway that allowed St. Patrick to walk to Ireland. Since

St. Patrick existed after Jesus, and the rising ocean levels ceased to rise well before his time, one is forced to believe it is either pure fantasy or an updated ancient tale with new names.[7]

Today there are still tales of vast submerged forests off the coast of Cornwall and walls rising from the sea in Wales's Conway Bay. In the Channel Islands separating England and France, there are tales of church bells ringing underwater from submerged towns.

The rising sea, the product of melting ice, rose about three to six feet per century. This was not exactly enough it would seem to create a flood. The sea, however, would form sand ridges and the rivers would form natural banks and levees, which would prevent flooding. But then a distant earthquake, or a sudden prolonged storm, or a severe winter creating spring floods would breach such a ridge or bank. Just how severe the effect would be of such an event is unknown.

The Mediterranean Sea and the North Sea were inland seas until a sudden breakthrough of ocean flooded most of the preclassical world. Dating the Flood is a tricky business, as the Ice Age had its first serious melting period around 12,500 B.C. Water raged through the rivers of Europe, and flooding occurred everywhere, all the way to the Black Sea and Caspian Sea. There is a great amount of evidence that this early flood stage submerged a huge portion of the Sahara desert.[8]

The geologist Dr. Robert Schoch believes that the Sphinx was actually constructed much earlier than historians accept. He points to erosion damage at the base of the monument that would have only happened if it were underwater for a prolonged period—much longer than a spring flooding of the Nile. Schoch validated the research of John Anthony West, a pioneer in setting back the date for the Sphinx. His research in turn was validated by the endorsement of his colleagues at the 1992 convention of the Geological Society of America.[9]

There was a second melting spike around 9500 B.C. that affected the Americas and not Eurasia. A third spike occurred 5600 B.C., and these meltings happened periodically due to climate change. The Black Sea had once been a freshwater inland sea, as was the Sea of Marmara. In 5600 B.C. the Black Sea, reacting to the sudden flood in the Mediterranean, overflowed its banks. It remained a freshwater sea, but the Sea of Marmara became a marine sea. Between 5600 and 1200 B.C. a third flood occurred, and the Black Sea was now marine as well. The world would never be the same.

Thousands of villages and hundreds of thousands of people were lost in the flood. And everywhere a racial memory was kept alive in stories of the Flood.

There could have existed many who survived through intuition, intervention of a god, or just the good fortune to own a boat, and floated to safety. The moral lesson and a good relationship with the deities may have been added later.

What separates the stories of Noah and the earlier story of Utnapishtim from the tales from around the rest of the world is that both claim a massive boat and a landing in Armenia. They can also be dated to around 1800 B.C. The evidence for the Hebrew Noah, an Aryan Manu, the Sumero-Babylonian Utnapishtim, and the Greek Deucalion all point to a flood that may have been responsible for emigration from the Black Sea area.

The second question: did Noah exist?

The biblical story as recorded in Genesis tells of a good man, Noah, who was tipped off by an angry God. Genesis 6 has God declaring, "I will destroy man, who I have created, from the face of the earth." It was punishment for humankind's wicked ways, including intermarriage between "sons of God" and "daughters of men." Prepared to seek vengeance against the sinful, he made one exception: "Noah found grace before the Lord."

He told Noah to construct a vessel with fairly exact dimensions. The Ark was to be made of timber planks with numerous rooms within. It would be three hundred cubits by fifty cubits and thirty cubits high. It would have one window. A door would be set in the side that would open to three levels. Noah was further instructed that a pair of every living creature was to be placed aboard, even fowls, and things that creep upon the earth. Even more specifically the "clean" beasts were to be brought seven and seven, male and female. He was also allowed to take his own family.

Soon all the work was completed. Once every person and animal were aboard, God let loose with a planetwide flood. The flood covered the earth and is described in Genesis as being fifteen cubits higher than the highest mountains. The rain itself lasted forty days (and nights). The waters didn't subside for 150 days.[10] Noah learned of dry land by sending off doves who would presumably not return if there was land anywhere. The Ark itself did not rest until the twentieth day of the seventh month. Then it rested "upon the mountains of Armenia." Noah made a sacrifice to thank God for his safety. God then promised that he would not again flood the earth. To make a sign of that promise, "I will set my bow in the clouds . . . this will be the sign of the covenant which I have established."[11]

There are, of course, a few parts of the tale that require a great deal of faith to accept. For one, Noah was six hundred years old. Assuming his sons, who were not born until he was five hundred years old, did most of the heavy lifting, the idea of four men building a 450-foot boat, five to ten times the size of some of the ships that explored the world in the fourteenth to sixteenth centuries, is still difficult. The boat had no sails and no rudder and one window to air out the smell of Noah's zoo. Their ability to trap live pairs of polar bears and kangaroos also lends a bit of difficulty to a completely literal interpretation.

Even accepting that the story of Noah had a bit of added color, there remains a few tough questions. Was there a universal flood so great it covered the earth? How are the numerous other flood stories in Babylonian, Greek, and Hindu to be reconciled?

Utnapishtim and the Ark

"For six days and six nights the winds blew, torrent and tempest and flood raged together like warring hosts. When the seventh day dawned, the storm from the south subsided, the sea grew calm, the flood was still."

These are the words of Utnapishtim. Long after the Bible was read throughout the world, the story of Noah and the flood was known to Jews and Christians everywhere. But it was not until 1839 when an English traveler in Asia unearthed the tablets containing this story. They dated back thousands of years, and no one at that time could read the strange wedge-shaped marks that were used to record the story. In the 1870s another Englishman, George Smith, began a translation of this flood story. He had works unearthed from the buried library of Ashurbanipal and from the buried cities of Nineveh and Nimrud that had not seen daylight for literally thousands of years. They provided a means of verifying the writing and translating the language. Soon the tale emerged in full.

It was a Babylonian story, handed down from the Sumerians and part of what is today called the *Epic of Gilgamesh*. Gilgamesh is the hero of the story. He is of royal birth, part god and part man. He had all the attributes an ancient king could want—strength, attractiveness, and power, but he was mortal. Seeking the meaning of life, Gilgamesh travels around with a companion named Enkidu who was raised in the wild. They slay the giant Humbaba, and then Gilgamesh manages to incur the wrath of the goddess

Ishtar by refusing to become her lover. She turns the Bull of Heaven loose on the two, and Gilgamesh's companion Enkidu is killed. In sadness, the hero takes to dressing in animal skins and embarking on Hercules-like travels to search for the one human to whom the gods have granted immortality.

He crosses the ocean and meets Utnapishtim, who tells him the story of the flood.

This Sumerian Noah had been tipped off by the god Enki that the most powerful god, Enlil, had plans to end the world with water. Utnapishtim tears down his house and uses the material to build a giant ship to very exacting standards, the breadth and length equal. This giant square box is six stories high and has seven separate compartments. This description, it should be noted, would seem to describe a vessel that is anything but seaworthy. The Hebrew Noah was not known to be a seafarer, but his Ark had much more sound dimensions than launching in a cube. This is even more surprising when the fact that the Sumerians were seafarers is taken into consideration. They built long boats, not square, with sails and ventured into the Mediterranean Sea as well as through the gulf along the coast of Africa. Utnapishtim's boat is covered with a large amount of bitumen inside and out to keep out the water.

It is also large enough to gather his family and the seed of life of every sort. As soon as his task is complete a terrible storm starts sending the gods to take refuge in the heavens. The rain begins, and the flood ensues, in this case lasting seven days. Like the biblical Noah, the Babylonian Noah also sends out birds, including doves, ravens, and swallows, which fail to return, letting him know that there is dry land.

> "I sent forth a dove . . . it came back"
> "I sent forth a swallow . . . it came back"
> "I sent forth a crow. . . . It went, the crow, and beheld the subsidence
> of the waters; it eats, it splashes about, it caws, it comes not back."[12]

Utnapishtim's ark then lands, and like Noah, he makes a sacrifice. In his case the gods are petty. They are hungry because no one left food at their drowned temples. When they smell his sacrifice, "like flies the gods gather." There is obviously little reverence for these Sumerian gods, and the sacrifice is meant to keep them from destroying the earth again. Utnapishtim then begins the task of repopulating the planet.

For Gilgamesh too there was to be no answer. Utnapishtim told him if he could stay awake for seven days and nights he would reach immortality. Gilgamesh fails to stay awake and in fact sleeps for seven days. Utnapishtim's wife tells him of a plant that grows beneath the sea that could allow him to live forever. After great toil he reaches the sea bottom, recovers the plant, only to have a serpent steal it from him before he could eat it. In near despair our hero finally gets the message. There is no immortality for man. The real meaning to life is to eat, drink, and enjoy every day.

While the moral message that is conveyed in the Bible and in flood stories from India to Ireland is not present in the *Epic of Gilgamesh,* there is one important clue. The odd-shaped ark of Utnapishtim was said to have landed on the tall Mount Nezir, which is, once again, in Armenia.

The epic flood was recorded in Sumerian documents from 2000 B.C. Very much like the Bible, ten antediluvian kings are mentioned, having a lengthy reign of 456,000 years. After the flood the very large numbers remain, although they are not as extreme. Twenty-three kings live 24,510 years in the first two dynasties after the flood. Sumerian documents do not treat Gilgamesh as a mythical person, however. While it is clear that the translation of the dating process is not accurate, there was at least a high degree of belief that these were not mythical stories.

Archaeologists have little problem proving that the area between the Tigris and the Euphrates rivers had occasional severe floods. These floods were so severe that in more than one instance a city was lost forever or the course of a river changed. Deep silt deposits over an ancient town in many cases separate it from a newer town built above. When Sir Leonard Woolley excavated the city of Ur, where Abraham was born, there was an eleven-foot silt level. Underneath were houses of the Ubaid Period that dated as old as 5000 B.C. It failed to make the case however for a universal flood, as the same deep silt levels were found in other locations with different dates. The level at Shuruppak, where Gilgamesh was king, was much closer to that of biblical times. This new date 2800–2300 B.C. would provide evidence that at least that flood was the basis of the Gilgamesh, and possibly the Noah, story.

These dates would fit with the flood story preserved in India.

Mani and the Ark

The Rig Veda is one of four Vedas that records the knowledge of the Aryan people who arrived in India before 1500 B.C. *Veda* simply means "knowledge," and the Rig Veda is the oldest. It is a collection of over a thousand hymns passed down for centuries and recorded in written form before 100 B.C. Most of the stories told in these hymns are of heroic individuals with moral undertones. They are not unlike the Bible or the Greek myths.

One of the tales contained in the collection has a hero, Manu, who is warned by a fish of the impending end of humanity. Mani is actually the seventh Manu, first name Vaivasvata, who is to become the father of the postflood race of humankind. Vaivasvata was praying on the bank of the river when a fish by the name of Matsya approached and asked for his protection. A larger fish was seeking to eat him. The holy man places the fish in a jar to keep him safe from the larger fish. It is perhaps the god Vishnu who sent Matsya to Manu, and Manu acted in charity, thereby distancing himself from the rest of humankind, who were at best less charitable. Manu builds an ark, and Vishnu makes sure that the ark survives the deluge.

The Hindu religion has changed over the centuries, and to a non-Hindu it can be confusing. Hindus believe in one god but have many. It is simple. Each god is a representation of the one God. Piety and reverence to any god brings one closer to the Supreme God. Hindu's believe their religious texts to be less literal than many Christians regard the Bible. It is possible that the tale of Manu is an allegory. The fish itself represents the male but also purity. Jesus, Vishnu, and Bacchus are also represented by the fish symbol. Jesus, like Vishnu, is the Savior. In a less allegorical sense, the tale of Manu has him landing on the peaks of the northern mountains. As the ancestors of the Eurasian continent, the Indo-Europeans spread from a central location. It is unlikely that they too were somehow living between the Tigris and Euphrates rivers. This area, known as the Fertile Crescent, may have provided for the Sumerian population and the emigrating Semite population as well, but it is more likely that the great Flood covered a wider area. Could this again be the Black Sea region, where the Flood demonstrated its fearful devastation on the population? It is then possible that the Aryan ancestors had too been effected by floods that occurred before 1800 B.C. and therefore migrated away?

Deucalion and the Ark

The Greeks too have their similar flood story. The god Zeus is angered because his people apparently are backsliding to less-civilized days. Lycaeus, or Lycaon, is the person who brought civilization to Arcadia, but unfortunately when he worshipped Zeus, he did it in a primitive way. He sacrificed a boy. One recalls the biblical lesson where Abraham is all set to sacrifice his son, when God intervenes. The message is that human sacrifice is no longer acceptable in a civilized world.

Zeus disguises himself as an itinerant traveler and visits Lycaon's sons, who number according to the tale somewhere between twenty-two and fifty. They had killed one of their brothers and cooked him in a soup along with goat and sheep meat. Zeus wasn't fooled and punished them by changing them into wolves. His anger, however, was not appeased by the punishment. On his way back to Mount Olympus he decided it was time to start over. He would destroy all humankind in one flood.

Prometheus was a Titan, which was a god who had human children. He went to the Caucasus region to warn his son Deucalion, who was the king of Phthia. Prometheus told him to build an ark, stock it with food, and be ready for the flood. When it came, it started with a storm, and soon the rivers overflowed and washed away every city and town. The entire world was covered, with the exception of a few mountain peaks. The only survivors reported were Deucalion and his wife, Pyrrha. They floated above the flooded earth for nine days and then let out a dove, who helped assure them the worst was over. Their landing was on Mount Parnassus, Mount Aetna, Mount Athos, or Mount Othrys in Thessaly, depending on where the myth is retold.

Upon landing they offered a sacrifice to Zeus. The asked him to repopulate the world, which was somehow accomplished by throwing stones over their shoulders who grew into humans. In this way both the Greek and Hebrew tales are creation myths of sorts, and the wife of Deucalion, Pyrrha, is regarded as a mother goddess. In Babylon she is Ishtar, part of the Gilgamesh story. In Palestine she is Pyrrha, meaning "fiery red," an adjective used to describe wine. A Hebrew folktale has Noah as the inventor of wine. A Greek myth has Amphictyon, a son of Deucalion, having something to do with introducing wine. The Hellenic version is notable in both its similarities and its differences. Deucalion was not the only survivor in the Greek tale. Others from various mountainous areas survived, but in Arcadia they reverted to human sacrifice despite the punishment.[13]

This story originally came from Asia, as the Hellenes were people who migrated to Thessaly around 2300 B.C. Hellen was either the son or the brother of Deucalion and the progenitor of three races of Greeks—Dorus (Dorians), Xuthus (Ionians), and Aeolus. Thessaly was originally named Pyrrhaea after Deucalion's wife. The story as it is retold has the flood taking place in Greece, although the evidence places its origin in the Black Sea area.

There are numerous other flood stories around the world. The stories of Sumer and Babylon, of the Hebrews, and of the Aryans and the Greeks have a great degree of uniformity. In addition to the man who was good enough to please at least one of the gods, these stories also all have the ark land in a place that is very likely to be in the area later called Armenia. And in two cases Ararat is named. That the Greeks provide a list of their own mountaintops as landing spots displays an obvious provincialism.

The discovery of a biblical flood tale written and based on an older Sumerian tale does not discredit the possibility of either an actual flood or a pious survivor of that flood. The collection of surviving flood stories were tailored by the wise men, priests, rabbis, and shamans. As these stories were passed from one generation to the next, they would pick up themes and occasionally new names. To many, the plot and often the moral point are true; the names and details are of less consequence.

To others, the Bible is correct, Noah and the Ark were real, and the Ark itself still lies in mountainous Ararat.

Modern Explorers

The fact that Ararat lies on the Turko-Russian border has been a serious hindrance to exploration and limited the amount of serious investigation. It also opened the door to self-styled Indiana Jones types. One was Ron Wyatt, whose audacious goals and claims have often been criticized by serious investigators. Mr. Wyatt was a nurse from Kalamazoo, Michigan, who had bigger plans. In 1977 he set out to find the Ark during his two-week vacation. Since traveling time used up three days, he had to find it fast. And did, or at least that is what he claimed. On the first day he found the "anchor stones." On the second day he found the house of Noah and the area where he took care of his herd of animals. He also claimed to see a series of inscriptions on a stele depicting scenes from the biblical story, complete with eight faces and two ravens. On the third day he found what was described as the "boat-shaped object." Samples from the wreckage of Wyatt's Ark he would claim were petrified wood.[14]

In subsequent expeditions Mr. Wyatt was in search of the Red Sea crossing point of Moses, the true location of Sinai where God appeared to Moses, and the locations of Sodom and Gomorrah. He was suspected of being an Israeli spy after crossing illegally into Saudi Arabia, and he was accused of stealing and smuggling artifacts of the Ark from Turkey. In 1985 Ron Wyatt and David Fasnold, a salvage diver, returned from Turkey with evidence that the location of the buried Ark was showing traceable lines of iron. They had used a CAT scan on the boat-shaped mound. Sadly, Wyatt passed away in 1999, and just as sad is the fact that his adventurous style had the scientific community view him as an intruder.

In the 1980s the NASA astronaut James Irwin added a degree of respectability to the search, and it was hoped that his name would pave the way to allow the search. Irwin was born in Pittsburgh, Pennsylvania, in 1930 and was commissioned in the air force upon graduation from the Naval Academy. In the early days of the space race he would begin his career in the Air Force Aerospace Research Pilot School and complete Experimental Test Pilot School as well. Starting in 1971 he would serve as a pilot on lunar modules and then become the commander of such missions. On the moon he would photograph the Apennine Mountains and spend much time on the surface, collecting samples.

In July 1972 he would resign from the air force to found and serve as chairman of the board of a religious organization called the High Flight Foundation. It was designed to help people become ambassadors for Jesus Christ in whatever profession they had chosen. Irwin was not the only one who felt closer to the presence of God while visiting the moon, but he may have been the most activist in his postastronaut life. He would conduct several hands-on expeditions searching for the Ark of Noah as well as the Ark of the Covenant.

Irwin too has passed away, and the 1990s did little to advance his research.

In 1991 the map of central Asia changed as Russia and the numerous republics of the Soviet Union separated. While Ararat is in Turkey, the wider interpretation of the biblical location says that the entire mountainous area could have served as the landing spot for the Ark. Armenia was not called by that name in 2000 B.C., but the area was called by that name when the Bible was put together. The new country of Armenia claims the Ark is in their country. To drive home the point, the new Armenian flag consists of three equal stripes of red, blue, and orange. In the center on a shield is Mount Ararat, complete with the Ark of Noah.

In the world post–September 11, 2001, eastern Turkey finds itself the staging area for war, which makes that area even less available for scientific exploration. Technology, however, generally advances at such junctures in history, when there is a need to develop new military tools, and the even more sophisticated spy satellites of 2002–2003 may be adding greater detail to what is known of Ararat.

Discovery from an "eye in the sky" or an intrepid Indiana Jones on the ground could be part of the not-to-distant future.

12

THE ARK OF THE COVENANT

The Timkat is a wild celebration that takes place in the African country of Ethiopia in mid-January. It is a combination of the Epiphany and the feast of Ethiopia's favorite saint, St. Michael. Almost everyone dresses in pure white garments except the priests of the Ethiopian Orthodox church, who wear ceremonial satin and velvet and carry sequined umbrellas. In every city the priests bring wooden chests called *tabots* from their churches. They are carried to the nearest water source amid ringing bells, blowing trumpets, and swinging incense censers. Feasting, singing, and dancing continue all day and night. The next day these *tabots* are again brought into the safety of the churches.

The *tabots* represent the Ark of the Covenant. Among Ethiopian peoples there is a blend of isolated Christianity, equally isolated Judaism, tribal religions, and Islam, which is the latecomer. In this tolerant society all are welcome, and not surprisingly, some of the varied major religious celebrations occur at the same time. In January the celebration that includes the *tabot* occurs throughout the country.

The Ark of the Covenant is one of the oddest items described in the Bible and one of the most sacred. Built of incorruptible acacia wood and pure gold, it has the power to communicate the words of God almost like a radio and to kill, very much like an extreme flash of radiation. The author Michael Drosnin claims in *The Bible Code* that in at least six instances where the Bible code is decoded, the Ark is translated as being a computer.

Depending on who is searching, it has been lost for over two thousand years. From the Knights Templar to the *Raiders of the Lost Ark,* the tale of the search for the Ark has many twists and turns. It may be in a secret chamber of the temple in Jerusalem, according to some. To others it is safely stored in Rosslyn Chapel in Scotland. It may be part of a Cathar treasure buried in the south of France. So far, no one can claim with any authenticity to have the Ark. Except the 67 million Ethiopians who celebrate their ownership of the Ark every year.

But don't ask to see it. While hundreds of *tabots* are paraded from town to city, only one is the real *tabot,* and it may be safe under the protection of a secret society of hereditary guardians.

Creating the Ark of the Covenant

The story of the Ark of the Covenant begins in the Torah, the first five books of the Bible. In Exodus 25 God speaks directly to Moses, and in verse 9 he says he will show Moses the likeness of the Ark. Then Moses should gather the required materials that God prescribes and build another Ark. "Frame an ark of setim wood" begins God. Setim is an incorruptible form of acacia wood. God states the dimensions, two cubits by one and one-half cubits with a height of one and one-half cubits. From there it is overlaid with the purest gold, both inside and out. Four golden rings are placed in the corners so that two acacia wood poles can be used to carry it. Moses is told that the poles are to be covered in gold and should never be taken out. Even when the Ark is set in a sanctuary, the poles remain.

Above the golden box, two cherubim, made of beaten gold, are placed facing each other. Exodus 25:20 specifically states that their wings should be spread in a fashion that together they cover the oracle, which is how the box is referred to. God then says this mechanism will allow him to instruct the people of Israel. In the next chapter the instructions get further complicated and include numerous loops of brass and gold as well as forty sockets of silver.

At least one writer has made the observation that the box had at least a rudimentary form of radio communication capability. In the movie *Raiders of the Lost Ark,* the fictional French archaeologist, Rene Belloq, sitting with Indiana Jones says, "Jones, do you realize what the Ark is? It's a transmitter. It's a radio for speaking to God." The "God" doing the communicating to man was not a god in the same sense that organized religion normally intends. In Exodus, the word *Dvir* (which means "the speaker") is used for the person the Ark will assist for contacting his people. This "speaker" could be an interplanetary visitor. The Ark was a two-way communication device that allowed man to ask a question or God to instruct.

The instructions did not stop here by any means. God further instructed that the people who would make and use the box must wear certain clothes. They also must bathe in a basin specifically made of copper. Copper is mentioned in more than one magical instance in the Old Testament. Sinai had copper mines from a very early date, and the priests of Israel used copper serpents to protect the people against the pestilence God wrought on the Egyptians. An initiated priesthood would be the only ones allowed to handle the Ark. The priesthood would be under the control of Aaron and his brothers.

Immediately after the Ark is completed, the people of Israel build an idol, presumably with the excess gold that had been melted. This Golden Calf is then worshipped by the people, possibly a backsliding to a more ancient culture. Moses puts the blame on Aaron. It is possible that the people were not as convinced as Moses is by his God. To squelch any doubt, the Ark was placed in the tent known as the tabernacle. Moses entered the tent, and within minutes a "pillar of the cloud" descended from the skies and stood at the door of the tent and "spoke with Moses" (Exodus 33:10–11). Moses asked to see the face of the Lord but was told if he saw it he would die.

Moses then went into the desert and spent forty days with the Lord. When he returned "he knew not that his face was horned" (Exodus 34:29). In fact even Aaron was afraid to come near him. Moses took to wearing a veil. Shortly thereafter, all of the items God ordered were fashioned. Censers of gold, sockets of silver, cups in the shape of nuts, lamps, and crowns. When all was complete, the cloud of God hung over it by day and a fire by night.

A Weapon of Mass Destruction

In the book of Numbers the instructions for traveling with the Ark are given. One stands out: the priests of Aaron must always pitch their tents around the tent of the Ark. When the Lord wanted the people of Moses to travel, the cloud was removed and headed in the direction they were to go. After days of traveling the people were tired and murmured "against the Lord." For their complaining the "fire of the Lord . . . devoured them that were at the outermost part of the camp" (Numbers 11:1). Only the prayers of Moses could get the fire to stop.

It was not the last time that the Lord showed his people that complaining could be hazardous to their health. Other occasions recorded in the book of Numbers have the ground opening to swallow up the ungrateful and fiery serpents flying out to bite the complainers. There is more than one case of spontaneous combustion. The cloud of the Lord also leads Israel into battle, where a very vengeful God orders all of the opposing peoples killed (Numbers 22). In the book of Joshua, God instructs the Israelites to march around the walls of Jericho with the Ark and seven trumpets. The walls, of course, came tumbling down and Jericho was taken.

But then something went wrong. In 1 Kings (also known as the first Book of Samuel) the people of Israel go to war with the Philistines. They fail to bring the Ark, and the tide of battle turns against them. They go back and retrieve the Ark, yet they are still defeated in battle. It is unexplained why the Ark failed to help them. No lessons of guilt serve as catalyst for their defeat. There is no record of their God deserting them for any particular reason. In fact the horrible powers of the Ark are still evident and not to be simply captured like a genie in a bottle. The Philistines soundly defeated the Hebrews and also captured the Ark. If the biblical account is correct, thirty thousand footmen were killed and the rest fled for their homes, deserting their army. A soldier of the tribe of Benjamin runs back to tell Heli of their defeat and the loss of the Ark. Upon delivering the bad news, he falls over dead. The fourth chapter of Kings then concludes, "the glory is departed from Israel, because the ark of God was taken" (1 Kings 4:22).

The Philistines soon found the Ark was not to be their talisman of power. They brought it to Azotus, where they placed it in the temple of their god Dagon. In the morning Dagon's statue had fallen. The next night they tried again, and this time Dagon was again tumbled and his hands broken. Then a plague of mice was upon the Philistines accompanied by sickness. For seven months the Philistines held on to the sacred object. Everywhere they brought the Ark it caused death. They offered it gifts and made sacrifices to it, but still it killed. Chapter 6 of Kings has the death toll at over fifty thousand. Soon the Philistines had enough. The Ark was brought to Cariathiarim, where the Jews were free to take it back.

The Hebrews brought the Ark by wagon. Despite the instructions given by God and passed down by the priests, not everyone may have been aware of the danger. Two brothers known as Oza and Ahio are recorded as driving the cart. When Oza saw the Ark was leaning, he attempted to right it with his hand. He was struck dead upon touching it.

A Home for the Ark

Around 1000 B.C., it would be King David who decided a temple should be built to house the Ark. He made an alliance with the Philistines that gave him the area called Judah. He took the sacred site where a Jebusite god called Salem was worshipped. Salem was a god of prosperity, and the city was already wealthy. He devoted his energies to starting work on the temple.

He turned over the instructions to his son Solomon, who would complete the work. The third book of Kings (of the Douay Rheims version of the Bible), chapter six, describes the building of the temple with almost the same detail as was used in describing how the Ark was built. Nothing was left to chance, everything was done to meet specific standards. Timbers cut from the cedars of Lebanon, purest gold from Ophir, and copper mined in Solomon's mines were brought in to fit with the exacting instructions. Iron could not be used. It took seven years to complete the task.

What is not mentioned in the Old Testament is how the rock underneath the temple was treated. It is a huge natural table of rock, and the builders of the temple cut the stone. Long straight cuts were made into the face of the natural stone, and niches were created. Inside the rock there are caverns that may too have been expanded by man. A stairway still descends from the temple to the cavern, and tunnels off the main cavern exist. Today the temple is in the hands of Muslim authorities who will not give permission for the temple to be explored.

The temple itself had three important inner sections above the rock. The Ulam was the outside area, the sixty-foot nave was next, and then the *debir,* the most holy place. This Holy of Holies was a thirty-foot cube cordoned off by golden chains. Only a few would be permitted to enter.

The temple was built in the style of a Canaanite temple, and for good reason. David and Solomon had employed Phoenician architects and workers to design and build the temple.

At the dedication of the temple, the God of the Hebrews again showed he was present in the Ark. A cloud descended upon it and remained. The cloud was such that the priests were afraid to minister in the presence of the cloud.

Jerusalem had already been a wealthy city, but now it became the center of wealth. Solomon ruled in splendor like a king and married the daughter of the pharaoh of Egypt, as well as the daughters of other kings. By employing Hiram's fleets, Solomon's ships sailed the Mediterranean and the Red seas. It was then that the queen of Sheba, also referred to as Saba, visited him.

The Lost Ark

Soon afterward the Ark is simply no longer mentioned. There are numerous traditions. An Assyrian conquest in 722 B.C. had Israel paying tribute to their hostile neighbors in the north. In 597 B.C. the Babylonian armies that were victorious against Israel were known to have looted all the gold and silver they could find, as well as taking the people of Israel into captivity. There is no record that the Ark was among the spoils, but a Babylonian theft of the Ark might be possible.

Jeremias claims that the Ark was brought to a cave near the place where God originally appeared to Moses. After he placed the Ark in the cave others came by to mark the trail. They told Jeremias they could not find the cave. Jeremias said that no one would find the Ark until God once again gathers his people (2 Maccabees 2:4–8 in the Douay Rheims version of the Bible).

A third tradition in the Talmud has King Josias hiding the Ark in a secret chamber in the Temple of Solomon where the king had provided for such a tragedy as the temple being taken or set ablaze by Israel's enemies. Certainly the caverns below the city were known to have tunnels for both water and others that exist even today.

Then the Ark was simply never mentioned again.

A fourth tradition grew out of the visit of the queen of Sheba. She brought many gifts to the king and returned home with one: a son. She bore her son Menelik I, who would become the first emperor of Ethiopia. Menelik means the "Son of the Wise Man." Menelik was born in Ethiopia, but at age twenty he headed to Jerusalem to visit his father. He was treated like a prince and given many gifts. Solomon sent many of the first sons of Israel's elders with him. One of them, Azarius, is recorded as taking the Ark with him to Ethiopia. When Menelik found out, he decided the Ark would not have been able to be taken unless it was God's will. So he kept it.

This story is actually more than a tradition. To Ethiopians it is recorded history in a sacred text called the Kebra Nagast. This thirteenth-century document is accepted as dogma by Ethiopia's large population of Christians, who celebrate the event to this day.

The Raiders of the Lost Ark

Not everyone is convinced by the Ethiopian tradition of the Ark story, and over the centuries several expeditions have attempted to locate the sacred artifact.

Perhaps the earliest was a small band of nine knights that would constitute the first Knights Templar. They were all from the Champagne area of France and related by family ties or alliances. The man who would later be called St. Bernard was actually the nephew of Andre of Montbard, one of the original nine. This handful of men made their way to Jerusalem and told Baldwin II that they were there to protect the highways and make the way safe for new pilgrims. A large task for a small group, yet they received Baldwin's permission and the right to make the temple their headquarters. While the king's chronicler Fulk of Chartres does not ever mention the small band of knights doing anything in the decade they spent in Jerusalem, they had been busy.

The Qumran document called the Copper Scrolls contains a list of at least twenty-four separate treasures stashed underneath the temple. Could a much earlier document have somehow survived and been among the first plunder brought back from the Holy Lands and Constantinople? It is possible that the Knights Templar, as they would later be known, came for a treasure hunt. There is no record of them finding an Ark of the Covenant or anything else.

When they returned to France, Andre's nephew Bernard was in a position, as the head of the Cistercian order of monks, to make the Templars heroes. Everywhere he preached, the sons of wealthy nobles rushed to give away their estates to join the order. The order survived two hundred years before the French king and Catholic pope had the Templars arrested and tortured into confessing to all sorts of iniquities. They were then disbanded officially, although many would survive in other entities—some historical, some secretive. In Portugal they became the Knights of Christ. In Scotland they joined the rebellion of Robert the Bruce. As a result of the help given by the Knights Templar, the crucial battle of Bannockburn was a victory for Robert the Bruce, and Scotland gained its independence.

One of the more secretive entities was early Freemasonry. In Scotland the ancient Lodge of Killwinning may represent Masonry's first and most prestigious lodge. Four hundred years after the end of the Templars, a descendent of Robert the Bruce and a member of the lodge would travel to Ethiopia. Eleven years before he left Scotland, James Bruce studied Ge'ez, the classical language of the country. He wrote a book about his travels to that country and mentioned that he searched for the Ark in the first church of St. Mary of Zion. He brought back three copies of the book of Enoch, a mystical text that had never been seen in Europe. He also brought home a copy of the Kebra Nagast. He witnessed the Timkat ceremony in 1770, but if he brought home the Ark, there is no evidence.

While there are some who believe the Templars or James Bruce may have taken the Ark, the evidence contradicts this theory. If the Templars did have it, many believe Bruce would be privy. If the Templars were aware of evidence that the Ark had been brought to Ethiopia, this would be a motive for Bruce's trip. While the Lodge of Killwinning is in Edinburgh, just outside that city is the Rosslyn Chapel. Here concealed in stone carvings are numerous messages only the initiated would understand. Underneath Rosslyn is a temple just as sacred to Freemasonry as Jerusalem is sacred to Israel. Though excavations there have found a subbasement where Knights Templar were buried, no treasure has been unearthed.

In 1867 the British were in Palestine, and the Royal Engineers received permission to conduct a survey under the area outside and to the south of the temple. What was called the Palestine Exploration Fund was set up to investigate archaeology, natural history, geology, and geography in Palestine. Its members included a former prime minister and a prominent statesmen. The public contributed, and even Queen Victoria chipped in 150 pounds sterling. Lieutenant Charles Warren was assigned to lead the expedition, although he was refused permission, however, to go under the Temple Mount. He was only twenty-seven years old at the time, although he already had done extensive fieldwork that had started during his stay at the Rock of Gibralter, where he had helped build the fortifications. He was an expert in all phases of military mining. If he could not accomplish something directly, he could sink shafts from various angles to get there indirectly. He would come in contact with water tunnels built circa 1000 B.C., when Jerusalem was still owned by a Jebusite farmer. Warren's Shaft, as it would be called, reached the ancient Hezekiah's tunnel and from there the Gihon Spring. He also encountered entrances to unexplored caverns.

He had to work fast, as rumors were spread that he was mining underneath for the purpose of planting gunpowder. As the resistance to his exploration began to heat up, he began only working at night. Even so the noise of the labors of his men caused a rock-throwing riot, which ejected them from the area.[1]

His reports to the British newspapers kept readers spellbound, and legendary names in travel literature like Karl Baedecker and Thomas Cook rushed to print guides to the Holy Lands.[2]

In 1894 a contingent of the British Army under Lieutenant Charles Wilson of the Royal Engineers made their own expedition into the tunnels under the Temple Mount. They are not on record as finding any treasure, however they did bring back some telling evidence. Their treasure included a Templar cross, a Templar sword, a spur, and a lance. What is also intriguing is that these artifacts are in the custody of Robert Brydon, who is a Templar archivist. Robert Brydon's grandfather was in communication with a Captain Montague Brownslow Parker, who was part of the 1894 expedition and later returned in 1911. Parker was a thirty-year-old aristocrat fresh out of the Grenadier Guards when he got started in archaeology. The 1909–1911 Parker expedition had been conducted after a Finnish biblical scholar studying in Sweden claimed a coded passage in Ezekial described the location of the temple treasure, which according to his work included the gold-covered Ark of the Covenant. Just how reliable the coded message might have been is questionable, since the scholar, Valter Juvelius, hired a clairvoyant to assist in finding the treasure. Parker was the son of the earl of Morley and had numerous connections with Britain's royals who contributed to his expedition. He even managed to enlist the support of Chicago's wealthy Armour family.[3]

His 1911 expedition spared no expense and even traveled with hired chefs. He hired the leading authority on the archaeology of Jerusalem, a Dominican scholar named Louis Hughes Vincent, to throw off suspicion that they were on a treasure hunt.

Parker found another secret tunnel not discovered earlier. But he did not find out if he was on the brink of any new discovery, as an Islamic mob chased him and his expedition away.[4]

Parker stepped on toes as soon as he reached the Holy City. Jews felt he threatened the tombs of David and Solomon. Baron Edmond de Rothschild, of the international banking family, openly led the way to prevent Parker from desecrating the site. Christians felt that he had duped them with his intentions. Complaints to the Turkish authorities were met with bribes to the governor, who allowed them to dig but gave them a short timetable to complete their work. Despite having the permission of Sheik Khalil, the hereditary guardian of the mosque, Parker and his men were still forced to disguise themselves as Arabs. Permission or not, on the night of April 19, 1911, the group working in the dead of night was caught and had to flee for their lives. April, of course, was the time when the greatest number of pilgrims were in the city. Muslims celebrated Nebi Mussa, Jews observed Passover, and Christians celebrated Easter. Riots broke out in Jerusalem, and the expedition members fled to Jaffa, where they had a yacht.

When rumors emerged that they had stolen the Ark, Jaffa police seized their baggage and questioned them. They were allowed to spend the night on the boat under the condition that the interrogation would continue the next day. Parker and his crew fled in the middle of the night and made it safely to England.[5]

In the 1920s an American named Antonia Frederick Futterer found an inscription that a scholar translated as giving directions that located the Ark under nearby Mount Nebo. Nebo is just across the border of Israel in Jordan. It was not until 1981 that Tom Crotser and a small team brought Futterer's map to Nebo to investigate. The team included Jim Bollinger and the astronaut Jim Irwin.

First they visited a Franciscan monastery that sits on top of Mount Nebo and owns the property. They received permission from the monastery and from the local military commander to photograph the area. They said a plaque was found claiming the Ark to be buried underneath. At night they entered a thirty-five-foot tunnel. The tunnel ended with a wall.

They illegally cut through the wall and entered another chamber carved out of rock. There they claim they found the Ark of the Covenant. They photographed a box and two packages that they believed held the cherubim. They claim they would not touch anything, as a result of the biblical warnings of what might happen. They brought back a series of slide photographs so poorly done that only two showed anything of value. Crotser refused to show anyone the pictures outside of a select handful. One of these was an archaeologist, Siegfried Horn, who claimed the box was machine produced and had at least one modern nail.

The author Graham Hancock was one of the most recent to search for the Ark. In 1991 he was a writer for the *Economist* when he traced the object to Ethiopia. His travels took him to the city of Axum, where St. Mary's Church of Zion is located. Hancock determined that it had been moved from Jerusalem during the time of King Solomon, and the queen of Sheba brought the Ark to her land, where the Falasha people practice a more ancient form of Judaism. These members of what could be described as a lost tribe of Israel survived in a hostile environment that included such natural enemies as famine and drought for hundreds of years. In A.D. 330 the Falasha Jews saw their ranks thinned by Christianity, which divided the country. They still kept their identity and retained certain unique ceremonial aspects of worship that are not practiced in Israel. Despite the differences between Israel's Judaism and that of the Falasha people, this distinction apparently is not considered a serious split, however, with more modern Judaism. In 1991 civil war in Ethiopia threatened them again. Ambassador Asher Naim, who had been posted by Israel to Addis Ababa, got wind of the danger to the Falasha as they were caught between rebel forces and the country's savage dictator Mengistu Haile Meriam. He negotiated support from several governments as well as funds to save the Falasha. The Israeli military, in a miraculously modern version of the Exodus, airlifted to safety fourteen thousand Falasha in twenty-five hours. They did not possess the Ark, however. In the fourth century it had passed to Ethiopian Christians, a sect unto themselves, who Hancock believes may hold the Ark today. The annual celebrations of the Ark that are held in many Ethiopian churches and their representations of the Ark lead many to believe Hancock's theory is correct. He, however, was never allowed to view the actual Ark itself and concluded that the *tabots* or Arks being paraded were all replicas.

His book, *The Sign and the Seal,* tells an almost Grail-like story of how one family is the Guardian of the relic, and its protection is a responsibility passed through generations. Not everyone agrees with Hancock.

From ancient to modern, there is no shortage of theories.

The Ark in Ireland

One of the earliest traditions has Jeremiah, a scribe named Baruch, and two princesses fleeing Jerusalem with the Ark and a coronation stone known as Jacob's Pillow. Jerusalem was under siege by the Babylonians, who were known to be unsparing. Before the assault was over, the temple was burned, and thousands were killed, blinded, or thrown into slavery. The Bible records a huge territory completely devoid of population for hundreds of years as a result. Archaeology backs up the Bible. In 1926 many excavations revealed that during the period called the Babylonian Captivity there was no occupation of numerous cities, towns, and fortresses.[6]

But there were many that had escaped the slaughter. They went to Egypt and, if traditions can be relied upon, much farther.

Jeremiah and company picked up a Tarshish-bound ship in Egypt.

Tarshish has been likened to Tartessus, a civilization that once traded with the Phoenicians and the fleets of Solomon. It was most likely located at the mouth of one of Spain's rivers but has never been found. Spain was a link in the Canaan-Ireland and England trade, and it is not impossible even in 700 B.C. for an Atlantic trade to have been met with mariners plying the Mediterranean Sea. At about this time numerous weapons made with newly introduced metals began being produced in Ireland.

With Spain and the Straits of Gibraltar serving as a gateway between the Mediterranean and the northern lands, the seafaring people called by the name of Dan ranged far and wide. Egypt fought with and then hired as mercenaries the Shardan. In Israel there was the tribe of Dan. In Greece there existed the people of the goddess Danae. In Ireland there were the people of the goddess Danu (Tuatha de Danaan). And farther into the Baltic Sea were the Danes. The linguistic connection also is interesting, as (H) I-biru (Hebrew) sailors trade with I-berian Spain and Portugal and ultimately with (H) Ibernian Ireland. The word *Hebrew* is supposed to have referred to the people of the "crossing," but it may have been more than a simple river crossing.

From the city-state of Tartessus, Jeremiah and his small group head north to Ireland. The year was 583 B.C., and in Ireland an account of the person the Irish call Ollam Fodhla, meaning the "learned seer," and his group is recorded. Jeremiah as the seer is no stretch, as he is a prophet. Jeremiah as the Patriarch, it is said, was the basis for the legend of St. Patrick, although there are other indications that he could have had his origin in the Roman god Liber Pater.[7]

Patrick was said to have come to Ireland as a slave about one thousand years after the "Patriarch."

Jeremiah's companion is the Princess Tamar Tephi. A translation of her name is the "Beautiful Palm Tree" of Judah. *Palm* in Ireland is *ailm*. It is strange that the Irish would even have a word for palm, a tree not indigenous to the island.[8] Being the granddaughter of Jeremiah, Tamar has a royal lineage in Judah, which in turn allows her to marry well in Ireland. She becomes the wife of the High King of Ardagh, Heremon Eochaidh. His home base is County Meath, which is the center of the five kingdoms. Legend has it that when she died she was buried on the Hill of Tara, the crowning place of Ireland's kings, along with the mysterious box she brought from her homeland. The buried chest contains, it is said, two documents brought from Judah. And the place is now called the Place of the Law, just as Tara is known as the Hill of the Law. Recalling this myth would not be complete without the comparison between the Jewish law, the Torah, and the Irish sacred center, Tara. Tara's ancient Celtic name is Teamhair na Riogh, Tara of the Kings.

There is not much to corroborate this tale. Around Tara is a passage grave, often the burial place of an important king, but it dates to 1800 B.C., more than one thousand years too early for the prophet Jeremiah. Other legendary places have assimilated so much of the layered culture that is Ireland that nothing around sacred Tara can be definitively categorized with any certainty. This has not stopped anyone from believing. Near this "Rath of the Kings" is the Rath of the Synods. Once, a ring wall had surrounded it. Today it is badly damaged after a group of British Israelites performed an amateur excavation in the early 1900s in search of the Ark of the Covenant.[9]

More systematic excavations began in 1952. The only discovery was that the entire area was the scene of a cult ceremony at some time in history.

Jeremiah is buried on the Holy Isle of Devenish near modern-day Enniskillen. Today there is not much to be seen there other than the ruins of a sixth-century monastery founded by the Irish Saint Molaise. A twelfth-century round tower and a ruined Abbey of St. Mary's are also nearby.

It is not known what became of the scribe Baruch, who became Simon Brugh or Brach, once in Ireland or of the other princess. Legend says they did bring a stone that the Irish call Lia Fail (the Wonderful Stone), and the more ancient name was Jacob's Pillow. The stone is also said to have been brought to Scotland, where it also served as the Coronation Stone of Scone until being taken to Westminster by the English army.

The princess of Judah and her husband had a son, Aedh, who died while still a teenager. At that time a crypt was built under Tara. The princess would later also be buried in the chamber. A second son, Aengus, grew up to be an arrogant king and had an elaborate tomb constructed for himself on the Boyne River. It is said that at Teltown games were instituted in honor of the princess.

The story has certain holes, as it seems to be based on more ancient Irish hero tales. There is no doubt that an Indo-European people expanded and settled from Ireland to India. The worship of Baal in Sumeria and Bel in Ireland, of Lugal in Sumeria and Lug in Ireland, and of Sin and Terah as moon goddesses in the Middle East and Shannon (Shin-An) and Tara in Ireland, are more than coincidental. Proof of Jeremiah bringing the Ark to Ireland, however, requires more.

The mounds that have been considered to play a role in the adventures of Jeremiah's granddaughter and her family date to two thousand years before the time Jeremiah lived. The stone too is problematic. It was known that *fals,* or sacred stones in the shape of the male phallus, were used in coronation ceremonies. This, however, was not a custom among Hebrews.

This has not stopped would-be modern-day archaeologists from proposing a dig at Tara. The *Catholic World News* carried a story of John Hill in the November 9, 2000, issue. Mr. Hill claimed to be studying the Ark of the Covenant for sixteen years and believed it to be buried under Tara and to still contain the two tablets of the Ten Commandments. Permission to dig was not granted.

The Ark in Rome

The period known as the Babylonian Captivity would not be the last time that Jerusalem fell to invaders or that the temple itself was victim to an enemy.

When the legions of Titus destroyed Jerusalem in the first century, it is recorded that they plundered the temple. The conflict had started in A.D. 70 when Israel was still in the hands of three factions. One of these was led by John of Giscala, who had his men disguise themselves as pilgrims to infiltrate and seize the temple. While this was going on, Titus landed and set up camp three-quarters of a mile from the city. He then ravaged the countryside, chopping down every tree that stood in a ten-mile radius. His men surrounded the city and demanded surrender.

Jerusalem, whose usual population numbered 100,000, may have then had five times that number, as pilgrims and refugees had packed the city. Deserting the starving city was not an option, as those who tried were crucified outside the walls for the besieged citizens to view. When the army of Titus, which was 65,000 strong and well provisioned, finally breached the walls, a street-by-street battle began that raged for days. Last to fall was the temple, where John of Giscala and his militant faction had barricaded themselves. When the battering rams and wall-scaling ladders didn't work, Titus had the doors set on fire. A battle ensued, and the temple itself did not fare well.

For the Jews the timing of the destructive fire in the temple could not have been worse, because it had been on the same day centuries before that the Babylonians had set the temple on fire. The implication served as a rallying cry, as the situation of the Jews was desperate. The garrisoned Jews waited for a lull in the fighting to counterattack the Romans, who were putting out the fire in the inner court. The Romans outnumbered them badly, and one soldier threw a blazing brand through a golden aperture that brought the fire to the chamber surrounding the sanctuary.

Titus sent a larger force, and they took over the sanctuary and put out the fire. The scene was described as a river of blood.[10] When the fighting again stopped, Titus took his staff into the holy place of the sanctuary. What they saw went "far beyond the accounts circulating in foreign countries."[11] "So laden with plunder was every soldier that all over Syria the value of gold was reduced by half."[12] But the attack on Jerusalem was still not over.

While hundreds hid in the tunnels underneath the city, the walls were burned and battered until they fell to the ground. The mopping-up effort took days, and prisoners were dying of starvation in their temporary detention camp. In all, the siege lasted four months and over one million Jews died.[13] Many of the wounded were simply killed; many who survived were brought to Italy as captives. The prisoners at one point numbered 97,000, but many of these died of starvation. Whatever could be carried—the surviving prisoners, the temple loot, the sacred relics—was taken aboard ships for Rome. The Arch of Titus in Rome depicts the looting of the temple and shows the seven-branched menorah as just one of the trophies of his victory, but there is no specific mention of the Ark other than one reference in the account of Josephus, who was the historian of the day. A traitor to his own people, he joined the Roman war effort against the Jews. He also recorded the war in great detail.

In his book *The Jewish War* he listed the treasures stolen—"the most remarkable being those that had been taken from the Temple of Jerusalem, the Table of Gold that weighed several talents."[14] Since Josephus, like many historians of his time, were frustratingly inexact, it is not certain if he is referring to the base under the Ark or the Ark itself. There is one very important clue that might indicate that the table was the Ark. In his discussion of the table and the seven-branched lamp, he says the procession of stolen artifacts ended with the Jewish law.[15] Historians believe he is referring to the Pentateuch, the scrolls of law, which many believe were housed in the Ark itself. It would make sense that in the booty procession the law would follow the Ark, which might have been the very heavy Table of Gold.

On way to board his ships and head home, Titus ordered the complete demolition of the city. If the Ark was not already part of the booty, then it may have remained in the tunnels, in a chamber undiscovered by the Romans. If it was part of the stolen artifacts taken to Rome, it would not stay in Rome forever. Rome itself would be looted within a few centuries.

The Ark in France

Stronger invaders from the East and the unrest caused by Roman rule uprooted many peoples who had served as a buffer between Rome and the barbarians. The Goths were one such people, and they split in two as they headed to Europe. One of these tribes, the Visigoths, attempted to settle on the eastern borders but were excessively taxed by Rome. Soon they revolted and began a series of wars while on the move. Rome was much weaker at home and unable to deal with the expenses of maintaining her government or her far-flung empire. Depending on mercenaries only made Rome worse, and soon her excesses came back to haunt her.

In 410 the Visigoths, led by Alaric, headed to Rome. Alaric plundered Rome, including the Imperial Treasury, where the treasures of Jerusalem were stored. His people under Ataulphus carried their treasure across Gaul and established their own kingdom in the southwest of France, in the borderline area between modern France and Spain, and across much of Spain itself. Their main capital was at Toulouse, but the Spanish city of Toledo, the French city of Carcassonne, and a present-day tiny Rhedae would play important roles. Much of this area had been controlled by Rome, but in order to bolster the weak center of the empire, many troops of Roman soldiers had been called back home. When the Visigoths reached the area, there was no resistance.

Their own culture was then overlayed on an area that had seen pre-Celtic tribes, Phoenicians, Celts, Greeks, and Roman invaders. The result was an amalgamation of beliefs that were further blended with the odd religion of the Visigoths. They had been converted to Christianity during their hundreds of years migrating from Asia. Along the way they had picked up a particular blend of beliefs that would be considered heretical by the church in Rome. Arianism wasn't known only to exist in the south of France, but hundreds of years after proponents of this blend of Christianity were rooted out elsewhere, this system was still thriving in the area that would be called Languedoc.

From the north, the Franks followed the Visigoths into France. The dynasty of the Merovingians and the descendents of the Carolingians were content with simply hemming the Visigoth kingdoms in the south. They had little reason to take their land and concentrated their power base in the north. They also recognized the value of intermarriage with Visigoth royalty. An early royal marriage took place between a princess, Giselle de Razes, and the king of the Frankish Merovingians, Dagobert II. It took place at Rhedae, which would later be called Rennes-le-Château.

But the Visigoths would face invasion from the south. In 711 Spain was invaded by the Moors, the armies of Islam from North Africa. The leader of the invasion was Jabel al Tariq, who would give his name to Gibraltar. The Islamic leader knew the Visigoths held a great deal of treasure and knew it to be stored at Toledo. However, by the time they conquered Toledo, the treasure had been moved to safety.

Islam and the Visigoths then shared a tolerant peace. Arian Christians and long-exiled Jews were treated fairly by the Moors. Science, literature, medicine, and music thrived under Moorish rule. Then the Moors tried to reach too far into Europe and were turned around by Charles Martel, the grandfather of Charlemagne. Martel's Franks also knew of the treasure and believed the Visigoths to hold it at the city of Carcassonne. They too would be disappointed.

The area between Spain and France was called Septimania, from the Seventh Legion of Rome, which had once held the territory. It thrived as a center of learning for a while and even claimed a Sephardic colony of Jews who held dear traditions about Mary Magdalene and an even earlier Jewish community. Under Roman rule the number of Jews had grown. The Visigoths had a minimal effect on the Jews, and there is evidence of intermarriage between Jewish and Visigothic families. The brief Islamic rule too did not threaten the Jewish community.

Before a new reign of intolerance would return to Septimania, a handful of Merovingian, Visigothic, and Jewish families shared the rule of the area and a secret. The treasure of the Temple of Jerusalem was held at Rhedae. One of these families was that of Hautpoul-Blanchefort, which would play a role in keeping the treasure hidden.

Disaster would strike the area with the defeat of the Moors. The Jews would be the scapegoats, and the Hebrew colleges, which shared an early Renaissance with Arab scholars, were closed as the Jews were painted as anti-Christian by the returning Europeans. The charge was that they sided with the Arab invaders, an indictment that could have applied to all of Septimania's residents.

The Arian-Christians would fare worst of all. Their religion had a dualistic belief that all was good or evil. God in heaven was good. A Christ on a material earth was a human, therefore he could not be divine. The cross was not an object of devotion but one of a horrible cruelty. This part of their belief was certainly not in line with the church in Rome. But it would get worse. The people called Cathars, the Pure Ones, would institute their own sacraments. Their ceremonies could be conducted by either man or woman. Often they were conducted by the *perfecti*, those Cathars who chose celibacy for their faith. The *perfecti* were a distinct minority, and often one would become "perfected" only after a life of enjoying earthly pleasures. The most serious offense, as far as Rome was concerned, was that no priests, bishops, or popes could come between man and his God.

From a theological viewpoint, it was problematic; but from the point of view of a church that depended on taxation of the faithful, it was a serious heresy. The church had grown to be the most wealthy and powerful institution on earth by defending its turf, and it was not going to allow such authority to be challenged by peasant farmers. St. Bernard was sent to investigate the Cathars for the church. He insisted that they posed no threat and were among France's most pious. Despite his judgment, the church was threatened.

At the same time Crusaders in the East were killing Christians and destroying their cities on their way to fight Arabs, a smaller but equally vicious Crusade was called for in France. Crusaders here were free to slaughter and pillage, and leaders could keep the lands they took. An Islamic enemy was not even considered. City by city, town by town, the Cathars were massacred. The genocidal rage would start at Beziers. The mercenary armies from the north of France had a limited conscription, so a long siege of the town was to be avoided. The town, however, dug in while surrounded by the threatening army.

On the feast of Mary Magdalene, a handful of Cathars were outside the city, separated from the army by a bridge. Insults were exchanged over the safe distance of the bridge until one soldier crossed over to make a point. The Cathars killed him. An unorganized brawl ensued, but the mercenary leaders quickly seized on the breach of security to organize a rush into the city.

The citizenry too was not ready for an attack and ran into the churches. The military officer reported to the representative of the pope that there were thousands of women and children in the churches. He asked what he should do with them. The papal legate replied, "Kill them all, God will recognize his own." The doors were burned and the indiscriminate massacre began. The legate Arnald-Amalric gleefully reported that twenty thousand men, women, and children were killed.[16]

The massacre strategy continued for years, culminating in the siege of Montsegur. There the "Safe Mountain" held a formidable fortress. Some believe it was the Grail castle, the center of the Cathar faith, as well as the site of the treasures brought to the south of France by the Visigoths. The siege here included the Knights Templar who fought alongside the Cathars. There is much evidence to believe their loyalties were along family lines moreso than along religious lines. After a while a fifteen-day truce was negotiated. At the end the captives had the choice of professing obedience to Rome or being burned at the stake. Most of the Cathars took their last sacrament and would freely go to their death by fire.

Before their surrender, however, four escaped, it is said, with the sacred treasures.[17]

The legend that there was treasure in the area would never go away. The Grail writer Wolfram von Eschenbach would say that the Grail was an object that could only be approached by the pure. He claimed to have heard the story from a scholar, Kyot of Provence, who learned of it while studying rare parchments in Toledo, the first repository of the Visigoth treasure. He described a Grail family that guarded the object, including Repanse de Schoye. The name *de Schoye,* translated back to French, could be *de Choix,* meaning "of the Chosen (People)."

Hunting for treasure, gold, or silver of holy grails has been going on for centuries. Occasionally something would add fuel to the fire. In the mid-fourteenth century counterfeit gold coins began turning up in the Languedoc area. Even though they were counterfeit, the coins had a higher gold content than the authentic coins. The king's investigator traced their origin to a cave where he found minting equipment and a store of gold.[18] The counterfeiters were members of a handful of local noble families. The pope himself, Clement VI, would intercede to get the noble criminals pardoned.

Published in 1759, a book titled *Le Dictionaire Historique de Moreri 1759* told of the Visigothic treasure. In 1860 a poorly minted gold ingot consisted of partially melted ancient gold coins was found in a field. But no greater story exists than the tale of Father Berenger Sauniere. Posted to the village of Rennes-le-Château in 1885, Sauniere apparently stumbled onto a massive treasure in 1891 while restoring the village church. In the churchyard was the burial monument of Marie, the Marquise de Hautpoul. Her family, mentioned above, linked prominent Visigothic-Jewish and Merovingian roots from one thousand years before. Her headstone was a code that helped Sauniere decipher texts he would find in the church's altar. Shortly after his discovery he was soon spending the equivalent of millions in today's money on renovations to the church, the town's infrastructure, and his own Tower Magdala. The church itself is one of Christianity's more bizarre, with a statue of the demon Asmodeus who is a pagan "custodian of secrets and guardian of sacred treasures" and St. Anthony of Padua. Perhaps Father Sauniere was showing his thanks to St. Anthony, who helps recover lost items. Whatever treasure Asmodeus and St. Anthony helped the parish priest find, Sauniere's secret died with him in 1917.

The Pyrennes mountain villages, however, would still be the site of treasure hunters into modern times. When Hitler took control of Germany, an odd collection of occultists, some very wealthy, had helped his early rise to power. His dark collection of disciples would grow to include an Otto Rahn, who had been obsessed with the Holy Grail since childhood.[19] Rahn may have made his first trip to Languedoc in 1931, where he conducted research in depth. In 1933 he published a book of his experience that found favor with the ruling Nazi party.[20] He was recruited into the SS, despite his mother being Jewish, and joined the staff of Heinrich Himmler. Both Hitler and Himmler shared a deep interest in the Knights Templar and modeled the SS after the order. They had a dream of building a Grail castle at Wewelsburg, where the sacred items they found would be held and SS knights would hold court around a round table. No sacred items were brought there, but it was not for a lack of trying. Several Nazi expeditions were sent that included miners to recover treasure in the caves. Even the composer Wagner would make his own pilgrimage to Rennes-le-Château before writing his last opera, *Parsifal.*[21]

Twice the Nazis would send Otto Skorzeny into Languedoc to search for the legendary treasures. Skorzeny would later be responsible for setting up ODESSA, a worldwide organization to protect SS agents from prosecution. Martin Bormann, a close friend of Skorzeny, was one of those who benefited from the ODESSA organization. When his wife, who would stay behind, was arrested by the Allies, she was holding 2,200 ancient gold coins.

But the Nazis did not rely on new discoveries for amassing treasures. They had simply chosen to loot everything that did not go into hiding, from private collections to those of Europe's finest museums. But there is no solid evidence that they had taken a Visigothic horde from the villages and mountains of the Languedoc.

What secrets remain around the Rennes-le-Château region? Recent studies by Henry Lincoln are recorded in his book, *The Holy Place*. He makes the connection between some historic castles, Templar precept houses, and sacred mountaintop churches that appear to form a five-pointed star on an ancient landscape. Within this enigmatic formation are some clues as to just what might be concealed in this area. Valdieu is one place-name, which would translate as the Valley of God. Arques, of course, can be said to point to the location of the Ark of the Covenant. A château at Arques serves as one of the pivotal links to the maze of sacred intersecting lines.

Blanchefort, or White Fort, is the home of the Hautpoul family. It was the last descendent of the Hautpoul family whose tomb served to point Sauniere to his secret treasure. L'Homme Mort, or the Dead Man, and Fauteuil du Diable, the Devil's Seat, also lie within this mysterious geography.

The Ark in Scotland

If the Cathars did hold the Ark of the Covenant, there can be two theories about its location after Montsegur. The first is that it remains hidden in the south of France. The second is that it was taken away. Proponents of the second theory believe the Knights Templar, which had a pro-Cathar bias despite being under the control of the pope, took the Ark. It may have gone to Paris to their headquarters, or it may have gone beyond Paris, to the domain of the Sinclair family in Scotland, Rosslyn. The Sinclairs of France, as St. Clairs, were among the founding members of the Templar order and would become the hereditary guardians of Scotland's Freemasons. As guardians the Sinclairs would be responsible for hiding Templar treasures, from gold and silver to the Ark and the Holy Grail.

The Rosslyn chapel is a most holy site to Freemasonry, and Masons make pilgrimages to this once ostensibly Catholic chapel built by the Sinclair family. When Protestant mobs inspired and incited by the preaching of John Calvin swept through Scotland, destroying Catholic churches and their relics, Rosslyn's chapel was spared.[22]

Rosslyn has recently begun renovations to preserve the integrity of the chapel walls. It has also been the subject of a great deal of excavation, in the hopes of revealing whatever secrets it may or may not hold. Through oil-exploration techniques, radar, and radio pulses, as well as good old-fashioned digging, there is evidence of still undiscovered chambers and vaults, but so far no treasure, or Ark, or Holy Grail.[23]

• • •

Locating the Ark of the Covenant presents insurmountable problems. It disappeared nearly three thousand years ago and is as elusive as the Holy Grail. While archaeologists search for a wood and gold box, scientists have avoided the discussion of the box itself. It was at once: a transmitter that allowed Moses to communicate with God; an energized box so powerful it destroyed many who came near or physically touched it; a gift from a god so radiant that the face of Moses was burned. For modern scientists, a serious discussion of the nature of the Ark can be as toxic to a career as the Ark itself was to those who got too close.

13

THE HOLY GRAIL

The quest for the Holy Grail has been going on for at least a thousand years. For some it is personal, an initiation into the mysteries of Christendom or even pre-Christian realms. For others it is a real object. It is the cup used at the Last Supper or a receptacle used to preserve the blood of a dying Christ. To the ancient Celts the Grail is the Horn of Plenty, the Cornucopia, the Cauldron of Bron, all of which provided endless bounty. To the alchemist the Grail is the philosopher's stone, the stone that fell from heaven that can turn base metal into gold. And in recent times speculative historians claim it is not an object, it is the bloodline of the family of Jesus, Sangre Réal, the Sacred Blood.

Some believe the Grail is the unattainable. It is the search for the sacred, the answer to the mystery of life. Others believe the Holy Grail was never actually lost and still exists, safe and sound, in a cathedral in the Spanish city of Valencia.

The Holy Grail of Valencia

The Valencia Grail is one of many that claim to be the chalice used by Jesus at the Last Supper, but it differs from all of the others in that it has never been shown to be anything else. Its provenance is unbroken from the first century until modern times, and it can be traced historically during the twenty centuries it has survived.

Seekers of the Grail need simply find the cathedral in Valencia. There is a small chapel, the Capilla del Santo Caliz, devoted only to the Grail. There the chalice used at the Last Supper sits. It is seven inches high, and the cup is as small as a teacup. It has acquired gold and jewels, which may have been added after the Last Supper. A continuous mass is said in the chapel, and visitors often feel compelled to sit or kneel to get a better view.[1]

The church tradition of the mass starts with Jesus transforming bread and wine into his own body and blood. This miraculous transformation is called the transubstantiation and is one of those things that is taken on faith. Jesus broke bread and drank wine with the apostles and instructed his disciples to do this in remembrance of him. This is the basis of the modern mass and is repeated every Sunday in churches worldwide.

Tradition has St. Peter keeping the chalice and bringing it with him to Rome, where he was the first bishop of that city. It remained in Rome, and the first twenty-four popes used it to keep that same tradition. Sixtus II was the last. Times had already been rough for the popes, as their average ten-year reign shows, but the Roman emperor Valerian was particularly cruel. He was also in need of funds, and as other kings would do later in history, he targeted a convenient scapegoat—in this case the Christian church. Sixtus II was the first target of Valerian. Anticipating his execution, he gave the chalice to St. Lawrence to protect it.

For Lawrence it was a death sentence, and he too acted to protect the chalice. He gave it and other important relics to a Spaniard to protect from the avaricious Romans. Lawrence then made his appearance to the emperor, who had demanded he surrender the treasures of the church. Pointing to his coterie of homeless Christian Romans, he said that these were the treasures of the church.[2] Within four days he would follow Sixtus II to a martyr's death. The chalice was on its way to Huesca in Spain.

The chalice would be safe in post-Roman Spain for four hundred years until the Moorish invasion in 711. It was brought to safety in the Pyrennes mountains, which served as a border between future Spain and France. The small towns of San Pedro de Siresa, Santa Maria de Sasabe—then San Juan de la Pena—served as repositories for the Grail.

After the *reconquista* the chalice remained at this protected monastery along the pilgrimage route to Santiago de Compostella until 1399. In that year the monks gave it to Martin the Humane, who was caught up in the mania of collecting relics. Martin passed it to his successor, Alphonse the Magnanimous, who brought it to the city of Valencia. For a while it was kept at his palace but was soon entrusted to the cathedral in that city, where it has remained until modern times.

Valencia was regarded in ancient times as "a piece of heaven fallen to earth,"[3] an interesting appellation, as the Grail too is regarded as having fallen from heaven. The Moors called the city Medina bu-Tarab, the "city of joy." They built a mosque over the foundation of a Roman-built Temple of Diana. The cathedral in Valencia was then built over the site of the mosque in the thirteenth century. Remodeled in the eighteenth century, it contains paintings by Goya, Palomino, and pupils of Leonardo da Vinci. The Grail has remained in its chapel in the cathedral for centuries, with the exception of a brief period during the Spanish Civil War when it was carried to safety and hidden in the mountainous village of Carlot, southwest of Valencia.

In 1982 Pope John Paul II celebrated mass with this most celebrated relic. He was the first pope to do so since St. Sixtus II, eighteen hundred years before.

The Genoa Grail

Valencia may have the chalice that is widely acknowledged as being the Holy Grail, but it has competition. In Genoa the Holy Grail is at the treasury of the Cathedral San Lorenzo. The cathedral, which was started in the twelfth century, has a sculpture of that saint, a chapel of St. John the Baptist with some of his bones, and in a tiny museum behind the sacristy, a hexagonal cup brought back by Crusaders. In this Italian city it is called the Sacro Catino, the Sacred Bowl, and it looks more like a goblet than a chalice. While there is no record of the cup in the Last Supper being green, and none of the Grail writers claim the Grail was a goblet or green, Genoa has the green Grail. There are several stories that tell of just how the emerald cup came to Genoa. Genoese soldiers and sailors were among the first Crusaders. They took part in the raid on Antioch in 1098 and on Jerusalem the year after. At the city of Caesaria, the green cup, thought to be carved from a single emerald, was taken. A second tale has them being given the cup as a reward for being the ferrymen of the Crusades. A third tradition has it coming from Spain and being the cup that St. Lawrence had protected.

The first two may be a blend of the truth, the third tradition patently false, especially if one is from Valencia. The Genoa Grail also proved to be made up of something less valuable than emerald. When Napoleon captured Genoa, he had the goblet sent to Paris for analysis. While it did not take long to determine that the emerald goblet was actually glass, proving that the goblet was not the Grail was another matter entirely. Genoa's Duomo di San Lorenzo has a carving of St. Lawrence being roasted on the grill, a sarcophagus with relics of St. John the Baptist, a blue chalcedony dish said to have held the head of St. John the Baptist, a reliquary arm of St. Anne, and their own version of the Grail.

The Nanteos Cup

Throughout Europe there are several cups, plates, and chalices that supposedly are the Holy Grail, but there is little basis for these claims. There is a Grail in France referred to as Abbot Suger's Chalice and another in Belgium called the Bruges Grail. In England there is the Nanteos Cup.

During the period known as the Dissolution, when Henry VIII shut England's monasteries, monks from Glastonbury fled. They ended up in Wales and sought refuge at Nanteos House, owned by the prominent Powell family, which was able to protect the monks. When the last of the monks was near death, he told a member of the Powell family of their treasure. He said it was the Grail and had been carried to England by Joseph of Arimathea, who entrusted it to his family as hereditary guardians. The Powell family displayed their treasure and held it until 1952, when the last Powell died. It was sold to a Major Merrill, who is said to hold it in a bank vault.[4] This Grail is made of wood, not fitting in with most artistic conceptions of the drinking vessel used at the Last Supper.

The New York City Grail

American seekers of the Grail only need to find their way to the magical island of Manhattan. By bus, train, or even car, the most northern reaches of that island contain the medieval wonder called the Cloisters Museum. Here is preserved the Antioch chalice, believed by some to be the Holy Grail.

It was discovered in one of the most important first-century cities for Christians, Antioch. The seven-and-a-half-inch silver goblet depicts ten of the apostles and Jesus, as well as a rabbit, an eagle, and a lamb. A Paris firm restored the cup for the Kouchakji Freres, who owned it, and it was shown at the Chicago World's Fair in 1933. It was then sold to the Rockefeller-funded Cloisters in 1950.

It does not take a high degree of skepticism to realize that most likely Jesus or the apostles did not have a commemorative cup made to use during the Last Supper. Neither the Cloisters nor the church regard this as the chalice of the Last Supper.[5] In fact, research into the Antioch chalice showed that it more likely would have been used as a church lamp in the sixth century.

The Grail of the Celts

Ancient Ireland was the repository of mysterious beliefs called from several civilizations. Well before the Celts, the builders of New Grange, an unusually large mound built to serve as a calendar and a place of awe, demonstrated a more sophisticated degree of knowledge than any other group outside of their contemporaneous cultures in Egypt and Sumer. They did not record their knowledge or traditions. Successive waves of civilizations, including Druids, Celts, and possibly Iberians and Greeks, created a blend of culture that defies any attempt to be deciphered in any order. We are left with several bodies of tales, called cycles, that create the image of a mystical Ireland but also are as complex and contradictory as the Grail literature that would come much later.

Ancient Ireland had four very sacred treasures in the four provinces. The Stone of Destiny, known as the Lia Fail, was in Falias. In Finias and Gorias were two magical spears, one said to be that of Apollo, in Gaelic known as Lugh. The most sacred was the Cauldron of Dagda, which provided a never-ending supply of food, but only for brave warriors.

Dagda's cauldron was known as Bran's and Bron's cauldron as well. Under these names the cauldron was the Celtic cauldron of regeneration. An allegory for life and rebirth, Bran's cauldron would bring to life dead warriors and provide food anytime it was needed. It is not too much of an allegorical stretch to transfer the properties of a Celtic Grail to a Christian Grail. The cup of the Last Supper was to be used not by warriors but by the faithful, those who spread a new message of peace. It provided food, and that food was the body of Christ. It also provided rebirth—salvation to those who believed.

Students of the Grail literature believe the Grail guardian story to be a twelfth-century invention, and the relation between the "cor" (body) of Jesus and the Grail to reflect an ancient tradition. Before there was a Greece there was a goddess Kore. She was worshipped between Britain and the Middle East, most likely until patriarchal invaders from Asia brought their own male gods. Kore was also known by similar-sounding names including Car, Cor, and Ceres. In Rome she provided the "Cor"nucopia, the Horn of Plenty, which was very much like Bran's magical platter. She was the basis for the word *corn,* as well as the word *cereal.* The "kern" was her sacred womb, where she gave birth, and the basis for the word *kernel.* The goddess name provides other derivations—*cardiac, carnal, carnal,* and *core.* Her celebration was the Carnivale, surviving thousands of years past her worship, although possibly as licentious then as now. In Egypt the Coptic Christians incorporated her feast, called the Koreion, with another feast, called the Epiphany.

From the grain goddess of pre-Celtic Eurasia, to a grain god Bran in Celtic times, the mystery of death and rebirth became an allegory with Jesus. The Corpus Christi, the body of Christ, was now the path to salvation. Chrétien de Troyes was the first to mention the "graal," and it is uncertain exactly what he meant. The French believed it to be a chalice that held the host.[6] *Gawain and the Green Knight* was one of the later Grail romances and harkens to primitive Britain paganism. Gawain and the knights of the Round Table are visited by a huge green man with an axe and a holly bough. It is Christmastime, and the green man, a not-too-disguised Celtic vegetation god, invites Gawain to chop off his head with the axe. He does, and the green man rides away, Ichabod Crane style, with his head. But in return, Gawain must then offer to have his chopped off. Not only does Gawain's power wax and wane like a sun god, but the coincidence of the Celtic birth-of-the-sun ritual occurring at the winter solstice and Christmas blends pagan myth and Christian doctrine without apparent motive, at least for modern readers.

The Medieval Grail

There is a gap of a thousand years between the Crucifixion and the emergence of Grail literature. Chrétien de Troyes in France was not the first to create the word, or possibly even the myth, of a Grail. Some writers believe his stories were based on Welsh tales, as they exhibit a great deal of Christianizing of Celtic myths. He began writing in 1180 when he was in the employ of Marie of Champagne. It is important to note that Hugh of Champagne was one of the first Knights Templar. There appears to be an agenda in place, with a goal as minor as glorifying those who risk all in the holy wars, or as conspiratorial as providing a connection between the Grail family of France and the bloodline of David, which passed through Jesus.

The work of Chrétien ended suddenly, possibly as a result of his death. Other writers picked up the task, however, writing several sequels to the story. Though many details remained the same, much was created anew.

Characters introduced were related to biblical figures by word or implication.

Joseph of Arimathea now figured in the story, and somehow he had a companion named Bron who brought the Grail to England. There is little masking of the close relationship between the Irish and Welsh traditions and medieval literature.

The Sacred Bloodline

One of the early Grail texts called the Grand Sainte Graal regards the Holy Grail as a book. The author of that work writes in Old French, the language of the northern half of the country, but is anonymous. He claims that Jesus appeared to him seven hundred years after the Crucifixion and presented him with a book that Jesus himself had written. The unknown author claims to be descended from the family of Jesus and names Lancelot and Perceval as being in the Davidic line as well.[7] Robert de Boron had brought Joseph of Arimathea into the story and invented the concept of a Grail family. Wolfram of Eschenbach wrote *Parzival,* adding to the Grail family but allowing in other guardians of the Grail. Some romances, like that of Robert de Boron, required that only the pure could participate in the Grail ceremony or sit at the Round Table. Others, like that of Wolfram, allowed for sinners to participate. The Templar order was said to allow sinners to join, as Christ welcomed the sinners as needing him the most. Wolfram called the Knights of the Round Table, the Knights Templar.

In all, between 1180 and 1230 there were ten versions of the Grail story, and in some cases they appeared to have an agenda. Because writers were either cloistered monks or hired scribes, they generally, like artists, required patrons during this period. The patrons of the Grail romances would have certain aspects of their own family blended in with the story, just as artists often painted portraits of their patrons, including them as part of a group in their depictions of the life of Jesus.

The Grail agenda of some may have been to establish their own family as the descendents of a Grail family. This Grail family might be descended from Joseph of Arimathea or even from the family of the bloodline of David, which included Jesus. A Grail family was also the guardian of the Grail, implying a divine right to rule and protect their kingdom. There is also the possibility that the agenda need not be conspiratorial. As mentioned above, it was custom among patrons of important artists to occasionally have themselves included in a religious painting.

The Grail Castle

A different version of the Grail existed in Spain and the Languedoc area of France. This borderline territory of the Pyrennes mountains blended Moorish tradition with Christian myth and stirred in bits and pieces of the Hebrew Kaballah as well. The Grail castle was a repository of jewels and a model of the universe. Called the Mount of Salvation or the Mount of Joy, it was located in various places, mostly mythical, but often centered around the Pyrennes mountains.

The Kaballah acknowledges the female principle in the divine, the spirit referred to in Genesis that was knowledge. This female presence, Shekinah in Judaism, Sophia to early Greek Christianity, was even part of early Islam as Sakina. But church fathers and orthodox rabbis rejected the principle. Eve with her knowledge of good and evil allowed the devil to bring sin to man. And as Lucifer, the "light carrier," brought light he also brought a jewel that was given to him when he fell from heaven. The *lapsit exillis,* the stone that fell, had some incredible powers, one of which, like the Cauldron of Bran, was to return man to life. A German poem, "The Contest of the Singers at Wartburg," refers to it as the luminous stone of the crown of Lucifer, torn from his head by the Archangel Michael.

This remarkable stone was preserved in a Grail castle. Montsegur of the Cathars was to be their last stand—a sacred mountain where they were surrounded by the armies of the Christian church in Rome. Their crime: the quest for God without using the intermediaries of the church. It was their own Grail quest, and reputedly the Knights Templar had fought alongside the heretics. Montsegur was the last Grail castle of the Cathars, as they chose death by fire than conversion.

It was the Parzival of Wolfram von Eschenbach[8] that created the stone that fell from heaven. He inserts his stone in the story, and although it may have a basis in myth, it is not the Celtic myth. There were always stones that fell from heaven, most likely meteors. The most famous may be the Kaaba, a black stone housed at Mecca. The stone and the Grail castle guarded by the Chevaliers of the Graal in Wolfram's *Parzival* may have had their origin in Islamic myth carried back by Crusaders. His poem was written between 1200 and 1210.

Students of the Grail literature can only conclude with the feeling that as an object of desire, the Grail never fills the void. It is at once many things and nothing. More likely the Grail is an allegory, rather than a chalice, a stone, or even an earthly reward.

In another sense the true Grail is the search for the divine within. The search leads to knowledge, it brings experience, and in the end harmony. For some it is an initiation to a higher plane of awareness. It may require finding a path on one's own, guided by an inner light. To others it may require the assistance of an intermediary, a shaman, a priest, or the guidance of an entire religious body. It requires honesty and pure intentions, and the ideal is that the journey itself is the reward. The Tao, or the Way of Eastern religion, the straight and narrow path of Western religion, the Golden Rule, may all point to the same thing—the way to find God is not by forsaking the world but by finding God in it.

14

THE MODERN RELIC TRADE

At the beginning of the twenty-first century, the demand for relics may be as strong as it was in medieval times. The ability to find and possess a personal artifact that will bring the owner a sense of closeness to their patron saint has never been easier. The ability to make a pilgrimage to the shrine of a favorite saint or holy cities, from Rome to Jerusalem, is less arduous than ever. For the stay-at-home collector, one needs simply to search a computer for a site where relics are offered.

This new facility combined with an affluence not found in previous centuries has opened up a wider market and a greater demand. To meet the demands of this new marketplace in which relics are regularly bought and sold, relics need to be discovered, sometimes created, and even unfortunately stolen. A host of characters, from men and women of the cloth to people in more shadowy occupations, may now find themselves competing either to preserve the sanctity of the sacred objects or obtain a great price.

If the church is hesitant to call relic theft a "sin," there are those who do. They include the FBI, Interpol, and in Italy, a special police force called the Digos. They are in constant battle with the *tombaroli,* the tomb raiders. Italy is a rich treasure trove of Christian and pagan catacombs and Roman and Etruscan tombs. From gold work to skulls, the rewards for getting one's hands dirty are great, if you don't mind the night shift.

That is when the *tombaroli* come out. They know the police do not have the manpower to hide a man behind every bush, and even in a cemetery it is often an easy matter to drop a pickaxe and shovel and pose as a stroller out for a walk. The greatest tombs are not part of large cemeteries. Tomb raiders usually spend a lifetime in this business, and they can distinguish a mound from a hill, and often an Etruscan tomb will yield treasures far greater than bones.[1]

Numerous dealers will gladly buy up the harvest, acting as middlemen whose next stop can occasionally be Italy's more organized criminals or friendly buyers for Europe's museums. The trade in relics and objects of archaeological significance is a large business, and like the war on drugs, police have attempted to curb the demand. But the tide refuses to be held back as museums and wealthy collectors proliferate.

Italy's greatest case of alleged relic theft is the work of a modern Indiana Jones, Vincenzo Cammarata. Described as tall, dark, and flamboyant, he is not the type to wear shabby clothes and engage in nighttime digging. Instead he is very visible, a popular lecturer who tours Italy, popping out a handful of ancient gold coins to dazzle his listeners. His villa, near an Etruscan ruin in Sicily, was the scene of his recent arrest. Leaving behind a treasure trove worth $30 million, he escaped through a tunnel and fled on a motor scooter. He then agreed to turn himself in, possibly expecting a quick release on bail. Instead he was locked in a Bologna jail, and his home in Sicily was descended upon by the Italian police. What they found was one of Italy's largest collections of art and ancient artifacts outside the Vatican. To the consternation of his family, his estate was then toured by some of Italy's important politicians, including Prime Minister Massimo D'Alema, who favorably compared the estate to Italy's museums. The estate was better endowed, and many of the valuables were from nearby sites.[2]

While it is said that Cammarata revels in the Indiana Jones role that journalists have given him, there appears to be a case in his favor. His accusers were envious professors, a real Mafia chieftain, and a convict looking for a deal. His "gang" was not the Mafia chieftains that the press claimed. Instead they were a handful of others with impressive credentials, two in fact were also professors. A close friend was Silvio Raffiotta, the prosecutor in the city of Enna, in Sicily, who is credited with waging war against tomb raiders. He had used Cammarata's talents to appraise stolen art but soon found himself under suspicion.

Cammarata's clients included New York's famed money manager Michael Steinhardt and the Paul Getty Museum in Malibu. Neither dealt with him directly, and both are considered the victims. In the case of two recent acquisitions the Getty Museum turned over the disputed property willingly, but Steinhardt fought back. A collector in Italy by the name of Vincenzo Pappalardo traded a gold phiale (a chalice or a libation bowl) to Cammarata in 1980. The estimated purchase price was $20,000. A Catania University professor, Giacomo Mangararo, wrote a paper on the chalice, which may have helped increase its value. He would be one of those arrested after the treasures in Cammarata's home were confiscated. In 1991 a Hungarian coin dealer, Michael Veres, traded Cammarata artwork worth $90,000 for the object. Veres put it up for sale in New York through a reputable dealer who sold it to Steinhardt for $1.2 million.[3]

While the real crime might be price gouging, the sale violated Italy's artifacts exportation laws. The chalice is now waiting in New York's Custom House for Steinhardt's case to be heard. While it is up to the court to determine if Cammarata's treasures were validated by honest paperwork, the high profile of the case influenced the Vatican to reiterate their position on treasures of the church.

While both past and present canon law forbids the sale, the Vatican wishes to slow the modern "translation" of everything, from bones to class-three relics. Like the daunting task faced by the police, from Italy's Digos to Interpol, there is apparently strong demand.[4]

A Romanian citizen living in Reading, Pennsylvania, recently confessed to his role in smuggling Catholic relics that were stolen in France to the United States. Sebastian Zegrean, a twenty-three-year-old security guard, and an accomplice were named in the theft of three relics valued as high as $130,000 U.S. Rather than attempt to smuggle them aboard an airline flight, Mr. Zegrean simply sent by FedEx a relic of St. Maxellendis back to the States.[5]

In A.D. 670 Maxellendis was a Frankish noblewoman who had joined an order of nuns in France to avoid being married to a pagan, Lord Hardouin. Insulted, the rejected lord killed his intended and was instantly struck blind. Three years later he wept at her gravesite and was cured for his penitence. The miracle was enough to launch the young nun on the way to canonization. Revered in her hometown of Caudrey, France, the theft of the relic of St. Maxellendis was nothing short of an international incident. It took fifteen months, but St. Maxellendis was on her way back to France.

Outside of Italy, the FBI and Interpol lead the fight against art theft, and while it often is seemingly un-newsworthy, there are at any one time twenty thousand stolen artifacts and artworks on the CD that is published and updated regularly by Interpol. Italy seems to rank highest in stolen art. But countries like Cambodia do not always update Interpol, and while massive theft has been going on in that country in the post–Pot Pol years, the Interpol CD in 2002 lists only two items. Russia and the former Soviet Union states are among the latest countries to see rampant looting of sacred treasure. It was reported that two thousand artifacts have been reported stolen in 2001 alone, and occasionally the thefts appear to be organized. Treasures of both the Orthodox Church and of Russian history are simply taken by the ruling class.

None other than Michael Jackson, the pop star, was stopped at the airport attempting to leave Russia with a ceremonial saber. He claimed it was a gift from General Alexander Korzhakov, Boris Yeltsin's bodyguard. This explanation was enough to allow him to leave but not the sword, as it was considered a treasure.[6]

One of Russia's oldest and most famous churches, the Church of the Intercession, was robbed of precious icons as well as gold and silver crosses and medallions. The church was undergoing renovations, and the budget left it without enough to pay for even one security guard. A breakdown in law and order left such treasures in danger everywhere in the country. The Federal Security Service responsible for such protection has made several large recoveries, including discovering four hundred icons in one St. Petersburg apartment.

The Russian Orthodox Church is not the only church under siege thanks to political events. The Turkish side of the island of Cyprus has seen everything from icons to church doors stolen from the Greek and Cypriot Orthodox churches. The Church of Cyprus has recently filed suit against a Dutch icon seller, Robert Roozemond. In his country he is a respected art dealer as well as an author on religious art. In Cyprus and the United States his reputation is less stellar. Just whom the Hague, the arbiter of such cases, rules in favor of is yet to be seen. In 1990 Roozemond sent twenty photographs of artwork to authorities in Cyprus that he was buying in the hopes of getting further proof of authenticity. While Cyprus was apparently slow or negligent in responding, they became a bit more concerned when the Royal Doors of the Ayios Anastasios Church in Peristerona were sold to a college in Japan through the religious art dealer. Cyprus, acting through the Hague, attempted to sue Roozemond over the ownership documents. Hedging their bet on the outcome of that case, they asked the Kanazawa College of Art in Japan to return the doors. As of this time no response has been given.[7]

For Roozemond, it was not the first run-in with the courts or the law. In 2000 he ended a five-year battle over another icon painting, *St. George Fights Evil*, with the Netherland's number one tennis player, Richard Krajicek. Sight unseen, the sports star had paid 450,000 guilders to buy the work. The deal between the two was that Roozemond would then resell the icon for 900,000 guilders. He instead sold it for less. The case was settled out of court, with the dealer refunding the original investment. Roozemond also appeared on an FBI list as being under suspicion of trading in undocumented art.

Because of the numerous laws concerning just what can be considered a national treasure, and just what this entails in numerous countries, there is little that can be regarded as black and white even for legitimate buyers and sellers.

Peg Goldberg, an Indiana social worker turned gallery owner, went to Amsterdam to buy a Modigliani and instead came home with four Greek Orthodox icon mosaics. To some they are simply ancient works of art. To others they are sacred icons who can weep, speak, bleed, heal, and otherwise exhibit supernatural powers. She paid $1.2 million for depictions of the apostles Matthew and John, Jesus, and an icon titled the "North Arkangel" from an Aydin Dikman. She did not realize that these had been marked up in a secret transaction by her "partners," who paid Dikman $350,000 only to mark them up considerably. One icon broker, Geza von Habsburg, an archduke in the imperial line, attempted to interest the Getty Museum for $20 million. The museum informed the Greek Cypriot Department of Antiquities.[8]

Before Ms. Goldberg could sell her icons, the men in black showed up, black collars that is. They sued Ms. Goldberg in her home state of Indiana. Swiss law, where the transaction officially took place, determines that if a good-faith buyer acquires articles five years after they are stolen, they have ownership. Indiana law says one cannot get title from a thief, although provision is made for goods that the original owner never sought to have returned. The laws get murky, as Cyprus went ten years without informing anyone, including Interpol, that the mosaics were stolen. In the case of *Cyprus v. Goldberg*, it even appeared that not only did the church know the seller, an Aydin Dikman, but also it may have had dealings with him. It didn't matter.

Peg Goldberg lost her mosaics during the civil trial, lost an appeal, and was refused a hearing in front of the Supreme Court.

In the quasi-legal world of trafficking in religious relics and art, the dangers are great. Questionable provenance, questionable authenticity, unfounded price markups; suspicious traders, contentious parties, and a myriad of law that vary from country to country and state to state make up the quicksand that can ruin an honest dealer.

The United States has its share of religious relic theft. The FBI Web site, which lists stolen religious artifacts and occasionally those recovered, does not have room for every crime. Recently it highlighted the San Antonio, Texas, archdiocese, which had been the victim of a series of thefts, including prayer books, statues and paintings, one of the Virgin Mary that dated to the eighteenth century. Some of the items were recovered, others are still in the hands of thieves.

The FBI maintains the National Stolen Art File that can be accessed at local offices by other police agencies. To be listed on the computerized file an object must be valued at $2,000 or more or have artistic or cultural significance.[9]

Ebay: Collectibles>Religious>Christianity

For the American collector of relics, whether a local bishop or an individual, it appears that one need no longer resort to stealing. Pious theft or otherwise.

Search "collectibles: religious" for Christian relics on ebay any day and there may be hundreds of offers, from holy cards to the milk of the Blessed Virgin to the True Cross. To believers it is just one more modern intrusion into the sacred. To others it is cause for a new crusade. To others it is fakery that pushes the envelope of both belief and just how far bad taste can go. The largest group opposing such sales is called the International Crusade for Holy Relics (ICHR). They have singled out the online auctioneers, the largest three being ebay, Yahoo!, and Amazon, to halt the trade. ICHR is the reaction of several faiths to the sale of relics. In attempting to reach a suitable compromise, ebay has agreed that no body parts will be allowed (anymore), but it has not gone as far as accepting the class designations of the Catholic Church. As a result, ebay regularly misses items that include bone fragments or even flesh, as there is a certain amount of coding that is used. While the code is not complicated, it can confuse a buyer or a seller and thereby allow the auctioneers to facilitate trade in the forbidden. One such coded reference is the church's own designation of "class one" relics. These range from items of the Crucifixion to bones of the saints. They imply a bone fragment is within the reliquary being sold, and while the description will avoid being too specific, generally the saint whose bone is housed in the reliquary will be named.

Ex-ossibus isn't exactly a code, it is simply a Latin description, letting the buyer know there is a bone. Buyers and sellers know what this means, as most likely does the company taking the listing, but apparently at the time of this writing, avoiding being blatant is a suitable compromise.

On one day (March 12, 2003) several unusually significant items were offered: "Ex. Velo BVM" refers to a piece of the veil or clothing of Mary, the mother of Jesus. While such a rarity might have been reason enough to build a cathedral, today the bid starts under $100.

A regular "power-seller," that is a person with over $2,000 per month in ebay sales, lists a reliquary holding a piece of the True Cross and separately a piece of the Crown of Thorns. The starting bid again was $99, with a reserve over $800. Steep in comparison to other online auctions but not in regard to prices, "authentic" relics have brought when trading hands. The power-seller, Clem73 of Hollywood, Florida,[10] did not respond to the author's questions as to the provenance of the items. Ebay, through its corporate spokesman Kevin Pursglove, explained that sellers do not have to respond. Authenticity is not ebay's concern, and fraud becomes a police matter.[11] So potential buyers need to know more Latin than just *ex ossibus;* caveat emptor is even more important.

Another seller offered *Ex Lacte BMV.* In case potential buyers were challenged by the Latin, the seller explained it meant "Of the Milk of Our Lady." While it seems like it may violate ebay's rules, many such listings are quickly posted and sold. The transactions occur before ebay even views the transaction. They refrain from allowing most human bone and body offerings, however, it is near impossible to review each listing. Often a complaint will have ebay responding by delisting the item, such as parts of the shuttle disaster and crime "memorabilia." In the case of the *Ex Lacte BVM* the seller's reserve of $445 was met, a bargain, considering he included a dozen other relics, including bone from St. Andrew. Like all relic sellers, he reminded buyers that it was the reliquary they were bidding on. The milk of the Blessed Virgin and assortment of saints' bones were a gift.

Ebay will allow certain items such as skulls to be listed, if marked for scientific or educational purposes.[12]

The Catholic Church plays opposing roles in the trade. On the one hand it commands that each altar in every church have two relics, a mandate from the authority of the Gospels. On the other, it does not allow the sale of relics. A church obtains its relics by receiving gifts from other churches. Often a church named St. Andrew will have a relic of that saint. As individuals, Catholics are forbidden to trade in the sacred for money, thus the disclaimer is commonplace. Thus the seller tells the buyer that the reliquary (the holder) is being purchased; the relic is a gift.

Not good enough, according to Tom Serafin of the ICHR, who blames the Internet for the revival of the relic trade. According to him it was dormant for five hundred years. He also established the Relic Foundation, which buys relics and puts them on a mobile display that tours the country. Serafin's Ichrusa.com Web site says ebay remains "a veritable online charnel house of holy bones."[13] According to ebay, men of the cloth have been among the buyers.

EPILOGUE: RELICS—THE LAST WORD

In a cynical (or scientific) sense the priest, the shaman, and their religions sell omnipotence. People want control, often that which is beyond their ability. When it is perceived that such control is possible, it relieves stress. The medical community peddles the same product. It is estimated that in one half of the millions of doctor visits each year in the United States, there is no real problem requiring the necessity of seeing a doctor. And in the other half, many illnesses are often cleared up without treatment.

The act of visiting the doctor, however, often produces a palpable result. The doctor, representing science, inspires and reassures the patient that the situation can be controlled by the doctor's intercession.

When the person needing help feels the problem is beyond the ability of such help, faith and prayer may be called upon. The intercession of a particular saint, from a patron saint such as St. Anne, who guides seafarers, to the saint of the last resort, St. Jude, can also provide a palpable result.

Does prayer work? A Duke University study of prayer concluded that it actually does work. Both petitionary prayer, for one's self, and intercessionary prayer, for someone else, increased the chances of surviving an illness. A Dartmouth study of heart patients and prayer came to the same conclusion. How surprising should this be?

The benefits of a doctor's role can often be measured. The results of faith and the actions of saints for the benefit of the relic bearer cannot. It does not mean that the miraculous does not exist. While it may seem that science and religion are at odds, in the future that may change. For now, science is just too young to understand.[1]

NOTES

INTRODUCTION

1. Herbert Thurston, *The Catholic Encyclopedia,* vol. 12 (New York: Robert Appleton Company, 1911). Viewed 10/2/2002, New Advent—Catholic Encyclopedia Online, www.newadvent.org/cathen/12734a.htn "Relics."
2. Paul Johnson, *A History of Christianity* (New York: Atheneum, 1976), 107.
3. Xinhua News Agency, December 15, 2002, via COMTEX.
4. Gregory of Tours, *The History of the Franks,* Betty Radice, ed., Lewis Thorpe, trans. (New York: Penguin Classics, 1974), 227.
5. Will Durant, *The Reformation* (New York: Simon & Schuster, 1957), 337.

1. THE ENIGMA OF THE SHROUD

1. Kenneth F. Weaver, "The Mystery of the Shroud," *National Geographic,* June 1980, vol. 157, no. 6.
2. The Holy Bible, Douay Rheims version (Rockford, Ill.: Tan Books and Publishers, 1899), John 20:1-6.
3. Ibid., Luke 24:12.
4. Eusebius, *The History of the Church,* translated by G. A. Williamson, edited and revised by Andrew Louth (New York: Penguin, 1989), 30-31.
5. H. LeClercq, "The Legend of Abgar," translated by Michael Tinkler, *The Catholic Encyclopedia,* vol. 1 (New York: Robert Appleton Company, 1907); online copyright © 1999 www.newadvent.org/cathen/01042c.htm, viewed 4/18/2000.
6. Ian Wilson, *The Blood and the Shroud* (New York: The Free Press, 1998), 267.
7. Dr. John H. Heller, *Report on the Shroud of Turin* (Boston: Houghton Mifflin, 1983), 72
8. Steven Runciman, *A History of the Crusades,* vol. 3 (Cambridge, England: Cambridge University Press, 1951), 123.

9. Wilson, *The Blood and the Shroud,* 273.
10. Ibid., 134.
11. Lynn Picknett and Clive Prince, *Turin Shroud, In Whose Image* (New York: HarperCollins, 1994), 120.
12. Heller, *Report on the Shroud of Turin,* 2.
13. Colin Evans, *The Casebook of Forensic Detection* (New York: John Wiley & Sons, 1996), 122.
14. Dr. Kenneth E. Stevenson and Gary R. Habermas, *Verdict on the Shroud* (Ann Arbor: Servant Books, 1981), 36.
15. Mike Fillon, "The Real Face of Jesus," *Popular Mechanics,* vol. 179, no. 12, December 2002, 71.
16. Heller, *Report on the Shroud of Turin,* 2–3.
17. Picknett and Prince, *Turin Shroud, In Whose Image,* 60–61.
18. Wilson, *The Blood and the Shroud,* 99.
19. Ibid., 98.
20. Stevenson and Habermas, *Verdict on the Shroud,* 82–83.
21. Heller, *Report on the Shroud of Turin,* 3.
22. Ibid., 140.
23. Picknett and Prince, *Turin Shroud, In Whose Image,* 13.
24. Evans, *The Casebook of Forensic Detection,* 197–198.
25. Ibid., 29.
26. Rodney Hoare, *The Turin Shroud Is Genuine* (London: Souvenir Press, 1994), 99–100.
27. David Van Biema, "Science and the Shroud," *Time,* vol. 151, no. 15, April 20, 1998.
28. Sue Benford, "New Evidence Refutes Medieval Origin of Shroud of Turin," Catholic Online, www.catholic.org/prwire/headline.php?ID=246, viewed 12/9/2002.
29. Dr. Leonicio A. Garza-Valdes, *The DNA of God* (New York: Berkley Books, 1999), 17.
30. Patrice Bousel, *Da Vinci* (New York: Konecky and Konecky, 1989), 27.
31. Picknett and Prince, *Turin Shroud, In Whose Image,* 151.
32. Dr. Kenneth E. Stevenson, *Image of the Risen Christ* (Toronto: Frontier Research Publications, 1987), 197.
33. The Holy Bible, Douay Rheims version, Matthew 27:51–54.

2. THE SACRED FACE

1. The Holy Bible, Douay Rheims version, John 20:6–7.
2. Michael Grant. *The Ancient Historians* (New York: Barnes & Noble, 1970), 347.
3. Ibid., 357.

4. Eusebius, *The History of the Church,* translated by G. A. Williamson, edited and revised by Andrew Louth (New York: Penguin, 1989), 233.

5. Elsdon Smith, *The Story of Our Names* (New York: Harper and Brothers, 1950), 173.

6. Tacitus, *The Histories,* translated by Kennet Wellesley (New York: Penguin Books, 1964), 253.

7. Kenneth Walker, *The Story of Medicine* (New York: Oxford University Press, 1955), 99.

8. Will Durant, *Age of Faith* (New York: Simon & Schuster, 1950), 986.

9. William K. Klingaman, *The First Century* (New York: Harper Perennial, 1990), 209.

10. F. Heinrich Pfeiffer, "Story and Truth in the 'Relatione historica' about the Veil of Manoppello," Sanctuario Del Volte Santo, Web site: www .Voltosante.It/english/the_story/p_pfeiffer/rel_storicapf.htm, viewed 10/26/2002.

11. Dante, *Paradiso,* canto 31, verses 103–111.

12. Joan Cruz, *Relics* (New York: Huntington, Our Sunday Visitor, 1983), 56.

13. Ean Begg, *In Search of the Holy Grail and the Precious Blood* (London: Thorsons, 1995), 106.

3. THE TRUE CROSS AND THE RELICS OF THE CRUCIFIXION

1. Jacobus de Voragine, *Golden Legend, Readings on the Saints,* translated by William Granger Ryan (Princeton, N.J.: Princeton University Press, 1993), 283.

2. The Holy Bible, Douay Rheims version (Rockford, Ill.: Tan Books and Publishers: 1899), Matthew 26:64.

3. Ibid., Matthew 27:11.

4. Steven Runciman, *A History of the Crusades,* vol. 2, 89.

5. Ibid., vol. 2, 132–133.

6. Ibid., vol. 2, 153.

7. Ibid., vol. 2, 166.

8. Ibid., vol. 2, 339.

9. Ibid., vol. 3, 17.

10. Anneli Rufus, *Magnificent Corpses* (New York: Marlowe and Company, 1999), 6.

11. The Holy Bible, Douay Rheims version, Zach 14:20.

12. Charles Homer Haskins, *The Renaissance of the 12th Century* (Cleveland: Meridian Books, 1957), 235.

13. Kristin Lawson and Anneli Rufus, *Weird Europe* (New York: St. Martin's Griffin, 1999), 39.

14. Ean Begg, *In Search of the Holy Grail and the Precious Blood,* 64.

15. Charles Homer Haskins, *The Renaissance of the 12th Century*, 235.

16. Pierre Riche, *Daily Life in the World of Charlemagne*, translated by Jo Ann McNamara (Philadelphia: University of Pennsylvania Press, 1974), 272.

4. THE SPEAR OF DESTINY

1. Jacobus de Voragine, *Golden Legend, Readings on the Saints*, translated by William Granger Ryan (Princeton, N.J.: Princeton University Press, 1993), 184.

2. C. W. Previte-Orton, *The Shorter Cambridge Medieval History*, vol. 1 (Cambridge: Cambridge University Press, 1977), 85.

3. Pierre Riche, *Daily Life in the World of Charlemagne*, 274.

4. Ibid., 276.

5. Peter Levenda, *Unholy Alliance* (New York: Avon Books, 1995), 49.

6. Ibid., 148.

7. Lynn H. Nicholas, *The Rape of Europa* (New York: Alfred A. Knopf, 1994), 40.

8. Ibid., 328–331.

9. Trevor Ravenscroft and Timothy Wallace, *The Mark of the Beast* (York Beach, Me.: Samuel Weiser, 1997), 135.

10. Charles Lawrie, " 'Dr. Stone' Walter Stein and the Holy Grail," in *The Household of the Grail*, John Matthews, ed. (New York: The Aquarian Press, 1990), 35.

11. Trevor Ravenscroft, *The Spear of Destiny* (York Beach, Me.: Samuel Weiser, 1982), 13.

12. Guy Patton and Robin Mackness, *Web of Gold: The Secret Power of a Sacred Treasure* (London: Sidgwick & Jackson, 2000), 125.

13. Michael Baigent, Richard Leigh, and Henry Lincoln, *Holy Blood, Holy Grail* (New York: Dell Books, 1983), 404.

14. Michael Baigent, Richard Leigh, and Henry Lincoln, *Messianic Legacy* (New York: Dell Books, 1986), 344.

5. THE SKULL OF JOHN THE BAPTIST

1. Francesca Ciriaci, "Controversy Aside, Wadi Kharrar Contains a Site Both Inspiring and Spiritual," *Jordan Times*, March 21, 2000, courtesy of Jordan embassy Web site: www.jordanembassyus.org/03212000010.htm, viewed 12/20/2002.

2. The Holy Bible, Douay Rheims version, Mark 6:29.

3. Maia Weinstock, "In Search of John the Baptist," *Discover*, December 2002, vol. 23, no. 12, 14.

4. The Holy Bible, Douay Rheims version, Mark 6:23.

5. Ademar of Chabannes, Chronicle of Ademar of Chabannes, Thomas Head

translation, courtesy of Hunter College Web site: http://urban.hunter.cuny.edu/~thead.ademar.htm, viewed 9/30/2002.

6. Jean Markale, *The Templar Treasure at Gisors* (Rochester, Vt.: Inner Traditions, 2003), 197.

6. THE BLESSED VIRGIN MARY

1. "Our Lady of Oz," *Fortean Times* FT 166 10, and "Pilgrims Flock to Weeping Virgin in Australia," *FarShores Para News,* posted September 8, 2002. Originally published News.com.au 9/8/2002 and viewed 2/13/2003.

2. Phillip Graham, *The Marian Conspiracy* (London: Sidgwick & Jackson, 2000), 148.

3. Douglas Adams, *The Beast Within* (New York: Avon Books, 1992), 106–107.

4. Michael Brown, *The Last Secret* (Ann Arbor: Servant Publications, 1998), 17.

5. Ibid., 31–32.

6. Ibid., 45.

7. Joan Carroll Cruz, *Relics* (Huntington, Ind.: Our Sunday Visitor, 1983), 97.

8. James J. Carney, *The Seton Miracles* (Woodridge, Va.: Mystical Rose Press, 1993), xi, 101.

7. CHRISTIANITY'S MOST SACRED WOMEN

1. Michael Baigent et al., *Holy Blood, Holy Grail,* 381.

2. Susan Haskins, *Mary Magdalen, Myth and Metaphor* (New York: Riverhead Books, 1993), 103.

3. Ibid., 111.

4. Ibid., 115.

5. Ibid., 123–124.

6. Baigent et al., *Messianic Legacy,* 100–101.

7. Eusebius, *The History of the Church,* 79.

8. Ibid., 81.

9. Ean Begg, *Cult of the Black Virgin* (London: Arkana—Penguin Books, 1985), 97.

10. Margaret Starbird, *The Goddess in the Gospels* (Sante Fe: Bear & Co., 1998), 38.

11. Baigent et al., *Holy Blood, Holy Grail,* 406.

12. Laurence Gardner, *Bloodline of the Holy Grail* (New York: Barnes & Noble, 1997), 164.

13. Susan Haskins, *Mary Magdalen, Myth and Metaphor,* 244–245.

14. Letter from Larry Haptas (administrator of the Shrine of St. Anne de Brighton) to author.

15. Courtesy of Society of the Little Flower, www.Littleflower.org/therese/faq, viewed 10/29/2002.

16. Rosie Cowan, *The Guardian,* "Saint's Remains Rekindle Ireland's Faith," April 30, 2001; www.guardian.co.uk/uk_news/story/0.3604,480479,00.htm, viewed 11/9/2003.

17. Judi Culbertson, and Tom Randall, *Permanent Italians* (New York: Walker & Co., 1996), 36–37.

18. Stan Griffin, "Stigmata," www.workersforjesus.com/stigmata.htm, viewed 11/9/2003.

19. Joan Cruz, *Mysteries, Marvels, Miracles in the Lives of the Saints* (Rockford, Ill.: Tan Books and Publishers, 1997), 121.

20. Ibid., 162.

21. Ibid., 38.

8. The Bones of Contention—the Relics of the Apostles

1. Colin Evans, *The Casebook of Forensic Detection,* 58–60.

2. Jacobus de Voragine, *Golden Legend, Readings on the Saints,* 340.

3. Eusebius, *The History of the Church,* 62.

4. Jacobus de Voragine, *Golden Legend, Readings on the Saints,* 347.

5. Joan Cruz, *Mysteries, Marvels, Miracles in the Lives of the Saints,* 359.

6. Marvin Meyer, *The Gospel of Thomas: The Hidden Sayings of Jesus* (New York: HarperCollins, 1992), 23.

7. The Holy Bible, Douay Rheims version, John 11:8–16.

8. The Holy Bible, Douay Rheims version, John 14:2–6.

9. Joan Cruz, *Mysteries, Marvels, Miracles in the Lives of the Saints,* 541.

10. Ean Begg, *In Search of the Holy Grail,* 90–91.

11. Joan Cruz, *Relics,* 109.

12. Omer Englebert, *Lives of the Saints* (New York: Barnes & Noble, 1994), 285.

13. Joan Cruz, *Relics,* 110.

14. Barbara Walker, *The Woman's Encyclopedia of Myths and Secrets* (San Francisco: Harper & Row, 1983), 460.

15. Prudence Jones and Nigel Pennick, *A History of Pagan Europe* (London: Routlege, 1995), 102.

16. Robert Eisenman, *James, Brother of Jesus* (New York: Viking, 1997), 411–416.

17. Hillary Mayell, "Jesus' Brother's Bone Box Closer to Being Authenticated," *National Geographic News,* April 18, 2003. www.nationalgeographic.com, viewed 11/10/2003.

18. Kevin Christopher, "A Forged James Ossuary?" www.Csicop.org/list/listarchive/msg00427.html, viewed 11/10/2003.

19. Eusebius, *The History of the Church,* 82.

20. Jacobus de Voragine, *Golden Legend, Readings on the Saints,* 267.

21. Joan Cruz, *Relics,* 130.

22. Barbara Walker, *The Woman's Encyclopedia of Myths and Secrets,* 482.

9. THE GOSPEL WRITERS (MARK, MATTHEW, LUKE, AND JOHN)

1. Olga Craig, "DNA Test Pinpoints St. Luke the Apostle's Remains to Padua," The Telegraph, courtesy of www.telegraph.uk/connected/main.jthml?xml=/connected/2001/10/25/ecnst25.xml, viewed 10/4/2002.
2. Patrick J. Geary, *Furta Sacra: Thefts of Relics in the Central Middle Ages* (Princeton, N.J.: Princeton University Press, 1978, rev. 1990), 88–94.
3. Jacobus de Voragine, *Golden Legend, Readings on the Saints,* 245.
4. Joan Cruz, *Relics,* 118.
5. Yury Razgulayev, "Return of the Relics of the Great Saint Mark to the New St. Mark's Cathedral," *Pravda.* Viewed courtesy of Online Pravda //english.pravda.ru/main/2002/08/29/35577.html, 3/21/03.

10. THE MIRACLES AND THE RELICS OF THE SAINTS

1. Michael Ott, "Oil of Saints," *Catholic Encyclopedia,* vol. 1, translated by Tim Drake (New York: Robert Appleton Company, 1907), online copyright 1999 www.newadvent.org/cathen/11228d.htm, viewed 10/28/2002.
2. Joan Cruz, *Relics,* 191.
3. Ibid., 192.
4. Mark Twain, *Innocents Abroad* (New York: Signet, 1966), 235.
5. Joe Nickell, *Looking for a Miracle,* 83–84.
6. Luigi Garlaschelli, "Chemistry of Supernatural Compounds 1," courtesy of CICAP, The Italian Committee for the Investigation of Claims on the Paranormal, www.cicap.org/en_artic/at101015.htm, viewed 10/22/2002.
7. Anneli, Rufus, *Magnificent Corpses,* 59–61.
8. Carol Myers, personal correspondence. See also: www.stnicholascenter.org.
9. Patrick J. Geary, *Furta Sacra,* 94–96.
10. Donald Attwater and Catherine Rachel John, *The Penguin Dictionary of Saints,* 3rd ed. (New York: Penguin Books, 1995), 260.
11. "Bones of Contention," *The Guardian,* December 22, 2000; www.guardian.co.uk/g2/story/0.3604,414584,00.html, viewed 12/27/2002.

11. NOAH'S ARK

1. David Fasnold, *The Ark of Noah* (New York: Wynwood Press, 1988), 30.
2. Ibid., 326–327.
3. Timothy Maier, "CIA Releases New Noah's Ark Documents," *Insight Magazine,* November 14, 2002; courtesy of the *Turkish Times* at www.theturkishtimes.com/f_ark.html, viewed 12/16/2002.
4. Bill Gertz, "CIA Spy Photos Sharpen Focus on Ararat Anomoly,"

Washington Times, 11/18/1997; www.noahsarksearch.com/anomaly.htm, viewed 1/18/2003.

5. Betsy McKay and Miriam Joredan, "US Satellite May Play 'I Spy' with Brazil Citrus Industry," *Wall Street Journal,* 1/28/2003.
6. Jean Markale, *Celtic Civilization* (London: Gordon & Cremonesi, 1978), 24–25.
7. Nicholas C. Flemming, *Cities in the Sea* (Garden City, N.Y.: Doubleday, 1971), 21.
8. William Ryan and William Pittman, *Noah's Flood: The New Scientific Discoveries about the Event That Changed the World* (New York: Simon & Schuster, 1998), 156–157.
9. Graham Hancock, *Fingerprints of the Gods* (New York: Three Rivers Press, 1995), 357.
10. Genesis 8:3.
11. Genesis 9:13–17.
12. C. Leonard Woolley, *The Sumerians* (New York: W. W. Norton, 1965), 124.
13. Robert Graves, *The Greek Myths: 1* (New York: Penguin, 1955), 138–143.
14. Mary Nell Wyatt, "Noah's Ark: The Story of Discovery," courtesy of www .biblerevelations.org/ronwyatt/noahsark1.htm, viewed 10/27/2002.

12. The Ark of the Covenant

1. Graham Hancock, *The Sign and the Seal* (New York: Crown Publishers, 1992), 390.
2. Thomas H. Flaherty, ed., *Lost Civilizations—The Holy Land* (Alexandria, Va.: Time-Life Books, 1992), 30.
3. Hancock, *The Sign and the Seal,* 391.
4. Christopher Knight and Robert Lomas, *The Second Messiah* (Boston: Element, 1997), 22.
5. Hancock, *The Sign and the Seal,* 394.
6. Werner Keller, *The Bible as History* (New York: William Morrow, 1956), 329.
7. Barbara Walker, *The Woman's Encyclopedia of Myths and Secrets,* 775.
8. Robert Graves, *The White Goddess* (New York: Farrar, Straus & Giroux, 1948), 190.
9. James Hogarth, *Baedeker's Ireland* (Stuttgart, Germany: Baedeker, n.d.), 191.
10. Josephus, *The Jewish War,* translated by G. A. Williamson (London: Penguin, 1970), 358.
11. Ibid.
12. Ibid., 363.
13. Ibid., 371.

14. Guy Patton and Robin Mackness, *Web of Gold: The Secret Power of a Sacred Treasure* (London: Sidgwick & Jackson, 2000), 6.

15. Josephus, *The Jewish War*, 176.

16. Oldenbourg, *Massacre at Montsegur* (London: Phoenix, 1999), 117.

17. Ibid., 361.

18. Patton and Mackness, *Web of Gold*, 59.

19. Ibid., 123.

20. Ibid., 137.

21. Michael Baigent et al., *Holy Blood, Holy Grail*, 41.

22. Andrew Sinclair, *The Sword and the Grail* (New York: Crown Publishers, 1992), 159.

23. Ibid., 190.

13. The Holy Grail

1. Paul Theroux, *The Pillars of Hercules* (New York: G. P. Putnam's Sons, 1995), 62–63.

2. Donald Attwater and Catherine Rachel John, *The Penguin Dictionary of the Saints*, 3rd ed. (New York: Penguin, 1983), 221.

3. Dr. Hans K. Weiler, *Baedecker's Spain* (Stuttgart: Baedecker, n.d.), 232.

4. David Nash Ford, "Holy Grail Candidates," www.earlybritishkingdoms .com, viewed 1/18/2003.

5. "The Antioch Chalice." Description courtesy of Cloisters, www.metmuseum .org/collections/view1.asp?dep=7&item=50.4, viewed 1/18/2003.

6. Roger Sherman Loomis, *The Grail: From Celtic Myth to Christian Symbol* (Princeton, N.J.: Princeton University Press, 1991), 28–29.

7. Norma Lorre Goodrich, *The Holy Grail* (New York: HarperCollins, 1992), 6–7.

8. Jean Markale, *The Grail, The Celtic Origins of the Sacred Icon*, translated by Jon Graham (Rochester, Vt.: Inner Traditions, 1999), 128–131.

14. The Modern Relic Trade

1. Rory Carroll, "The Ransack of Italy's History," viewed courtesy of www .dante-alighieri.org.au/Dante-News/SupplementStories/Italyshistory.htm on 3/9/2003.

2. Chris Endean, "Indiana Jones and the Temple of 'Stolen' Relics," appeared in Archeology Online, May 1, 1998, courtesy of www.museum-security .org/reports/003299.html, viewed 3/9/2003.

3. Andrew L. Slayman, "The Looting of Italy," *Archeology*, vol. 51, no. 3 May/ June 1958.

4. For a list of stolen and recovered art and relics, see www.interpol.int.
5. Tunku Varadarajan, "French Joyful as Stolen Relics Found," *London Times*, courtesy of Museum Security at www.museum-security.org/reports/02978.html, viewed 11/12/2003.
6. "Russian Customs Seize Michael Jackson's Saber," Canoe, courtesy of www.canoe.ca/JamMusicMichaelJackson/Sep19_Jackosaber.html, viewed 11/14/2003.
7. "Church Sues Dutch Icon Dealer," Cyprus News Agency, courtesy of Hellenic Resources Network, www.hri.org/news/cyprus/can/97-07-01 .can.html, viewed 11/14/2003.
8. Dan Hofstadter, *Goldberg's Angel* (New York: Farrar, Straus & Giroux, 1994), 49.
9. See www.fbi.gov and www.fbi.gov/hq/cid/artheft/arththeft.htm.
10. Item viewed as eBay item 719845541.
11. Interview with author 3/12/2003.
12. Interview with author 3/12/2003.
13. Jeff Sypeck, "Relics for Sale," source: www.ichrusa.com/courtyard/web-articles/relics-for-sale.htm, viewed 10/2/2002.

EPILOGUE: RELICS—THE LAST WORD

1. Dan Brown, *Angels and Demons* (New York: Pocket Star, 2001).

BIBLIOGRAPHY

Adams, Ansel. *The Negative.* Boston: Little, Brown & Co., 1981.

Adams, Douglas. *The Beast Within.* New York: Avon, 1992.

Andrews, Richard, and Paul Shellenberger. *The Tomb of God.* New York: Little, Brown & Co., 1996.

Ashe, Geoffrey. *Dawn Behind the Dawn.* New York: Henry Holt, 1992.

Attwater, Donald, and Catherine Rachel John. *The Penguin Dictionary of the Saints.* New York: Penguin, 1983.

Baigent, Michael, Richard Leigh, and Henry Lincoln. *Holy Blood, Holy Grail.* New York: Dell, 1983.

——. *Messianic Legacy.* New York: Dell, 1986.

Begg, Ean. *In Search of the Holy Grail and the Precious Blood.* London: Harper-Collins, 1995.

——. *The Cult of the Black Virgin.* London: Arkana—Penguin Books, 1985.

Blum, Howard. *The Lucifer Principle: A Scientific Expedition into the Forces of History.* New York: Atlantic Monthly Press, 1995.

Bousel, Patrice. *Da Vinci.* New York: Konecky and Konecky, 1989.

Brown, Michael H. *The Last Secret.* Ann Arbor, Mich.: Servant Publications, 1998.

Butler, John. *The Quest for Becket's Bones.* New Haven: Yale University Press, 1995.

Campbell, Joseph. *Occidental Mythology: The Masks of God.* New York: Viking Penguin, 1976.

Carney, James L. *The Seton Miracles.* Woodbridge, Va.: Mystical Rose Press, 1993.

Carroll, Donal, and Derek Davies. *Traveler's Turkey Companion.* Guilford, Conn.: The Globe Pequot Press, 1999.

Carston, Peter Thiede, and Matthew D'Ancona. *The Quest for the True Cross.* New York: Palgrave, 2002.

Case, Thomas W. *The Shroud of Turin and the Carbon 14 Dating Fiasco.* Cincinnati: White Horse Press, 1996.

Cosman, Madelaine. *Medieval Workbook.* New York: Facts on File, 1996.

Crossan, John Dominic, and Jonathan L. Reed *Excavating Jesus.* New York: HarperCollins, 2001.

Cruz, Joan Carroll. *Relics.* Huntington, Ind.: Our Sunday Visitor Inc., 1983.

———. *Mysteries, Marvels and Miracles in the Lives of the Saints.* Rockford, Ill.: Tan Books and Publishers Inc., 1997.

———. *The Incorruptibles.* Rockford, Ill.: Tan Books and Publishers Inc., 1997.

Culbertson, Judi, and Tom Randall. *Permanent Italians.* New York: Walker and Company, 1996.

Dalrymple, William. *From the Holy Mountain.* New York: Henry Holt, 1997.

Durant, Will. *The Story of Civilization: Age of Faith.* New York: Simon & Schuster, 1950.

Eisenman, Robert. *James, Brother of Jesus.* New York: Viking, 1997.

Englebert, Omer. *The Lives of the Saints.* New York: Barnes & Noble, 1994.

Eusebius. *The History of the Church.* Translated by G. A. Williamson and edited and revised by Andrew Louth. London: Penguin, 1989.

Evans, Colin. *The Casebook of Forensic Detection.* New York: John Wiley & Sons, 1996.

Fasnold, David. *The Ark of Noah.* New York: Wynwood Press, 1988.

Flaherty, Thomas H., ed. *Lost Civilizations—The Holy Land.* Alexandria, Va.: Time-Life Books, 1992.

Flemming, Nicholas C. *Cities in the Sea,* Garden City, N.Y.: Doubleday, 1971.

Frazer, Sir James George. *The Golden Bough.* New York: Collier Books, 1922.

Furneaux, Rupert. *Ancient Mysteries.* New York: Ballantine Books, 1977.

Gardner, Laurence. *Bloodline of the Holy Grail.* New York: Barnes & Noble Books, 1997.

Garza-Valdes, Leoncio A. *The DNA of God.* New York: Berkley Books, 1999.

Geary, Patrick J. *Furta Sacra.* Princeton, N.J.: Princeton University Press, 1978.

Gies, Joseph, and Frances Gies. *Life in a Medieval City.* New York: Thomas Y. Crowell, 1969.

Gilbert, Adrian, Alan Wilson, and Baram Blacknett. *The Holy Kingdom.* London: Corgi Books, 1999.

Goodrich, Norma Lorre. *King Arthur.* New York: Harper & Row, 1986.

———. *The Holy Grail.* New York: HarperCollins, 1992.

Grant, Michael. *The Ancient Historians.* New York: Barnes & Noble Books, 1970.

———. *Jesus: A Historian's Review of the Bible.* New York: Charles Scribner's Sons, 1977.

Graves, Robert. *The White Goddess.* New York: Farrar, Straus & Giroux, 1948.

———. *The Greek Myths 1.* Middlesex, England: Penguin Books, 1955.

Hancock, Graham. *Fingerprints of the Gods.* New York: Three Rivers Press, 1995.

———. *The Sign and the Seal.* New York: Crown Publishers, 1992.

Haskins, Charles Homer. *The Renaissance of the 12th Century.* New York: Meridian Books, 1957.

Haskins, Susan. *Mary Magdalen, Myth and Metaphor.* New York: Riverhead Books, 1993.

Heller, Dr. John H. *Report on the Shroud of Turin.* Boston: Houghton Mifflin, 1983.

Hoare, Rodney. *The Turin Shroud Is Genuine.* London: Souvenir Press, 1994.

Hogarth, James. *Baedeker's Ireland.* Stuttgart, Germany: Baedeker, n.d.

Jacobus de Voragine. *The Golden Legend, Readings on the Saints.* Translated by William Granger Ryan. Princeton, N.J.: Princeton University Press, 1993.

James, Peter, and Nick Thorn. *Ancient Mysteries.* New York: Ballantine, 1999.

Johnson, Paul. *A History of Christianity.* New York: Athenem, 1976.

Jones, Prudence, and Nigel Pennick. *A History of Pagan Europe.* London: Routledge, 1995.

Keller, Werner. *The Bible as History.* New York: Bantam/William Morrow, 1956.

Kersten, Holgar, and Elmer R. Gruber. *The Jesus Conspiracy: The Turin Shroud and the Truth about the Resurrection.* Shaftesbury, Dorset: Element, 1994.

Klausner, Joseph. *From Jesus to Paul.* New York: Macmillan Co., 1943.

Klingerman, William K. *The First Century.* New York: Harper Perennial, 1990.

Knight, Christopher, and Robert Lomas. *The Second Messiah,* Boston: Element, 1997.

Laidler, Keith. *The Head of God: The Lost Treasure of the Templars.* London: Orion, 1998.

Lawson, Kristan, and Anneli Rufus. *Weird Europe.* New York: St. Martin's Griffin, 1999.

Levenda, Peter. *Unholy Alliance.* New York: Avon, 1995.

Lincoln, Henry. *The Holy Place.* London: Corgi Books, 1991.

Loomis, Roger Sherman. *The Grail: From Celtic Myth to Christian Symbol.* Princeton, N.J.: Princeton University Press, 1991.

Mac Cana, Proinsias. *Celtic Mythology.* New York: Peter Bedrick Books, 1985.

Magnusson, Magnus. *Archeology of the Bible.* New York: Simon & Schuster, 1977.

Markale, Jean. *Celtic Civilization.* London: Gordon & Cremonesi, 1978.

———. *Merlin, Priest of Nature.* Rochester, Vt.: Inner Traditions, 1995.

——. *The Grail: The Celtic Origins of the Sacred Icon.* Rochester, Vt.: Inner Traditions, 1999.

——. *The Templar Treasure at Gisors.* Rochester, Vt.: Inner Traditions, 2003.

Matthews, John, ed. *The Household of the Grail.* New York: The Aquarian Press, 1990.

Meyer, Marvin. *The Gospel of Thomas.* New York: HarperCollins, 1992.

Nickell, Joe. *Inquest on the Shroud of Turin.* Buffalo, N.Y.: Prometheus Books, 1983.

——. *Looking for a Miracle.* Amherst, N.Y.: Prometheus Books, 1998.

Nicholas, Lynn H. *The Rape of Europa.* New York: Alfred A. Knopf, 1994.

Oldenbourg, Zoe. *The Crusades.* New York: Pantheon Books, 1966.

——. *Massacre at Montsegur.* London: Phoenix, 1999.

Patton, Guy, and Robin Mackness. *Web of Gold: The Secret Power of a Sacred Treasure.* London: Sidgwick & Jackson, 2000.

Phillips, Graham. *The Marian Conspiracy.* London: Sidgwick & Jackson, 2000.

Picknett, Lynn, and Clive Prince. *Turin Shroud, In Whose Image.* New York: HarperCollins, 1994.

——. *The Templar Revelation.* New York: Simon & Schuster, 1997.

Previte-Orton, C. W. *The Shorter Cambridge Medieval History,* vol. 1. Cambridge: Cambridge University Press, 1952.

Ravenscroft, Trevor. *The Spear of Destiny.* York Beach, Me.: Samuel Weiser, 1982.

Ravenscroft, Trevor, and Timothy Wallace. *The Mark of the Beast.* York Beach, Me.: Samuel Weiser, 1997.

Rees, Alwyn, and Brinley Rees. *Celtic Heritage.* London: Thames and Hudson, 1961.

Riche, Pierre. *Daily Life in the World of Charlemagne.* Translated by Jo Ann McNamara. Philadelphia: University of Pennsylvania Press, 1978.

Robinson, James M. *The Nag Hammadi Library.* San Francisco: Harper & Row, 1977.

Ross, Anne, and Don Robbins. *The Life and Death of a Druid Priest.* New York: Summit Books, 1989.

Rufus, Anneli. *Magnificent Corpses.* New York: Marlowe and Company, 1999.

Runciman, Steven. *A History of the Crusades.* Cambridge: Cambridge University Press, 1951.

Ryan, William, and William Pittman. *Noah's Flood: The New Scientific Discoveries about the Event That Changed the World.* New York: Simon & Schuster, 1998.

Schonfield, Hugh J. *The Passover Plot.* The Netherlands: Bernard Geis Association, 1965.

——. *The Jesus Party.* New York: Macmillan, 1974.

Sinclair, Andrew. *The Sword and the Grail.* New York: Crown Publishers, 1992.

Sklar, Dusty. *The Nazis and the Occult.* New York: Dorset Press, 1977.

Smith, Elsdon S. *The Story of Our Names.* New York: Harper & Brothers, 1950.

Smith, Asbury. *The Twelve Christ Chose.* New York: Harper & Brothers, 1958.

Starbird, Margaret. *The Goddess in the Gospels.* Sante Fe, N.M.: Bear & Co., 1998.

Stevenson, Kenneth E. *Image of the Risen Christ.* Toronto: Frontier Research Publications, 1987.

Stevenson, Kenneth E., and Gary R. Habermas. *Verdict on the Shroud.* Ann Arbor: Servant Books, 1981.

Strachan, Gordon. *Jesus, the Master Builder: Druid Mysteries and the Dawn of Christianity.* Edinburgh: Floris Books, 1998.

Sykes, Brian. *The Seven Daughters of Eve: The Science That Reveals our Genetic Ancestry.* New York: W. W. Norton, 2001.

Tacitus. *The Histories.* Translated by Kenneth Wellesley. New York: Penguin Books, 1964.

Theroux, Paul. *The Pillars of Hercules: A Grand Tour of the Mediterranean.* New York: G. P. Putnam's Sons, 1995.

Treece, Patricia. *The Sanctified Body.* New York: Doubleday, 1989.

Walker, Barbara G. *The Woman's Encyclopedia of Myths and Secrets.* New York: Harper & Row, 1983.

Walker, Kenneth. *The Story of Medicine.* New York: Oxford University Press, 1955.

Weiler, Hans K. *Baedeker's Spain.* Stuttgart, Germany: Baedeker, n.d.

Wilson, Ian. *Jesus: The Evidence.* San Francisco: HarperCollins, 1984.

———. *The Blood and the Shroud.* New York: The Free Press, 1998.

Woolley, C. Leonard. *The Sumerians.* New York: W. W. Norton, 1965.

INDEX

Aachen, Germany (formerly Aix-la-Chapelle), 7, 60, 69, 73, 143; Cathedral at, 11, 73
Abbey Church of Saint Mary Magdalene at Vezelay, 105, 109
Abbot Suger's Chalice, 209
Abgar V, King, 15–16
Abgar VIII, 17
Abu Saud, Effendi, 136
Acciaioli, Captain Leone degli, 129
acheiropoietoe (image made not by human hands), 16, 47
Acre, 59; bishop of, 57
Acts of Pilate, 76; on Veil of Veronica, 43, 44–45
Acts of Thaddeus, 17
Acts of the Apostles, 46, 140, 143, 145
Acts of Thomas, 127, 128
Adam, 93
Adana Air Base, Turkey, 170
Addai, 16
Adler, Alan, 26–27, 31
Aedh, 196
Aegeus (Roman proconsul), 124
Aengus, 196
Agrippina, 122
Ahio and Oza, 187
Aistulf, 47
Aix-la-Chapelle. See Aachen, Germany (formerly Aix-la-Chapelle)
Alaric, 67, 199
Albanopolis (now Baku), 142
Alexandria, Egypt, 81; St. Mark's body in, 146, 147, 148
Alfonso VI, King, 49
Alfred, the canon of Durham, 10

Alphonse the Magnanimous, 207
Amalfi, Italy, 126
Amaseno, Italy, 157–158
Ambrose, St., 4–5, 6, 8, 67, 157
American Commission for the Protection and Salvage of Artistic and Historic Monuments in War Areas (Monuments Commission), 74
Amiens, France, head of St. John the Baptist in, 82, 87–88
Amphictyon, son of Deucalion, 180
Anastasios, Emperor, 142
Andre of Montbard, 190
Andrew, St., 5, 11, 78, 123–126, 221
angels, 84
Anicetus, Pope, 122
Anjara, shrine of the Blessed Virgin at, 80
Annas (adviser to the Sanhedrin), 65
Anne, St. (grandmother of Jesus), 8, 11, 109–112, 209, 223
Annunciation, the, 91–92
anorexia nervosa, 117
Anthony of Padua, St., 159–160, 203
Antioch, Asia Minor, 208
Antioch chalice, 209–210
Antoninus of Piacenza, St., 76, 78
apocryphal Gospels, 62, 101, 102–103
Apollo, spear of, 210
Apollonj-Ghetti, Bruno, 120
apostles. See names of individual apostles
Apostolic Palace, Rome, 1

apparitions, 1, 2, 3; of Blessed Virgin Mary, 2, 90, 99, 131
Appollonea, St., 45
Apt, France, 110, 111
Aquitane, France, 88
Arameans, 86
Ararat, Mount, 4, 167–172, 181, 182, 183; geopolitical obstacles to exploration of the region, 168, 172, 181
Arbash Cipher, 89
Arch of Titus, 198
Aretas, King, 85, 86
Arguelles, Bishop Ramon, 114
Arian Christians, 66, 199, 200–201
ArkImaging, 167
Ark of Noah. See Noah's Ark
Ark of the Covenant, 95, 182, 184–205; creating, 185–186; Ethiopia and, 184, 185, 189, 190–191, 193–194; in France, 185, 199–204; Ireland and, 194–197; Knights Templar and, 184, 190–191, 204; powers of, 184, 186–187, 188, 205; in Rome, 198–199; in Rosslyn Chapel, Scotland, 185, 204; Temple of Solomon and, 188, 189
Armenia as landing site for Noah's Ark, 168, 175, 178, 181, 182
Arnald-Amalric, 202
Aroulf (French bishop), 17
Artemis, goddess, 151
Asclepiodotus, 52
Asclepius, 8
Ashurbannipal, library of, 176
Asmodeus (demon), 203
Assumption of Mary, 92–93
Assyrians, 189

Ataulphus, 199
Athanagild, King, 68
Athanasius, Bishop, 94
Athelstan (ruler of England), 70
Attila, 9
Augustine (church writer), 124
Augustine, St., 5, 45
Auspicius, St., 110
Austria, 71, 73
Autun, France, 106
Ayios Anastasios Church, Peristerona, 218
Azarius, 189

Babylonian Captivity, 116, 189, 194, 197
Babylonian story of the flood, 176–178
Bagatti, P., 136
Baima-Bollone, Pierluigi, 28
Bajazet, Sultan, 78
Baldwin, King, 56
Baldwin II, King, 58, 190
Ballestrero, Cardinal of Turin, 29
Bannockburn, battle of, 9, 190
baptism, 83
Barbet, Dr. Pierre, 23, 24
Barbujani, Guido, 144
Bari, Italy, 160, 165–166
Barnabas (cousin of St. Mark), 148
Baronio, Cardinal, 125
Baruch (Simon Brugh or Brach) (scribe), 194, 196
Basilica di Sant Antonio in Padua, 159
Basilica of Mount Sion, 76
Basilica of St. Justina, Padua, 145
Basilica of St. Mark, Venice, 147
Basilica of St. Thérèse of the Child Jesus, Normandy, 112
Basilica of the Holy Apostles, Rome, 141
Basilica of the Holy Blood, St. Basil's Chapel, Belgium, 60
Becket, St. Thomas à, archbishop of Canterbury, 100
Bede, St., 10
Benedict, St., 10
Benedict XIV, Pope, 78
Beneveto, Italy, 142
Benford, M. Sue, 31, 32, 36
Bernadette, St., 152–153
Bernadine, St., 45
Bernard, St., 108, 190, 201

Bernini, 122–123
Berosus, 169
Bertelli, Ruggero, 63
Bertz, Bill, 171
Bevilacqua, Cardinal Anthony, 113
Bible Code, The (Drosnin), 184
Biblical Archeology Review, 133
biofeedback, 8
Birth of Venice, 132
Black Sea, 174, 175, 179, 181
Black Virgin, 97
Blaise, St., 8–9, 45
Blessed Virgin Mary, 7, 11, 43, 80, 90–99, 109, 150, 151, 152–153; the Annunciation, 91–92; apparitions of, 2, 90, 99, 131; the Assumption, 92–93; feast days, 91–93; goddess role and, 93–95, 101; Immaculate Conception, 92; in the New World, 96–97; tomb of, 92, 93; Veil of Veronica and, 46; weeping statues of, 2, 90–91, 99
blood, 1, 5; of St. Gennaro, 154–157; of St. Lawrence (San Lorenzo), 157–158; thixotropy effect, 154–155, 156, 158. *See also individual relics*
bodies or body parts, incorrupt, 2, 3, 152–153, 158–159
Bollinger, Jim, 193
Bollone, Dr., 63
Bonaventura (sister of St. Catherine of Siena), 114
Bonaventure, St., 159
bones, 1, 2, 5; "manna" from. See "manna." *See also names of individuals*
Bonus (Venetian merchant), 147
Bormann, Martin, 203
Boston, Massachusetts, 9
Botolph, St., 9
Botticelli, Sandro, 132
Boulouge, chapel at, 96
Bramante, 122
Bran's cauldron (Bron's cauldron, Cauldron of Dagda), 206, 210
Bretons of France, 111
brigantes, 132
Brigit, Brigantine sea goddess, 131–132
Brigit, St., 132
British Society for the Turin Shroud (BSTS), 24
Brittany, 111

Bron's cauldron (Bran's cauldron, Cauldron of Dagda), 206, 210
Brookhaven Laboratory, 29
Brother of Jesus, The (Witherington), 137
Bruce, James, 190–191
Bruges, Belgium, 60
Bruges Grail, 209
Brugioni, Dino, 171
Bruse, Father Jim, 99
Bryce, Sir James, 169
Brydon, Robert, 192
Bucklin, Dr. Robert, 22
Buddha, 6
Burke's Peerage, 21
Bush, George H. W., 167
Byzantine armies, 47
Byzantine art, depictions of Jesus in, 17

Cabrini, St. Francis, 46
Caesarea, Christian library at, 42
Cahill, Dr. Thomas, 27
Caiaphas (high priest), 65
Caligula, 46, 122
Callahan, Dr. Philip, 98
Calvin, John, 62, 109, 143, 204
Cambodia, 217
Camino de Santiago, the Way of St. James, 129–130
Cammarata, Vincenzo, 216–217
Camorra, the, 156
Canale, Marcello, 28
Canterbury Cathedral, 142
Capilla del Santo Caliz, Valencia, 206–207, 208
Cappella Carafa, Duomo of Naples, 155
Cappella del Tesoro, Duomo of Naples, 155
carbon 14 dating, 40, 89, 135, 146; errors, 29, 30–31; of Shroud of Turin, 2, 13–14, 29–32, 33, 42
Carcassonne, France, 199, 200
Carmelite monasteries, 113
Carnivale, 211
Carolingians, 109, 146, 199
Carthusian monks, 100
Casanova, Baron, 110
Castle Church, Wittenberg, 9–10
Cathars, 19, 185, 201–202, 204, 213
Cathedral of Notre Dame, Amiens, 87–88
Cathedral of Notre Dame, Chartres, 94, 95

Cathedral of Our Lady of the Pillar, Sargossa, Spain, 11

Cathedral of St. John the Baptist, Chapel of the Holy Shroud, Turin, 14

Cathedral of St. Thomas, Mylapore, 128

Cathedral of St. Vitus, Prague, 146

Cathedral of the Sacred Heart, Newark, 113

Cathedral San Lorenzo, Genoa, 208–209

Catherine dei Ricci, St., 153

Catherine of Bologna, St., 153

Catherine of Siena, St., patron saint of Italy (Catherine di Benincasa), 114–117; *Dialogue* of, 116–117

Catholic Encyclopedia, 76, 93

Catholic World News, 197

Cauldron of Dagda (Bran's cauldron, Bron's cauldron), 206, 210

Cave of the Seven Sleepers, 103

Cedrono, Giorgio, 47

celibacy: the Cathar *perfecti* and, 201; St. Thomas' views on, 128

Celtic Grail, 206, 210–211

Central Intelligence Agency (CIA), 4, 167, 171

Charlemagne, 7, 60, 68–69, 73, 74, 78, 96, 105, 110, 111, 150; crown of, 109

Charles, Prince, 166

Charles Martel (Charles the Hammer), 68, 200

Charles of Borromeo, St., 60

Charles the Bald, king of France, 62, 95

Charroux Abbey, 62

Chartres, France, 94, 95

Chicago, Illinois, 160

Chinese belief in healing through gods, 8

Chios, island of, 129

Chosroes I Anushirvan, King, 17, 78

Chrétien de Troyes, 211

Christian Coptic Chruch, 146, 148, 211

Christians of St. Thomas, 128

Christina, Queen, 123

Christmas customs, 163–164

Chronicon Paschale, 78

Churchill, Winston, 75

Church of Cyprus, 218

Church of Our Lady of Fatima, Brighton Park, 110, 111–112

Church of San Bartolomeo, Rome, 142

Church of Santa Croce in Gerusalemme, Rome, 63–64, 129

Church of Santa Maria Sopra Minerva, Rome, 114

Church of St. Catherine's, Germany, 73

Church of St. Francis, Lanciano, 63

Church of St. Maria, Amaseno, 158

Church of St. Matthew, Trier, 150

Church of St. Sophia, Constantinople, 78

Church of the Holy Cross, Jerusalem, 63

Church of the Holy Sepulcher, Jerusalem, 55

Church of the Intercession, Russia, 218

Church of the Most Holy Virgin, Ephesus, 94

Cid, El, 49

Cistercian order of monks, 108; monastery of la Boissiere, France, 7, 57

Claremont-Gannueau, Charles, 136

Clare of Assisi, St., 153

Clarke, Douglas, 91

Clement (early church writer and bishop), 148

Clement I, Pope, 45, 46

Clement III, Pope, 105

Clement IV, Pope, 106

Clement VI, Pope, 202

Clement of Alexandria, 103, 134

Cleophas (brother of Joseph), 133

Cloisters Museum, 209

Clotilde, Princess of Savoy, 21

Coca-Cola advertisements, St. Nicholas and, 164

Codex Atlanticus (da Vinci), 34

Codex Valenciennes, 50

Coel, king of the Britons, 52

Comiskey, Bishop Brendan, 114

Commodus, Emperor, 17

Confucius, 6

Constantine, Emperor, 52, 78, 81, 102, 122, 123, 125, 133, 150, 162; importance to Catholic Church, 54–55; Spear of Destiny and, 66

Constantinople, 5, 58, 61, 78, 81–82, 103–104, 145; sacking of, 18, 56, 82, 103–104; St.

Andrew's remains and, 125, 126; Shroud of Turin in, 18, 31; Veil of Veronica and, 46

Constantius, Emperor, 52, 145

"Contest of the Singers at Wartburg, The," 213

Coon, Carleton, 22

Copper Scrolls, 190

Coptic Church, Christian, 146, 148, 211

Cordero, Gil, 97

Cornish legend of the Y's, 173

Cornucopia, the Horn of Plenty, 206, 210

Correnti, Verenando, 120

Council of Nicaea of 325, 54, 93–94, 162

Crispell, Tom, 171

crops, blessing the, 9

Crotser, Tom, 193

Crown of Thorns, 11, 41, 58–59, 60, 64, 82, 129; wounds made by, 24

crucifixion, 24

Crucifixion, the, 43–44, 54, 92, 142–143; Crown of Thorns (*see* Crown of Thorns); Gospel accounts of, 15, 24; nails of, 2, 11, 53, 58, 59–61, 64, 129; nail wounds, 23–24, 29; the reed, 61; sacred blood of Jesus, 60–61; scourging, 24, 43; sponge given to Jesus to drink, 58, 59, 60, 61; Stations of the Cross (Way of the Cross), 44; three crosses of, 52, 53, 65, 129; True Cross (*see* True Cross); wound from spear of Longinus, 24, 36, 43, 65, 76–77 (*see also* spear of Longinus)

Crusades, 3, 7, 18, 47, 56, 57, 58, 61, 82, 87, 201–202, 208

Currer-Briggs, Noel, 20–21

Cuthbert, St., 9

Cybele, goddess, 151

Cypriot Orthodox churches, theft of religious relics from, 218

Cyprus, island of, 218, 219

Cyprus v. Goldberg, 219

Cyril, Bishop, 55

Czestochowa, Poland, 96

da Bomba, Donato, 48

Dagobert, King, 95

Dagobert II, King, 200

Daguerre, Louis, 34

D'Alema, Massimo, 216

Damascus, Syria, 87
Dan (seafaring people), 195
Dan, tribe of, 195
Danae, people of the goddess, 195
Dandolo, Enrico, doge of Venice, 82
Danes, 195
Dante Alighieri, 47
Danu (Tuatha de Danaan), people of the goddess, 195
D'Arcis, Pierre, Bishop of Troyes, 19, 35
Dartmouth study on efficacy of prayer, 223
da Sangallo, Antoni, 122
David, King, 188
Davidic bloodline, lineage of Jesus and, 83, 106–107, 133, 212
da Vinci, Leonardo, 33–35
Dead Sea Scrolls, 83
de Boron, Robert, 212
Debretts, 21
de Charnay, Geoffrey, 19–20
de Charny, Geoffrey, 19, 20, 21
de Charny, Margaret, 20
de Charny family, 19, 20
de Fabritiis, Donato Antonio, 48
Defense Intelligence Agency (DIA), 171
Delage, Yves, 23
de Lille de Charpigny, Hugh, 19
de Mely, M., 78
de Molay, Jacques, 20, 35
de Pairaud, Hugues, 89
De pignoribus sanctorum (Guibert of Nogent), 60
de Roussillon, Count Girart, 105
de Sarton, Wallon, 87
de Schoye, Repanse, 202
Deucalion, 175, 180
Devan, Don, 27
de Vergy, Jeanne, 19, 21
de Vergy family, 20
de Villiers, Gerard, 21
di Clari, Robert, 18
Dictionaire Historique de Moreri 1759, Le, 202
Diego, Juan, 96
Digos (special Italian police force), 215, 217
Dikman, Aydin, 219
Diocletian, Emperor, 52, 162
Dionysus, Bishop of Alexandria, 42
Divine Comedy (Dante), 47

DNA testing, 82, 89, 118, 137, 144; Shroud of Turin and, 28, 38
Doctor at Cavalry, A (Barbet), 23
doctor visits, results of, 223
Dogubayazit, Turkey, 168
Dominican order, 115, 117
Domitian, Emperor, 107, 138, 150, 151
dove, symbol of the, 83
Drosnin, Michael, 184
Druids, 164, 210
Duke University, 223
Duomo di San Lorenzo, Genoa, 208–209

Eadgita, 70
ebay, 220, 221, 222
Edessa, 15–17, 18, 31, 128, 129
Edward the Confessor, 45
Egeria, 55
Egypt and Egyptians, 194–195; illness, beliefs about, 45; mummies, carbon dating of, 29
Eisner, Kurt, 71, 72
Elias, prophet, 80
Elizabeth (sister of Blessed Virgin Mary), 91–92
elution absorption method, 63
Emesa, Phoenicia, 81
Enrico, Giuseppe, 22–23
Ephesus and Ephesians, 93–94, 103, 151; council of 431 at, 94
Epic of Gilgamesh, 176–178
Epiphanius (4th-century Christian writer), 44
Epiphanius, Bishop (in Cyprus), 94
Epiphanius of Salamis, Bishop, 169
Epiphany, feast of the, 211
Erasmus, St., 45
Erzurum, Turkey, 168
Eschel, Hanan, 82
Eschenbach, Wolfram von, 74, 202, 212, 213
Essenes, 82, 83–84
Etheria of Galicia, 103
Ethiopia: Ark of the Covenant and, 184, 185, 189, 190–191, 193–194; Timkat celebration in, 184, 185, 191, 194
Ethiopian Christians, 194
Ethiopian Orthodox church, 184
Etschmiadzin, Armenia, 78
Eucharistic miracle of Lanciano, 62–63
Eucharius, St., 150

Eugenius III, Pope, 105
Euphemia of Chalcedon, St., 59
Eusebius, 16, 42, 44, 53, 95, 107, 121, 138
Eve, 93, 94, 95, 213
Evening Telegraph (England), 82
Evremar, Patriarch, 56–57
Exodus, book of, 185–186
Exuviae Sacrae Constantinopolitanae, 78
Ezekial, 66, 192

Falasha Jews, 193–194
Fasnold, David, 182
Father Christmas Foundation, 164
Fatima, 191
favors, relics given to provide, 2, 7
feast of Cana, wedding, 92
Federal Bureau of Investigation (FBI), 4, 215, 217, 218–220; National Stolen Art File, 220
Ferdinand and Isabella, 130
Fermin, St., 87
Ferrua, Antonio, 120
Festa, Giorgio, 153
Fillan, St., 9
Fitzmyer, Reverend Joseph, 135
Flavius Josephus, 169
flogging, 24, 43
Flood, stories of the great. *See* Noah's Ark
Florence, Italy, 117
Florida, 171–172
forgery of relics, 6, 11, 24
Forster, Dr. Edmund, 71
Foundation for the Preservation of Turkish Monuments, 164
Francis Assisi, St., 115
Franciscans, 59, 62–63, 159
Franks, 47, 56, 146, 199–200
Frederick Barbarossa, 70
Frederick II Hohenstauffer 70–71
Free Corps, 72
Freedom of Informatio 167
Freeh, Louis, 137
Freemasonry, 190–?
Frei, Dr. Max, 25, ?
French Revolutio
106
Freres, Kouch
Freud, Sigm?
Freund, Ri?
Fulk of Cl?

furta sacra, 10
Futterer, Antonia Frederick, 193

Gabriel, archangel of God, 91
Gaius (Christian writer), 122
Galician Holy Grail, 130
Garden of Eden, 16, 92
Garlaschelli, Dr. Luigi, 158
Garza-Valdes, Dr. Leoncio, 32, 36, 98
Gascoyne, Captain, 169
Gawain and the Green Knight, 211
Genesis, 213; Noah story in, 175–176
Genevieve, St., 9
Gennaro, St., 3, 154–157
Genoa Holy Grail, 208–209
Geoffrey (Cluniac abbot), 105
Geological Society of America, 174
Germanorden, 72
Gervase of Tilbury, 19
Gervasius, 4–5
Getty Museum, 219; Malibu, 216
Gibraltar, 200
Gilgamesh, 176–178, 180
Giselle de Razes, 200
Giuliani, Rudy, 137
goddesses, 93, 97, 151, 180, 210–211; Mary and goddess role, 93–95, 101; Mary Magdalene and goddess role, 101
Golan, Oded, 137
Goldberg, Peg, 219
Golden Calf, 186
Golden Legend, The (Voragine), 53
Gonella, Luigi, 29
Gospel of John. *See* John, St., Gospel of
Gospel of John the Evangelist, 83, 150
Gospel of Luke. *See* Luke, St., Gospel of
Gospel of Mark. *See* Mark, St., Gospel of
Gospel of Mary, 103
Gospel of Matthew. *See* Matthew, St., Gospel of
Gospel of Nicodemus, 44, 76
Gospel of Philip, 103
Gospel of Thomas, 103, 126–127
Goths, 67, 93, 123, 199
Grove, Dr. Harry, 28, 29
Grail castle, 202, 203, 213
Grand Sainte Graal, 212
Greek flood story, 179–181

Greek Orthodox Church, 140, 146, 218, 219
Gregory, Pope, 94
Gregory, St., 69
Gregory of Tours, 103
Gregory XI, Pope, 116
Gruber, Elmar, 35
Guadeloupe, Our Lady of, 96–99
Guarducci, Margherita, 120
Guibert of Nogent, 60
Guimont, Louis, 111
Gundafor, King, 128
Gypsies, 104

Habsburg, Geza von, 219
Habsburg, Dr. Otto von, 79
Habsburgs, 71, 73, 79
Hadad (sun god), 86
Hadrian, Pope, 68
Hagopian, George, 170
Hail Mary, 94
Haithon, Johan, 169
Hancock, Graham, 193–194
Hannah (mother of Samuel), 110
Hardouin, Lord, 217
Hart, Rob, 91
Hautpoul-Blanchefort, 200, 202–203, 204
healing power, 45; of relics, 1, 2, 7, 8, 46; sacramentals, 45, 46. *See also individual relics*
Hegesippus, 107, 108, 134, 138
Heinrich I the Fowler, 70
Helen, St., 19
Helena, St. (mother of Emperor Constantine), 4, 5, 51–53, 54, 55, 58, 60, 63, 77, 78, 81
Heller, John, 26–27, 36
Henri, Bishop of Troyes, 19
Henry II, King, 100
Henry VIII, King, 209
Heraclius II, Emperor, 55
Hercules Aerospace lab, 41
Heremon Eochaidh, High King of Ardagh, 195
Herod, 3; Jerusalem palace of, 81; John the Baptist and, 84–85
Herodias, 81, 84, 85
Herod of Agrippa, King, 130
Hickey, Barry, archbishop of Perth, 90
High Flight Foundation, 182
Hill, John, 197
Himmler, Heinrich, 72–73, 75, 203

History of the Church (Eusebius), 42, 138
History of the Crusades, 18
Hitler, Adolf, 2, 66, 70, 71, 72–73, 74, 75, 76, 203
Hoare, Rodney, 30–31
Hofburg Museum, Vienna, 71, 73, 76
"holy anorexia," 117
Holy Blood, Holy Grail (Baigent et al.), 89, 106
Holy Germanic Empire, 69–71
Holy Grail, 74, 95, 203, 206–215; Antioch chalice, 209–210; as bloodline of family of Jesus, 206, 211, 212–213; as a book, 212; of the Celts, 206, 210–211; chalice from the Last Supper, 157, 206–208; Galician, 130; Genoa, 208–209; the Grail castle, 202, 203, 213; literature, 19, 108, 109, 202, 210, 211–213; the medieval, 211–212; the Nanteos Cup, 209; as receptacle used to preserve blood of dying Jesus, 206; as search for the divine within, 214' Sinclair family and, 204; of Valencia, 206–208
Holy League, 79
Holy Place, The (Lincoln), 204
"Holy Relics of Charlemagne and King Athelstan, The," 75
Holy Roman Empire, 68–69, 73, 79
Holyrood, palace of, 57
Holy Shroud Congress of 2002, 58–59
Horn, Siegfried, 193
Household of the Grail, The, 75
Hugh of Champagne, 211
Hugh of Lincoln, St., 100, 101
Huns, 67

Ichrusa.com Web site, 222
Ieper, Belgium, 61
Immaculate Conception, 92
Impression of the Stigmata of St. Francis, 115
incorrupt bodies or body parts, 2, 3, 152–153, 158–159
India, flood story from, 178–179
infrared spectroscopy, 32
Innocent VIII, Pope, 47, 78
Institute of Technology, Zurich, 29–30, 31
International Crusade for Holy Relics (ICHR), 220

Internet, 3, 215; online auctions of relics, 3, 220–222
Interpol, 4, 215, 217, 219
Iraq, 9
Ireland: ancient, treasures of, 210–211; the Ark of the Covenant and, 194–197
Iron Cross of Lombardy, 60
Irwin, James, 182, 193
Isabella and Ferdinand, 130
Isaiah, 66
Ishodad of Merv, 50
Ishtar, 95, 97, 180
Isidore of Seville, 169
Isis, 95, 97, 109, 142
Islam, 55–56, 68, 86, 146, 184, 213; John the Baptist and, 86–87
isotropy, 154
Israel, rescue of Falasha Jews by, 194
Israeli Antiquities Authority, 41, 137
Israeli Government Geological Survey, 135
Italy and the trade in relics, 4, 215, 216–217

Jabel al Tariq, 200
Jackson, Dr. John, 27, 28
Jackson, Michael, 218
Jackson, Stonewall, 6
Jacob's Pillow, 194, 196, 197
James (brother of Jesus) (son of Alphaeus) (James the Lesser), 5, 95, 107, 132–137, 138, 140, 141; James bone box, 133–137
James (son of Zebedee) (James the Greater), 129–131, 150
Januarius, St. *See* Gennaro, St.
Jeremiah, 194–195, 196
Jeremias, 189
Jerome, St., 67, 81, 103
Jerusalem, 5, 31, 41, 52, 58, 59, 78, 81, 191–193; Crusades and, 18, 56, 208; excavations of family tomb in East Talpiot section of, 135–136; first temple, 188, 189, 194, 197; Knights Templar and, 20; second temple, destruction of the, 197–198; Temple Mount, 191, 192; Titus and destruction of, 24, 197–199; True Cross, 52–53, 54, 55
Jesus, 7; baptism of, 83; body parts of, 62; burial cloth of (*see* Shroud of Turin); Crucifixion of (*see* Crucifixion, the); Essenes and, 83–84; family of, 106–109, 133–134, 138–139, 149; Holy Grail as bloodline of, 206, 211, 212; lineage of, 83, 106–107, 133, 212; married-Jesus theory, 106–108; Mary Magdalene and (*see* Mary Magdalene); Jesus and miracle at wedding feast of Cana, 92; paintings of, 17–18, 35; resurrection of (*see* Resurrection, the); sacred blood of, 60–61; the sudarium and (*see* sudarium); the Veil of Veronica and (*see* Veil of Veronica)
Jesus Conspiracy, The (Kersten and Gruber), 35
Jesus the Magician (Smith), 77
Jet Propulsion Laboratory, Pasadena, 27, 28
Jewish War, The (Josephus), 198
John, St., 80, 83, 151; Gospel of, 15, 39, 40, 46, 50, 65, 76, 80, 84, 102, 141
John Damascene, St., 17
John of Damascus, St., 92
John of Giscala, 197
John Paul II, Pope, 1, 80, 87, 91, 151, 208
John the Baptist, St., 69, 80–89, 108, 150, 209; bones of, 81, 82, 208; connection between Mary Magdalene and, 89, 108, 109; cults centering on, 85–86; feast day of, 83; skulls of, 3, 5, 59, 60, 80–83, 87–89; story of beheading of, 81, 85
John the Evangelist, 92, 130, 150; Gospel of, 83, 150
John XXII, Pope, 59
John XXIII, Pope, 1
Jordan, 80, 81
Jordan River, 4, 11, 80
Joseph (husband of Blessed Virgin Mary), 92, 133
Joseph of Arimathea, 15, 61, 92, 104, 209, 212
Josephus, 133, 198
Joshua, book of, 187
Josi, Enrico, 120
Josias, King, 189
Judas (Jerusalem wise man), 52–53
Judas Iscariot, 36, 102, 142–143
Jude: A Pilgrimage to the Saint of Last Resort (Trotta), 139

Jude Thaddeus, St., 137–139, 140
Julian, St., 9
Julius II, Emperor, 145
Jumper, Dr. Eric, 27–28
Jupiter (god), 86
Justinian, Emperor, 67–68, 151
Juvelius, Valter, 192

Kaaba (sacred black stone), 55–56, 213
Kaas, Monsignor Ludwig, 120
Kaballah, 213
Kanazawa College of Art, Japan, 218
Keating, Bishop John, 99
Kebra Nagast, 189, 191
Kersten, Holgar, 35
"Keyhole" project, 171
Khalil, Sheik, 192
Kings: first book of (first Book of Samuel), 187; third book of, 188
Kirschbaum, Englebert, 120
Knight, Christopher, 35
Knights of Christ, 129, 190
Knights of Germany, 72
Knights of Malta, 88
Knights of the Holy Sepulcher, 59
Knights Templar, 20, 21, 35, 57, 59, 108, 192, 203, 204, 211, 212; Ark of the Covenant and, 184, 190–191, 204; Cathars and, 202, 204, 213; St. John the Baptist and, 88–89
Kolbe, Maximillian, 46
Koran, 85
Kore (goddess), 210–211
Koreion, feast of, 211
Korzhakov, General Alexander, 218
Krajicek, Richard, 218
Krakow, Poland, 74, 76, 78
Kyot of Provence, 202
Kyrgyz Academy of Sciences, 149
Kyrillos VI, pope of Alexandria, 148

la Boissiere, France, Cistercian monks of, 7, 57
Lanciano, Eucharistic miracle of, 62–63
Languedoc region, France, 199, 202, 203, 213
Lapa (mother of St. Catherine of Siena), 114
lapsit exillis, 213

Last Supper, 83, 84, 138, 139, 140, 143, 150; chalice from the, 157, 206–208, 209, 210

Lawrence, St. (San Lorenzo), 3, 157–159, 207, 208–209

Lawrie, Charles, 75

Lazarus, 35, 40, 102, 106, 148; the Lazarium, 103; St. Thomas and, 127

Lemaire, Andre, 133, 135

Leo, lector of Constantinople, 18

Leo III, Emperor, 18

Leo III, Pope, 68

Leo VI, Emperor, 103

Leonelli, Marzia, 48

Lia Fail (Stone of Destiny), 196, 210

Liber Pater (Roman god), 195

Life of St. Nino of Georgia, 50

Lincoln, Henry, 204

Lincoln Cathedral, England, 100

Lindsay, Brett, 91

Linoli, Dr. Odoardo, 63

Lirey, France, 19, 30

Lisbon, Portugal, 159–160

Lodge of Killwinning, 190, 191

Lomas, Robert, 35

Lombards, 47, 142

Longinus, 36, 65–66, 77; spear of. *See* spear of Longinus

Looking for a Miracle (Nickell), 97–98

Loomis, Laura Hibbard, 75

Lorraine, House of, 79

Los Alamos National Scientific Laboratory, 36

Louis I, duke of Savoy, 20

Louis IX, King, 58, 106

Louis XI, King, 109

Lourdes, 1, 112, 153

Lucifer, 213

Luke, St., 5, 95, 96; bones and body parts of, 3, 144–146; Gospel of, 15, 44, 65, 76, 80, 83, 84, 102, 145

Luther, Martin, 9, 60, 109, 118, 164

Maccabees, second book of, 189

McCrone, Dr. Walter, 26–27, 29, 30

Machaerus, fortress at, 81, 85

Magyars, 70

Mainz, archbishop of, 11

Majella, St. Gerard, 153

Malchus, centurion, 121

Malta, 88, 145

Mandeville, Sir John, 78

Mangararo, Giacomo, 216–217

"manna," 3, 124, 125, 126, 152, 160–161, 166

Manoppello, Italy, Veil of Veronica found in Capuchin monastery in, 39, 48

Manu, tale of, 175, 179

Ma'nu VI, 16–17

Marco Polo, 169

Marie, the Marquise de Hautpoul, 202–203

Marie of Champagne, 211

Marino, Joseph, 31, 32, 36

Mark, St., body of, 146–148; Gospel of, 65, 81, 83, 84, 85, 102, 133, 146–147

Markale, Jean, 89

Marsailles, France, 106

Martha, 104, 105

Martin, St., 132

Martin, St., patron saint of Tours, 10

Martin, Vito Terribile Wiel, 145

Martin the Humane, 207

Mary, Blessed Virgin. *See* Blessed Virgin Mary

Mary, wife of Cleophas, 133

Mary of the Blachernae, basilica of St., Constantinople, 18

Mary Celeste, 95–96

Mary Jacobe, 105, 110

Mary Magdalene, 100–109, 110, 200; connection between John the Baptist and, 89, 108, 109; in the Gospels, 102–103; the historic, 101; Jesus and, 101, 103, 104, 106, 109

Mary Salome, 105, 110

Masada, 107

mass spectrometry, 30, 32

Matera, Father, 166

Matthew, St., 124, 148–150; Gospel of, 65, 83, 84, 102, 121, 133, 143, 149; tomb of, 149–150

Mattingly, Stephen, 32, 36

Mauritius (commander of Theban Legion), 66

Maxellendis, St., 217

Maxentius, 52

Maximian, 66

Maximilla, wife of Aegeus, 124

Maximinus, St., 105

Mecca, 55–56, 213

Medina, 55–56

Mediterranean Sea, 174

Melnikoff, Sergey, 149

Melrose Abbey, 6

Memorial to Moses on Mount Nebo, 80

Menelik I, 189

Meriam, Mengistu Haile, 194

Merovingian dynasty, 108, 109, 199–200, 202–203

Merrill, Major, 209

Meryem, Queen of Persia, 55

Meryemana, 151

Mexico, 96–97

Michael, Archangel, 213

Michael, St., 95, 184

Michelangelo, 119, 122

microspectrophotometer, 28

Milvian bridge, 66, 132

miracles: church's stance on, 109–110; relics and, 2, 5, 7, 8, 152–153. *See also individual relics*

Molaise, St., 196

Monastery of Roncevalles, Augustinian, 130

Monastery of the Apocalypse, Patmos, 151

Monastery of the Ark, Phrygia, 169

Montenegro, 88

Montevergine, Benedictine Abbey of, 21

Montsegur, siege of, 202, 204, 213

Moore, Dr. Clement, 164

Moors, 6, 131, 200, 207, 208

Morrison, Jim, 6

Moses and the Ark of the Covenant, 185, 186, 205

Mothers Night, 163

Mount of Olives, 81

Muhammad, 55–56

Muhammad Ali, 126–127

Mukawaer, 80

Muntinlupa Prison, Philippines, 114

Muslims, 188. *See* Islam

Myra, Turkey, 160, 161, 162, 164–165

Nabatean people, 85

Nag Hammadi Gospels, 106

Nag Hammadi library, 126

nails of the Crucifixion. *See* Crucifixion, the, nails of

Naim, Asher, 194

Nanteos Cup, 209

Naples, 154–156

Napoleon, 21, 58, 71, 73, 88, 155, 208

Nast, Thomas, 164

Nathaniel Bartholomew, 140

National Geographic, 137

National Security Agency (NSA), 4
Navarra, Fernand, 170
Nazarius, St., 5, 8
Nazi Germany, 72–74, 75, 76, 203
Nazorean church, 107
Nebo, Mount, 193
Nero, Emperor, 121, 122
Neuvy, France, 61
New Amsterdam, 166
New Grange, 210
Nezir, Mount, 178
Nicaea, Council of, in 325, 54, 93–94, 162
Nicetas, 78
Nicholas, St., 160–166; bones of, 3, 160–161, 166; legend and customs associated with, 162–164
Nicholas V, Pope, 122
Nickell, Joe, 97–98, 137
Nicodemus, 44, 76
Niketas Choniates, 18
Nimrud, 176
Nineveh, 55, 176
Nino, St., 50
Noah's Ark, 4, 167–183; Babylonian story of the ark, 176–178; evidence of a great flood, 172–175; geopolitical difficulties in researching, 168, 172, 181; Greek story of the ark, 179–181; Indian story of the ark, 178–179; modern explorers and, 169, 181–183; size of, 167–168; story of Noah, 175–176; U.S. secret intelligence and, 4, 167, 170–172; witnesses to, 169–170
Normans, 160
North Sea, 174
Notre Dame Cathedral, Paris, 59
Nouri, Prince (an archbishop of Babylon), 169
novenas, 112
Numbers, book of, 186, 187

O Cebreiro, Spain, 130
ODESSA, 203
Odor of Sanctity, 153
Old Testament prophecy regarding the true Savior, 66, 106–107
Olearius, Adam, 169
Ollam Fodhla, 195
Order of the Star, 20
Origen, 103

original sin, 92
Ortona, Italy, 126
Osiris, 97
Otto I, 70
Otto III, 76
Otto the Great, 70
Our Lady of Guadeloupe, 96–99
Oxford Research Laboratory, 29–30, 31
Oza and Ahio, 187

Padua, Italy, 145, 159
Palestine Exploration Fund, 191
Pamphilus, 42
Pandora, 93
Papias, 149
Pappalardo, Vincenzo, 216
Paris, France, 9, 58
Parker, Captain Montague Brownslow, 192–193
Parsifal, Wagner's, 203
Parzival (Eschenbach), 74, 212, 213
Passover Plot, The (Schonfield), 35–36, 77, 89
Patmos, island of, 150–151
Patrick, St., 195
Patton, General George S., Jr., 74–75
Paul, Czar, 88
Paul, St., 4, 5, 122, 134, 140, 144, 145, 148, 151
Paul V, Pope, 48
Paul VI, Pope, 120, 126, 148, 151
Pelagius, Pope, 141
Pelayo, Bishop of Oviedo, 49–50
Pepin, 47
Perdono, 126
Persians, 17, 47, 55
Peter, St., 5, 15, 39, 46, 50, 68, 118–123, 134, 136, 143, 148, 150; chalice from the Last Supper and, 157, 207; crucifixion of, 122, 123; Mary Magdalene and, 101, 103, 107; wife of, 139
Petrucci, Pancrazio, 48
Pfeiffer, Father Heinrich, 39, 46
Pharisees, 134, 135, 149
Philip, Prince (husband of Queen Elizabeth), 118
Philip, St., 140–141, 141
Philip of Valois, 45
Philistines, 187
Pia, Secondo, 14–15, 22, 23
Piaf, Edith, 113
Piazza San Marco, Venice, 147
Picknett, Lynn, 34–35

Pietà of Michelangelo, 119
Pilate, 15, 53, 54
pilgrimages, 1, 6, 7, 11, 20, 51–52, 68, 81, 95, 96, 103, 105, 111, 112; to Bari, Italy, 165; for feast of St. Thomas in Ortona, 126; to Padua, 159; to Santiago de Compostela, 129–130, 131
Pillar of Scourging, 129
Pio, Padre, 46, 153
Pisterzi, Father Italo, 158
Pius XI, Pope, 112, 118, 119
Pius XII, Pope, 118, 119, 120
Poitiers, battle of, 68
Poletto, Cardinal Severino, 37–38
pollen sampling; of Shroud of Turin, 2, 25, 28, 29, 41; of sudarium, 41
Polycarp, St., bishop of Smyrna, 4–6
Polycrates, bishop of Ephesus, 141
Poor Clares convent, sisters of the, 21
Powell, Patty, 90, 91, 99
Powell family, 209
Powers, Gary, 171
Pozzuoli, Italy, 156
prayer, efficacy of, 223
Prince, Clive, 34–35
Priscillian, 126
Prometheus, 180
Protasius, 4–5
protective power, belief in relics', 2, 6, 9, 17, 223
Protestant churches, trade in relics and, 10
Protevangelism of Saint James, The, 110
Ptolemy, 141
Pullara, Vincenzo, 137, 139
Pursglove, Kevin, 220
Pyrrha, wife of Deucalion, 180
Pythagoreans, 8

Rabanus, archbishop of Mainz, 104
Raffiotta, Silvio, 216
Rahn, Otto, 203
RAI2 (Italian state television), 158
Raiders of the Lost Ark, 184, 185
Raphael, 122
Ravenscroft, Trevor, Spear of Destiny and, 66–76, 78, 79
Reading, abbey at, 11
reconquista, 56, 68, 131, 207
Reformation, 48, 118, 125

Refutation of All Heresies
(Epiphanius), 94
Relic Foundation, 222
religious relics, 118; classes of, 7,
25, 220; "multiplicity" of, 60;
powers attributed to, 2,
8–9; trade in (*see* trade in
religious relics); veneration
of, history of, 4–6. *See also
individual relics and categories
of relics*
Rennes-le-Château, France
(earlier called Rhedae), 199,
200, 202–204
Resurrection, the, 77; Shroud
of Turin and. *See* Shroud of
Turin, the Resurrection and
Revelations, book of, 150
Rhedae, France (later called
Rennes-le-Château), 199,
200, 202–204
Rig Veda, 178–179
Robert the Bruce, 6, 190
Rodoin, 69
Rohm, Ernst, 71, 72
Roime, 132
Roman Catholic Cathedral:
Edinburgh, 126
Roman Catholic Church:
altars, relic requirement for,
3, 7, 221; blood of St.
Gennaro and, 154; canonical
texts, 140; the Cathars and,
201–202, 213; classification of
relics, 7, 25, 220; collection of
relics, 1, 2–3; Constantine's
importance to, 54–55; on
manna of the saints, 152, 161;
Shroud of Turin and (*see*
Shroud of Turin, Catholic
Church and); storage of
relics, 1; trade in relics and, 3,
5, 217, 221; Veil of Veronica
and, 39, 40, 48–49;
veneration of relics and, 4–7;
women and, 93, 108
Romanovs, 118
Rome, Italy, 5, 47, 66, 67, 78,
123, 126, 142; Ark of the
Covenant in, 198–199;
catacombs, 93; chalice from
the Last Supper in, 157, 207
Romero, Archbishop Oscar, 1
Roozemond, Robert, 218–219
Roskovitsky, Lieutenant
Vladimir, 170
Rosslyn Chapel, Scotland, 185,
191, 204
Rothschild, Baron Edmond de,
192

Round Table, Knights of the,
211, 212
Royal Engineers, 191, 192
Royal Monastery of
Guadeloupe, Toledo, 25
Royal Ontario Museum, 133,
136
Rule, St. (or St. Regulus), 125,
126
Runciman, Steven, 18
Russia, looting of artifacts of,
217–218
Russian Orthodox Church, 218
Russian Revolution, 88, 170
Rusticus (Venetian merchant),
147

SA, 72
"sacramentals," healing
through, 45, 46
Sacred Sepulcher of Neuvy, 61
Sadducees, 134
St. Andrew's Cathedral, 125
St. Anne d'Auruy, 111
St. Anne de Beaupre, near
Quebec, 111
St. Anne de-la-Palue, 111
Sainte-Chapelle, Chambrey, 21,
31
Sainte-Chapelle, Paris, 57, 58,
59, 73, 88
St. Chaumont, Lyonnais, 88
St. Corneille of Compiegne,
church of, 143
St. George Fights Evil, 218
St. Gildard Convent, Nevers,
153
Sainte Gudule convent,
Brussels, 57
sainthood: process, 112–113, 152.
See also names of individual
saints
St. John's Basilica, Ephesus, 151
Saintes-Maries-de-la-Mer, Les,
104
St. Mary of Zion, Axum, 191,
193
St. Mary's, Krakow, 74
St. Maximin (previously Villa
Lata), 105, 106, 109
Saint-Medard de Soissons,
monks of, 62
St. Patrick's Cathedral, New
York, 113
St. Paul's Cathedral, London,
140
St. Peter's Basilica, Vatican, 47,
48, 68, 69, 78, 118, 119,
122–123, 140; chapel of
Veronica, 47, 48; search for

grave of St. Peter in the
Grottos beneath, 119–121, 123
St. Sylvester, church of, Rome,
88
St. Victor, church of,
Marseilles, 108–109
Saladin, 57
Saldarini, Cardinal (custodian
of Shroud of Turin), 38
Salome, 81, 84, 85
Samaria, 150
Samson-Purkinje effect, 98
Samuel, 110
Samuel, first Book of (1 Kings),
187
San Antonio, Texas,
archdiocese of, 220
Sandia Lab, New Mexico, 28
Sanhedrin, 54, 133
Santa Croce in Gerusalemme,
Rome, 63–64, 129
Santa Sophia, Constantinople,
82
Santiago de Compostela,
129–130, 131, 207
Saracens, 70, 110, 123, 147
Sarah (servant girl), 104, 105
Saul. *See* Paul, St.
Sauniere, Father Berenger,
202–203, 204
Savoy, House of, 14, 20, 21
Saxons, 68, 69–70
Schoch, Dr. Robert, 174
Schonfield, Guy, 42
Schonfield, Hugh, 35–36, 89
scientific investigation of
authenticity of relics. *See
specific scientific methods and
individual relics*
Scotland, 9, 125, 190
Sea of Galilee, 11
Sea of Marmara, 174
Sebaste, Samaria, 81
Sephardic Jews, 22, 200
Septimania, 200
Serafin, Tom, 221–222
Serra, Father Junipero, 1
Severus, Bishop, 155
Severus Alexander, Emperor,
128
Shahrbaraz (Persian general),
55
Shardan, the, 195
Sheba, queen of, 189, 193
Shiite Muslims, 56
Shroud Congress of 1989 in
Bologna, 41
Shroud of Turin, 13–38, 33, 82;
availability for study, 13, 29,
38; blood evidence, 28, 29, 63;

as burial cloth of Jesus, 13, 14, 21, 39; carbon 14 dating of, 2, 13-14, 29-32, 33, 42; Catholic Church and, 13, 37; contact method for creation of, 36; creation of, theories about, 32-37; DNA evidence and, 28, 38; fires endured by, 21, 31-32; "flash" theory, 37; folding of, 17; image depicted by, 13, 28; lining replacement in 1868, 21; painting, regarded as a, 14, 19, 26, 27, 35, 36; paranormal cause of image on, 37; photographing of, 14-15, 22-23; pollen sampling of, 2, 25, 28, 29, 41; provenance of, 15-22; religious bias and authenticity of, 13, 23; repairs to, 21, 31, 32, 37-38; the Resurrection and, 2, 11, 13, 37; scientific testing of, 2, 13-15, 22-32, 63; "scorch" theory for creation of, 36; size of, 13, 17; the sudarium, 41-42; textile testing of, 2, 27-28, 29; vapor-diffusion method for creation of, 36; the Veil of Veronica, properties shared with, 40
Shroud of Turin Research Project (STURP), 24-26, 27, 29, 36, 37
Siberia, 114
Sicarii, 142
Siegen, Germany, 74
Sign and the Seal, The (Hancock), 194
Sig runes, 72-73
Simeon, St., 11
Simocatta, Teofilatto (aka Theophylact Simocrates), 47
Simon Magus, 121-122
Simon of Cyrene, 43
Simon the leper, 102
Simon the Zealot, 139-141
Sinclair family, 204
sinning, punishment for, 45
Sixtus II, Pope, 157, 207, 208
Sixtus IV, Pope, 21
Skeptical Inquirer, 137
Skorzeny, Otto, 203
Smith, George, 176
Smith, Morton, 148
Society of St. Nicholas, 165
Soemundarson, Nicholas, 18
Sol Invictus of Constantine, 163
Solomon, King, 188-189

Sonnini, C. S., 140
Soviet Union, looting of artifacts of former, 217-218
Spanish missionaries in the New World, 96, 97
Spartacus, slave revolt of, 24
Spear of Destiny, The (Ravenscroft), 66, 75
spear of Longinus, 65-79; death of Jesus and, 24, 36, 43, 65; Hofburg Spear (lance of St. Maurice), 71, 73, 76, 78-79; in Krakow, Poland, 76, 78; Old Testament prophecy and, 66; other versions of the story, 76-79; power of, 2, 66, 69, 70, 75; Ravenscroft and history of, 66-76, 78, 79; in the Vatican, 76, 78
Speculum: A Journal of Medieval Studies, 75
Sphinx, 174
SS, 72, 203
Stations of the Cross (Way of the Cross), 44
stealing of religious relics, 6, 10-11, 47-48, 147, 160, 215. *See also* translation (taking of a relic)
Stein, Dr. Walter Johannes, 75
Steinhardt, Michael, 216, 217
Stephanus, St., 158
Stephen, St., 5, 69, 140
Stephen II, Pope, 47
Stephen IX, Pope, 105
stigmata, 2, 3, 115-116, 153; St. Catherine of Siena and, 115, 116
Story of a Soul (St. Thérèse of Lisieux), 112, 114
strega (Italian liquor), 142
Stuarts, 123
sudarium, 40-42; provenance of, 42, 49-50; scientific study of, 41; the Shroud of Turin and, 41-42; significance of, 39-40
Sufis, Indian, 8
Sumeria and Sumerians, 176, 177, 178, 179
Sunni Muslims, 56
Sylvester I, Pope, 107, 122
Synopsis de Apostol (bishop of Tyre), 140
Syriac Christian Church, 16

tabots, 184, 185, 194
Tacitus, 45
Talmud, 189

Tamar Tephi, Princess, 194, 195
Tammuz, 97
Tara, Irish sacred center, 196, 197
Tarshish, 194-195
Tartessus, 195
Taylor, Porcher, 167
Templar Treasure at Gisors (Markale), 89
Temple Mount, 191, 192
Temple of Artemes, 151
Temple of Solomon (first temple) (Jerusalem), 188, 189, 194, 197
Teresa of Avila, St., 153
Tessiore, Giorgio, 31
Thaddeus, 16
Theban Legion, 66
Theodoric I, 67
Theodosius I, Emperor, 5, 6, 67
Theophilus of Antioch, 169
Theresa, St., 1, 9, 46
Thérèse of Lisieux, St., 112-114
Thessalonica, 67
thin-layer chromatography test, 63
thixotropy effect, 154-155, 156, 158
Thomas, St., 92, 126-129
"three Marys" tradition, 104, 105, 110
Thule (secret society), 71-72
Tiberius, Emperor, 44-45, 46, 54
Timothy, 5
Titus, 24, 197-199
Toledo, Spain, 199, 200
tombaroli (tomb raiders), 215, 216
Tonantzin (Mexican goddess), 97
Tonsman, Dr. Jose Asta, 98-99
Torrija Lavoignet, Dr. Rafael, 98
Torrocella Bueno, Dr. Javier, 98
Toulouse, France, 199
tourism, religious, 1, 11, 81, 130. *See also* pilgrimages
Tower of St. Rule, 125
trade fairs, 7, 11
trade in religious relics, 3-4, 9-11, 215-222; Cammarata case, 216-217; conflicting laws, 219; criticism of, 6, 118, 220, 221-222; online, 3, 220-222
Trajan, 107
translation (taking of a relic), 10, 69, 103, 106, 117, 128-129, 217

transubstantiation, miracle of the, 62, 207
Treatise on Anatomy (Da Vinci), 34
Treatise on Relics (Calvin), 143
Trematore, Mario, 31
Trier, Cathedral at, 11
Trier, Germany, 60, 150
Trotta, Liz, 139
True Cross, 55–58, 59, 60, 82; churches and cathedrals containing a piece of, 7, 11, 55, 57, 63, 129; power of the, 2; St. Helena and, 51–53, 77; scientific testing of, 2; scroll hung over the head of Jesus, 54, 58, 64; story of discovery of, 51–53; today, 63–64
Turin, Italy, 21. *See also* Shroud of Turin
Turin Shroud, In Whose Image?, The (Picknett and Prince), 34
Turkey: Culture Ministry, 165; exploration for Noah's Ark, 170
Twain, Mark, 154, 155
"'Twas the Night Before Christmas," 164
Tyron, abbey in, 88

Uhlenhuth's zonal precipitation reaction, 63
Umayyad dynasty, 56
Umayyad Mosque, 86–87
Umberto II, 22
U.S. Conference of Research on the Holy Shroud, 24
University of Arizona, Tucson, 29–30, 31
Ur, city of, 178
Urban III, Pope, 105
Urban VIII, Pope, 48
Utnapishtim, 175, 176–178
U-2 spy planes, 170–171

Valencia, Holy Grail of, 206–208
Valerian, Emperor, 157, 207
van Boland, Father John, 47

Vandals, 67, 123
vaporograph, 33
Vatican, 22, 35; relics housed at the, 11, 48, 59–60, 76; St. Peter's Basilica (*see* St. Peter's Basilica, Vatican); Wadi Kharrar and, 80
Veil of Veronica, 112; copies of, 48; described, 39, 40, 47; the name of the pious woman, 42–43; provenance of, 42–49; scientific testing of, 2, 39, 40; the Shroud of Turin, properties shared with, 40; significance of, 39; size of, 39; the story, 40, 42–44
Venice, city of, 58, 60, 117; St. Mark's body and, 146–148
Venus, 132
Veres, Michael, 217
Vespasian, Emperor, 45, 107
Vesuvius, Mount, 155, 156
Vezelay, Burgundy, 105, 106, 109
Vianney, St. John, 153
Victor Emmanuel III, King, 22–23
Victoria, Queen, 191
Victricius, Bishop, 5
Villa Lata (later St. Maximin), 105, 106, 109
Ville du Pay, France, 88
Vincent, Louis Hughes, 192
Vinland Map, 26, 27
Virgin and Child with St. Anne, 33–34
Visigoths, 67, 68, 199–200, 202
Vittorio, Donato, 40
Vladimir, archbishop of Bishkek and Central Asia, 149
von Thurn und Taxis, Prince, 71–72
Voragine, Jacobus de, 53, 104–105, 108, 133, 134, 147
VP-8 image analyzer, 28
Vril (secret group), 72

Wadi Kharrar, Jordan, 80, 89
Wagner, Richard, 203
Waheeb, Mohammed, 80, 81
Walburga, St., in Bavaria, 152
Walsh, Father Finbarr, 91
Ward, Keith, 40
Warren, Lieutenant Charles, 191–192
Warren's Shaft, 191
Way of the Cross (Stations of the Cross), 44
Way of Seven Falls, 44
weeping statues, 2, 3, 90–91, 99
Welsh tales: of a great flood, 173–174; Holy Grail literature and, 211, 212
West, John Anthony, 174
Whanger, Alan, 41
Whitaker, Gary, 91
Willian the Conqueror, 9
Wilson, Ian, 15, 19, 20
Winchester Cathedral, Holy Sepulchre Chapel of, 19
Witherington, Ben, 137
women: Catholic Church and, 93, 108; goddesses. *See* goddesses. *See also names of individuals*
Woolley, Sir Leonard, 178
Woolsey, James, 167
Worldwide Congress "Sindone 2000," 31
Wyatt, Ron, 181–182

Xavier, St. Francis, 153

Yale University, 26
Yearam, Haji, 169
Yohanan (crucifixion victim), 51

Zacharias, prophecy of, 60
Zealots, 84, 139
Zegrean, Sebastian, 217
Zeus, 179–180
Zumarraga, Bishop, 96
Zwingli, Ulrich, 109